CLARENDON LAW SERIES

Edited by

A. M. HONORÉ AND J. RAZ

CLARENDON LAW SERIES

AN INTRODUCTION TO
ROMAN LAW

BY

BARRY NICHOLAS

FORMERLY PROFESSOR OF COMPARATIVE LAW
IN THE UNIVERSITY OF OXFORD
AND SOMETIME PRINCIPAL OF
BRASENOSE COLLEGE

CLARENDON PRESS · OXFORD

Oxford University Press, Walton Street, Oxford OX2 6DP

Oxford New York

Athens Auckland Bangkok Bombay
Calcutta Cape Town Dar es Salaam Delhi
Florence Hong Kong Istanbul Karachi
Kuala Lumpur Madras Madrid Melbourne
Mexico City Nairobi Paris Singapore
Taipei Tokyo Toronto

and associated companies in
Berlin Ibadan

Oxford is a trade mark of Oxford University Press

Published in the United States
by Oxford University Press Inc., New York

© Oxford University Press 1962

First published in hardback 1962
Reprinted 1972, 1975, 1977, 1979, 1982, 1984, 1987, 1988, 1990, 1991, 1992, 1995

ISBN 0-19-876063-9

Printed in Hong Kong

PREFACE

THIS is not intended to be a comprehensive textbook. The customary English elementary textbook of Roman law has been essentially an expansion of and commentary on the Institutes of Gaius and Justinian. My purpose has been somewhat different. The main framework of the Institutes has become a necessary part of any thinking about Roman law, and to some extent about law in general, and an account which abandoned that framework would not be an account of Roman law. But within that framework I have attempted a shift of emphasis. It was not the habit of the Roman lawyers to make explicit the fundamental assumptions and distinctions with which they worked; nor could they criticize and evaluate their own achievement in the way that we, with our knowledge of its subsequent history and of the contrasts provided by the English Common law, are able to. I have tried to do both these things and also to point very briefly to some of the ways in which Roman law still survives in modern Civil law systems.

I have tried, in the first place, to draw out the fundamental assumptions and distinctions of the Roman law and to delineate its most characteristic institutions. In doing so I have of course stated many of its detailed rules, since without them the skeleton would lack life, but I have omitted much that seemed to me to be, in a book of this size, of secondary importance. Those who are already acquainted with the subject will each, I fear, find that I have omitted something which to him is fundamental and included something else which is trivial or abstruse. Such readers will also find that on controversial points—and owing to the peculiar character of the surviving evidence they are many—I have either muted the controversy or, more often, have stated without qualification what is no more than one opinion. I have had to steer a course between two familiar dangers. On the one hand it would be an unjustifiable distortion to depict the Roman law of any period as clear and undisputed, and on the other hand it would defeat the purpose of an introductory book to express every qualification that strict scholarship would demand. Where I have made a choice

between conflicting opinions I have thought it right to err on
the side of conservatism even where my own preference might
be for a more radical view.

I have tried, in the second place, to show the Roman law as
a living system with both merits and defects, a system made by
men who worked within limitations imposed by the conditions
of the time and by their own methods of thought. And finally
I have attempted to provide some signposts to the more significant contrasts to be found in the Common law and to the salient
features of the Roman inheritance of modern Civil law. In a
book of this size they can be no more than signposts, and I have
made no attempt at exposition of the modern law. Moreover
within the Civil law I have confined myself to the French and
German systems, as being both the most divergent and the
most influential. I have made almost no mention of Scots law.
For this the explanation is in part my own ignorance and in
part a sense that the influence of English law has been strong
enough to blur the similarities and that of Roman law to blur
the contrasts which I was seeking.

I have said little about early Roman law, both because the
proportion of conjecture to evidence is very much higher than
in the classical and later law, and the risks of distortion in
a simplified account are correspondingly increased, and also
because the interest to be found in the primitive law is often
different in kind from that offered by the mature system, and
it is the mature system which has influenced subsequent law.

I have abandoned the main framework of the Institutes in
several respects, of which only one needs mention here. I have
given no separate treatment of Actions. This is not because I
think Actions unimportant. On the contrary, I am sure that
their main features are vital to an understanding of the law.
But I think that in an introductory book those main features
are best incorporated in the discussion of the sources and of
the substantive law.

I am indebted to a number of friends for criticism and advice.
From Professor F. H. Lawson I have derived more ideas and
insights over the past dozen years than I can now hope to
identify; and I am in particular grateful to him for reading the
manuscript of the book at a time when it had become overgrown
and for suggesting the points at which it could advantageously

be pruned. I am greatly in the debt of Mr. G. D. G. Hall, who subjected the final draft to a penetrating and detailed criticism which was all the more valuable because it came from one whose primary interest lies outside the field of Roman law. I am most grateful also to Mr. D. L. Stockton and Dr. W. A. J. Watson for their advice on particular sections, and especially to Professor P. Stein who read the proofs and saved me from a number of errors and obscurities. For those in which I have persisted he is of course not responsible.

BARRY NICHOLAS

Oxford, November 1961

CONTENTS

I. HISTORY AND SOURCES OF THE LAW

IV. LAW OF OBLIGATIONS

DATES

Republic

B.C.

451–450 Twelve Tables

367 Institution of (Urban) Praetorship

c. 242 Institution of Peregrine Praetorship

?*c.* 125 *Lex Aebutia*

Principate

27 Augustus regularizes his power

A.D.

14 Death of Augustus

117–138 Reign of Hadrian

c. 130 Consolidation of Edict

138–161 Reign of Antoninus Pius

?*c.* 161 Institutes of Gaius

161–169 Reign of M. Aurelius and L. Verus

169–180 Reign of M. Aurelius alone

193–211 Reign of Septimius Severus

211–217 Reign of Caracalla (Antoninus)

c. 212 *Constitutio Antoniniana*

Dominate

284–305 Reign of Diocletian

306–337 Reign of Constantine the Great

313 Toleration of Christianity

330 Transfer of capital to Constantinople

395 Final division of Empire

426 Law of Citations

438 *Codex Theodosianus*

476 End of Western Empire

527–565 Reign of Justinian

I

HISTORY AND SOURCES OF THE LAW

I. INTRODUCTION

1. THE CLAIMS OF ROMAN LAW

ACCORDING to tradition Rome was founded in 753 B.C. In the twenty-seven centuries since then Roman law has lived two lives and makes two claims on our attention. In its first life it was the law of the city of Rome and, in its ultimate maturity, of the whole Roman Empire. But it was more than this. It was the most original product of the Roman mind. In almost all their other intellectual endeavours the Romans were the eager pupils of the Greeks, but in law they were, and knew themselves to be, the masters. In their hands law became for the first time a thoroughly scientific subject, an elaborately articulated system of principles abstracted from the detailed rules which constitute the raw material of law. This process of abstraction is important not merely for the simplicity of formulation which it makes possible, but also because principles, unlike rules, are fertile: a lawyer can by combining two or more principles create new principles and therefore new rules. The difference between a system of principles and a system of rules may thus be likened to the difference between an alphabetic script and a system of ideographs such as the Chinese.[1] It was the strength of the Roman lawyers that they not only had the ability to construct and manipulate these abstractions on a scale and with a complexity previously unknown, but had also a clear sense of the needs of social and commercial life, an eye for the simplest method of achieving a desired practical result, and a readiness to reject the logic of their own constructions when it conflicted with the demands of convenience. If the law is 'practical reason' it is not surprising that the Romans, with their genius for the

---

[1] This observation, with others on this page, was made by Rudolf von Jhering in perhaps the most perceptive book ever written about the Roman law, *Geist des römischen Rechts* (*Spirit of the Roman Law*, 1st ed. 1852–65), unhappily never translated into English (French translation by O. de Meulenaere).

practical, should have found in it a field of intellectual activity to which they were ideally suited.

This first life of Roman law was summed up, and in the event brought to a close, by the Emperor Justinian in the sixth century A.D. It claims our attention for the intrinsic quality of its intellectual achievement. But five and a half centuries later the law books of Justinian came to be studied in northern Italy, and there began, at first in the universities and later in the courts, the astonishing second life of Roman law which gave to almost the whole of Europe a common stock of legal ideas, a common grammar of legal thought, and, to a varying but considerable extent, a common mass of legal rules. England stood out against this Reception of Roman law and retained its own Common law largely but not entirely uninfluenced by the Roman. Hence it is that in the world today there are two great families of law of European origin—the one deriving from the Common law of England and embracing the greater part of the English-speaking world, and the other rooted, or partly rooted, in the revived Roman law and including almost all the countries of Europe and a number of others besides.[1] In contrast to the Common law these Romanistic systems are commonly called Civil law, the name by which until quite recently the Roman law itself was known.

The Roman law thus makes this second claim on our attention, that it provides the Common lawyer with a key to the common language of almost every other system of law which traces its origin to Europe.

It is not for the whole of Roman law, however, that this claim can be substantiated. The Romans themselves made a distinction between public law and private law. The former was concerned with the functioning of the state, and included in particular constitutional law and criminal law; the latter was concerned with relations between individuals. It was the private law to which the Roman lawyers devoted their main interest, and it was the private law which gave to the second life of Roman law its great importance. It is with it alone, therefore, that we are here concerned.

[1] See further below, pp. 51 f. The two great non-European systems—the Hindu and the Mohammedan—are religious in character. In the field of commercial law they have been largely superseded by importations from one or other of the European systems, but in other fields they still regulate the lives of many millions of people.

2. THE CONSTITUTIONAL AND HISTORICAL BACKGROUND

No system of law can be fully understood in isolation from the history of the society which it serves and regulates. What follows can be, however, no more than a sketch of some of the salient features of the history of Rome in the thirteen centuries which end with the death of Justinian in A.D. 565.

The struggle between the Orders, and the Republican constitution. For the history of the first period, ending traditionally in 510 B.C. with the expulsion of Tarquinius Superbus, the last king, we have little reliable evidence, and for its law even less. From this period the Roman Republic emerges as a small city-state, based mainly on agriculture but already acquiring some commercial importance and showing signs of those military abilities which were to extend her frontiers far beyond the Mediterranean world. However, the first century and a half of the Republic (510–367 B.C.) was devoted largely to the internal struggle between the two Orders or classes into which the citizen body was divided—the Patrician nobility and the Plebeians who formed the bulk of the population. The struggle was for equality, partly economic but mainly political. It was important for the early development of the Roman constitution, but since it was finally over by at the latest 287 B.C., and the significant development of the private law did not begin for at least another century after that, we may be content merely to glance at the relevant features of the Republican constitution. This constitution consisted from the beginning of three elements—the magistrates, the Senate, and the assemblies.

The magistrates were the inheritors of the royal power. For the principal political consequence of the revolution which inaugurated the Republic was simply the replacement of the King by two magistrates, eventually known as Consuls. They were endowed with full executive power (*imperium*), subject only to three limitations: in the first place, though each had full power, each was subject to the veto of the other; in the second place, they held office only for a year; and lastly, their power might be limited by legislation. As Rome developed, other major magistracies were created to relieve the Consuls of their duties in specific spheres, but the principle of the *imperium* remained—each such magistrate had full power within his own sphere, subject to the same limitations and subject also to the veto of magistrates superior to him. How sweeping this power was can be seen from the fact that it was only by legislation that a citizen had the right of appeal to the Assembly from a magisterial order for his execution.

The magistracy which most vitally concerned the private law was the Praetorship, created in 367 B.C. to take over that part of the Consuls' duties which concerned civil (as opposed to criminal) jurisdiction. The Praetor was thenceforth responsible for the administration of the civil law, though the period of his great formative influence upon it was not to come for another two centuries. In about 242 B.C. a division of his functions became necessary and thereafter two Praetors were appointed. One had jurisdiction in cases in which both parties were citizens and was called the Urban Praetor (*praetor urbanus*), and the other had jurisdiction in cases in which at least one party was a foreigner (*peregrinus*), and was called the Peregrine Praetor (*praetor peregrinus*, or, in full, *praetor qui inter peregrinos ius dicit*). In the later Republic the number of Praetors was greatly increased, but only these two were concerned with the private law.

The two Curule Aediles, also appointed for the first time in 367 B.C., were the magistrates responsible for what might be called public works in the city, and also for the corn supply, but their importance for the private law lies in their control of the market place, in connexion with which they exercised a limited civil jurisdiction. This jurisdiction enabled them to make an important contribution to the law of sale.[1]

The Censors, first appointed in 443 B.C., were appointed every four or five years and held office for not more than eighteen months. They had no direct concern with the law, but they exercised a general supervision over morals which might form an important supplement to the law. This supervision of morals derived from their main function, which was the taking of the census. This involved the allotting of each citizen to his appropriate group for political and military purposes and for taxation. In carrying out this duty the Censors might place a mark (*nota*) against the name of any man of whose conduct, in public or in

[1] See below, pp. 181 f.

private life, they disapproved, and this would usually have the effect, *inter alia*, of virtually disenfranchising him. Their discretion was quite unrestricted: we hear of the affixing of the *nota* for abuse of paternal power, for luxurious living, for bad husbandry, for desertion in the army, or for improper conduct as a magistrate. This power was even more important in the discharge by the Censors of their function of revising the list of members of the Senate, a function which was transferred to them from the Consuls probably in the fourth century B.C. They enjoyed in consequence a prestige exceeding even that of the Consuls,[1] and from the middle of the third century B.C. they were drawn almost exclusively from among those who had already held the consulship. In the last fifty years of the Republic, however, the office was in decay, and no Censors were appointed after 22 B.C., though the Emperors continued to exercise the power of the *nota*.

The Senate was a council of elders, recruited in historical times almost entirely from the ranks of ex-magistrates and numbering until the last century of the Republic three hundred. In form its function was merely advisory, but it came in substance to be the most powerful element in the constitution. For the Assembly, as we shall see, had no power of initiative, and a magistrate, holding office only for a year, would rarely act against the assembled wisdom of the Senate, the more so as he could only do this to any purpose if he could carry with him his colleague.

The Assembly was a very different body from a modern legislature. Like all ancient assemblies it was composed not of representatives but of the entire citizen body. An even more important difference was its lack of initiative. It was presided over by a magistrate who alone could convene it and who alone decided what motions should be put before it. There were no 'private members' bills' and no power of amendment. The Assembly could only accept or reject a proposal put before it by the magistrate, and that proposal would previously have been debated and approved by the Senate. Further, though every citizen was entitled to vote, voting was by groups, not by heads: there was no principle of one man one vote. It was this group voting which had enabled the Patricians to retain their supremacy

---

[1] They had however no *imperium*.

during the struggle between the Orders. For the voting groups were so 'weighted' as to give the Patricians a majority.

To speak of the Assembly in the singular is in fact inaccurate. There were three assemblies of the whole people, differing in the unit on which the voting group was based. The precise nature of each voting unit is uncertain, and from the viewpoint of the private law unimportant. The earliest assembly was the *comitia curiata*, in which voting was by thirty *curiae* (perhaps a territorial unit), but in historical times this had only a vestigial political function. It retained, as we shall see, some formal importance in the private law, but for this purpose the *curiae* were simply represented by thirty lictors, the attendants of the magistrates. The politically effective assemblies were the *comitia centuriata* and the *comitia tributa*, the voting unit in the one having probably a basis of wealth related in some way to military organization, and in the other a territorial basis.

There existed also an assembly of the Plebeians alone, the *concilium plebis*, the voting unit of which had the same basis as that of the *comitia tributa*. It was presided over by special Plebeian magistrates, the Tribunes, but its resolutions (*plebiscita*) had originally no legal effect. Even this, however, was eventually conceded. For the last act in the struggle between the Orders was the *lex Hortensia* of 287 B.C., which enacted that *plebiscita* should have full legislative force. There were thus three effective legislative bodies: the *comitia centuriata* and the *comitia tributa* consisting of the whole citizen body, and the *concilium plebis* consisting of the Plebeians alone. The latter, however, came to be the normal legislative organ because the Tribunes had more time for such duties than the Consuls or Praetors who presided over the *comitia*.

This concession of legislative power to the inferior section of the population is at first sight surprising, but the Patricians must by this time have constituted only a very small proportion of the citizen body, and the old contrast between Patrician and Plebeian was already out of date. For the struggle between the Orders had been substantially settled eighty years earlier, by the *leges Liciniae Sextiae* of 367 B.C. This legislation conceded the main economic demands of the Plebeians and also their most important political demand, that one of the Consuls must in each year be a Plebeian; and it was not long before Plebeians were admitted to all magistracies. It was, however, only the wealthier Plebeians who benefited from this political emancipation, and what in fact emerged from the struggle was not a classless society, but a new nobility based on office. The distinction was now not between Patrician and Plebeian but between those families whose members had held one of the higher magistracies and those which could point to no such distinction. It came to be unusual for a man to secure election to one of the higher magistracies unless one of his ancestors had held such office, and since, as we have seen, the holding of office came also to be the key to admission to the Senate, there emerged a Senatorial nobility. New men, such as Cicero, might break in to this circle of governing families, but the achievement was one of which a man could be justifiably proud.[1]

The later Republic. The most important phase of internal political strife may therefore be said to have ended in 367 B.C., and in the next century and a half Rome turned her energies to territorial expansion. By 272 B.C. her control over Italy[2] was virtually complete—partly by direct rule, partly by nominal but unequal alliances—and Rome faced Carthage, her only rival for the control of the Western Mediterranean. In two wars (264–241, 218–201 B.C.) Carthage was eventually defeated, but at heavy cost to Rome in life and in the dislocation of Italian agriculture. As a result of these two wars, however, Rome acquired her first provinces—territories outside Italy which were placed under the government of a magistrate with *imperium*. The first province was Sicily, created in 241 B.C.; Sardinia was added ten years later, and two provinces in Spain at the end of the second war with Carthage. It is no coincidence that it was in this period also that the number of peregrines in Rome increased to such an extent as to make necessary, as we have seen, the appointment of the *Praetor peregrinus* to exercise jurisdiction in cases in which they were parties.

The final destruction of Carthage as a city and as a power did not come until 146 B.C., but in 201 Rome was clearly established

---

[1] Of the 200 Consuls of the century before the tribunate of Tiberius Gracchus (123–122 B.C.), 159 came from 26 families, and, of these, 99 came from only 10 families.

[2] In Roman terminology 'Italy' did not extend much to the north of the modern Florence. Beyond was Gaul.

as the dominant power in the Western Mediterranean. Almost immediately, despite the depletion of her resources, Rome found herself at war in the East, with Macedonia. War with Syria followed, and the result of some seventy years of intermittent fighting was the creation of new provinces in Greece and Asia Minor, and, after the final destruction of Carthage, in North Africa.

This period of territorial expansion in the second century B.C., and Rome's meeting with the older civilization and commercial wealth of the Near East, had far-reaching consequences in Roman history. Rome became a great commercial power, and capital flowed in from the East and from the other new provinces. And not the least important form that this capital took was slaves in vast numbers. This influx of wealth, coupled with the depletion of the citizen body at home—partly by constant wars and partly by emigration to the newly conquered territories—changed the face of Italy. It was no longer a country of yeomen farmers; the land came more and more into the hands of the rich, who cultivated it in large estates with slave labour. This replacement of the small holding by the large estate was accompanied by a radical change in the use to which the land was put. Egypt and North Africa could now supply corn in larger quantities and more cheaply than could Italy, and Italian landowners therefore concentrated on those products (principally the grape and the olive) which would find the best market overseas and which at the same time were best suited to exploitation by the farmer with capital.

All this in turn produced a great change in Roman society. The old compact citizen body had disappeared. There was now a gulf between the wealthy man of capital and the poor. Now for the first time there emerged a proletariat. For many of those citizens who had lost their land and who had not migrated drifted to Rome and existed as best they could, often as the 'clients', or hangers-on, of a wealthy man.

Rome also now felt the full impact of Greek culture. Roman literature, until now slight, began to grow. The models and the inspiration were Greek, the educated man learned Greek, and Greek philosophy began its influence on Roman life. But there was also a debit side to the account of Greek influence on Rome. Greek morals were laxer and more sophisticated than the simple

code by which the Roman had hitherto been guided. His introduction to this new world of wealth and loose standards was
too sudden, and a moral degeneration began.

In the later years of the second century the Republican
structure began to break down. It was plain that a state
dependent for her strength, as Rome was, on her citizen army
could not afford to see her citizen body degenerate into a land-
less proletariat dependent on the rich man's dole. But the rich
filled the Senate, and no reform was possible. Indeed a public
corn-dole was instituted for citizens, and this secured the per-
petuation of a proletariat interested only in 'bread and circuses'.
The next step followed before the century was out. Citizens were
no longer sufficiently numerous or sufficiently willing to fill the
army, and Rome had to resort to the use of a professional army
drawn from the lowest class of the citizen body. Henceforward
any ambitious general, with an army prepared to serve him as
long as he could pay them and with the means to secure by
largess the votes of the populace in Rome, could make himself
virtually master of the Empire. A succession of such generals
provides the pattern of the last century of the Republic. Further
sources of danger were a mutinous slave population on the great
estates, with little to lose by revolt, and Rome's Italian allies, re-
sentful at her refusal to grant them the citizenship. This griev-
ance came to a head in the frightful Social War of 91–88 b.c.,
which resulted militarily in victory for Rome but politically in
the concession of what she had fought to refuse—citizenship
for all Italy.

And yet in this period territorial expansion continued without
pause. The frontiers were pushed forward to the Channel, the
Rhine, the Danube, and the Euphrates, and each fresh conquest
brought in new wealth. In this period also and in the years immediately following came the finest flowering of Roman literature.

From the succession of contending generals, and from the
civil wars to which their contentions gave rise, there eventually
emerged alone Octavian, better known by his title of honour,
Augustus. The constitution had long been in effect in suspense,
but in 27 b.c., with peace restored, he claimed to have restored
constitutional government. The restored constitution was only
in form, however, Republican, and it is from this moment that
we date the beginning of the Empire.

The Empire is usually divided into two periods, that of the Principate (27 B.C.–A.D. 284) and that of the Dominate or absolute monarchy which followed.

The Principate. Julius Caesar had been assassinated because he made too naked an assertion of personal power. Augustus learned the lesson of Caesar's fall, and dressed his power in Republican forms. There was no ostensible alteration in the constitution. The magistracies remained; what was new was the concentration in the hands of Augustus of powers which had never before been held by one man, and the fact that he held them in practice for life. He was in form merely *princeps*—first citizen—but in substance his authority extended into every department of government. The popular assemblies were not abolished, but were allowed gradually to die. Their acts were never more than ratifications of the wishes of the Emperor, and they became progressively rarer as the Principate wore on, disappearing altogether by the end of the first century A.D. By contrast, the power of the Senate was, formally at least, enhanced. Political authority was shared between Emperor and Senate, so that the constitution of the Principate has been described as a dyarchy, but there was never any doubt as to which was the predominant member of the partnership. The legislative power which had formerly belonged to the assemblies passed now to the Senate, so that by the early second century A.D. it was beyond question that its resolutions (*senatusconsulta*) had the force of law. But here too the effective voice was that of the Emperor: the Senate was virtually his mouthpiece.

The Emperor's authority rested ultimately on the army and on the popular fear of what seemed the only alternative—a return to the disorder and civil war of the closing years of the Republic. The fact of the army's power was made plain in A.D. 69, when on Nero's death four generals were proclaimed Emperor by their troops in different parts of the Empire. But this was only a momentary glimpse of the truth. For the last of the four, Vespasian, succeeded in establishing a new dynasty, and there followed a hundred years of largely unbroken peace, prosperity, and good government. Yet the seeds of future troubles were being sown. The centre of balance of the Empire was being shifted from Italy and from the old Roman families.

Several of the successors of Vespasian came from provincial families—Roman by blood, but long settled in the provinces. (It was not until the end of the second century that the first Emperor of non-Roman blood, Septimius Severus, appeared, and he, ironically enough, was of Carthaginian descent.) The imperial civil service, on whom increasingly devolved the effective powers of government, was drawn largely from freedmen[1] or the descendants of freedmen—men, therefore, not of Roman stock. More important still was the change in the composition of the army. The recruits came increasingly not merely from outside Italy but from the frontier peoples of the north, peoples without Roman traditions and with more affinity with the potential enemies of Rome than with Rome herself.

The seeds which were thus sown bore fruit in the last hundred years of the Principate. Marcus Aurelius, the last of the great Emperors of the second century, died in 180. For nearly twenty years there had been trouble on the frontiers—invasions across the Rhine and the Danube, wars with Persia. Now, if ever, the Empire needed a good ruler, but it was disappointed. Commodus rivalled the worst excesses of Nero, even appearing in the arena as a gladiator, while the treasury was exhausted and the food supply in Rome broke down. His assassination in 192 was followed by a brief period of anarchy which was ended, as before, by the seizure of the throne by a soldier, Septimius Severus. Once again the army ruled the Empire and demanded its reward from the Emperor it had created. To meet these and other demands Septimius Severus and his successors resorted to wild taxation and devaluation of the currency. This period of economic crisis, accompanied by frontier wars, culminated in 235 in a collapse of imperial authority. The following fifty years saw a bewildering succession of Emperors or claimants to the title, very few of whom died a natural death. The Empire was torn by civil wars and subjected to invasions along its frontiers. The result was economic and political chaos. If Rome's enemies had been sufficiently politically developed to seize their opportunities, the history of Rome might well have ended in the third century. Towards the end of this period, however, a few strong Emperors began to restore order, and their work was completed

[1] i.e. slaves who had been given their freedom. See below, pp. 75 f.

by Diocletian (284–305), whose reign is customarily taken to mark the opening of the Dominate.

The Dominate. The Dominate is so called because the last vestiges of the Republican constitution and of the Emperor as merely the first citizen were cast aside, and the Emperor was openly accepted as *dominus,* as lord and master of the Roman world. In this, however, the division of history into periods is even more than usually misleading. The fact of the absolute power of the Emperor—that the constitution was, as it has been put, 'an autocracy tempered by the legal right of revolution'—had been manifest for a century and more. Diocletian's work was not, any more than that of Augustus had been, one of sweeping innovation. Both merely brought together what had grown up in the confusion of the age and made it into a system. The achievement of Diocletian, as of Augustus, was to take facts as he found them and order them into a constitutional form.

The Empire in the third century had suffered from three defects, political, administrative, and economic. Politically, the Emperor was at the mercy of the army; he had continually to be on his guard against the setting up of a usurper who would offer the soldiers more attractive terms. Administratively, a single central authority was not capable of ruling so widespread an Empire, still less of repelling invasions along perhaps ten thousand miles of frontier. Economically, the heavy increase in taxation, in a period when invasion and civil war had drastically weakened the ability of the tax-payer to meet the imperial demands, had led to a continual devaluation of the currency, with its attendant evils. The character of the later Empire is in part summed up in the remedies which Diocletian found for these three defects.

For the political defect the remedy was the completion of the Emperor's transformation from *princeps* to *dominus.* He was now a monarch in the oriental style, appearing rarely, hedged about with an elaborate ceremonial maintained by a numerous court, a figure whose every aspect was sacred and on entering whose presence even the highest in the land must prostrate himself. The forms of Republican government were finally discarded. All power was in the Emperor and was administered by him through a civil service responsible only to him. The Senate lost even the appearance of legislative power and dwindled to scarcely more than the municipal council of Rome. The Consuls survived, but their office was purely honorific. They could indeed claim a certain immortality because it was by their names that the years were still dated; and they had also the costly duty of providing the games for the city. So burdensome indeed did this duty become that in 541 Justinian abolished the office.

The administrative defect of overcentralization was met by a division and sub-division of the Empire. For future history the most important feature of this was Diocletian's sharing of his power with a co-Emperor, Maximian, Diocletian administering the Eastern part of the Empire and Maximian the West. This feature did not, however, become permanent until 395, and even then it was not a division of the Empire: it was a division of the rule of an undivided Empire. All legislation, even though the work of one Emperor, was issued under the names of both. Division was carried even further. For each Emperor appointed an assistant, a Caesar, who administered a part of his territory and was marked out as his successor. And under the Emperors and their Caesars there was an administrative hierarchy of four prefectures, each divided into dioceses, which were in turn divided into provinces.

To remedy the economic ills the Emperors resorted to compulsion and to state control. State factories were common, and the state regulated the internal and external commerce of the Empire. A rigid hereditary class system grew up. For example, the son of an artisan was bound to his father's trade, and peasants were commonly tied to the land in the manner of the medieval villein.

With Diocletian's successor, Constantine, the Roman Empire becomes the Byzantine Empire. He created in Byzantium a New Rome, thenceforth known as Constantinople, to which in 330 he transferred his capital. The shift in the centre of gravity of the Empire from West to East was thus finally recognized. And seventeen years earlier he had taken the far more momentous step of ending the persecution of the Christians and granting imperial favour to the new religion. There then began the close association of Emperor and Church which was to be so marked a feature of the Byzantine Empire.

By the end of the fourth century the Western Empire was

threatened. In 410 Rome was sacked by the Goths, and there-after successive invasions reduced the imperial power to a shadow. We place the end of the Western Empire in 476, when the Emperor Romulus Augustulus was deposed.

So it was that when, in 527, Justinian succeeded to the throne, he ruled over a Roman Empire of which Rome was no longer a part. But Justinian was a man with a vision, the vision of restoring the glory of the Roman Empire. He set out to recover its lost territories and to revive and perpetuate its greatest intellectual achievement, the Roman law. His territorial ambitions were only momentarily realized: he restored the imperial rule to Italy, North Africa, and southern Spain, but he had over-estimated the strength of the Empire, and his conquests did not last. The law, however, he did perpetuate, but in a way which he could not foresee.

II. SOURCES OF THE LAW

The term 'sources of law' is used in many senses. Here it denotes the ways in which law was made, as opposed to what may be called the literary sources, which are the historical evidence for what the law was. The sources of Roman law may be broadly classified under three heads: statutes, edicts of magistrates, and the *interpretatio* of the jurists.

I. STATUTES

Lex and plebiscitum. By 'statute' we mean an express enactment of a general rule by a legislator or a legislative body. We have seen that under the Republican constitution there were three legislative bodies—the *comitia centuriata*, the *comitia tributa*, and the *concilium plebis*. An enactment of the *comitia* in either of its forms was known as *lex*,[1] an enactment of the *concilium plebis*

---

[1] In contrast with *lex*, *ius* is the unenacted law. English does not possess two words for these two senses of 'law', and the use of one word to translate both *lex* and *ius* can therefore be misleading. (The word 'law' is not derived from *lex*.) On the other hand *ius*, at any rate in later usage, has two meanings, corresponding to the English 'law' and 'right' (as a noun). The same terminological features are found in modern European languages other than English. Thus, French distinguishes between *loi* and *droit*, but uses *droit* also to mean 'right'. It is the same with the Italian *legge* and *diritto* and (more surprisingly) the German *Gesetz* and *Recht*. It is therefore customary to qualify *droit*, *diritto*, *Recht*, &c., as 'objective' and 'subjective' when the distinction between 'law' and 'right' is intended.

as *plebiscitum*. But this terminology was not at all strictly observed, and *plebiscita* were commonly referred to as *leges*.

The layman when he thinks of law commonly thinks first of statute law. But in the history both of the Roman law and, at any rate until recently, of the Common law, statutes have played a very minor part in the development of the private law. It has been 'lawyers' law' in the sense that its formation has been left very largely in the hands of the professional lawyers—the courts in England, the jurists in Rome. And yet, paradoxically, to the Roman the foundation of all his law was the Twelve Tables, and they were pre-eminently *lex*.

The Twelve Tables were an early product of the struggle between the Orders. The law was at that time administered by Patrician magistrates, and evidently even the knowledge of its contents was denied to the populace at large. One of the demands of the Plebeians was therefore for the publication of the law. The traditional story—compounded in what proportions of legend and of fact we do not know—is that in 451 B.C., after a delegation had been sent to Greece to study the legislation of Solon, ten men compiled a code which was set up in the market-place on ten bronze tablets. A further two were added by another commission of ten in the following year (450). In a sense, therefore, the Twelve Tables were both a statute and a code, but one must beware of pressing either word too far. They were not a code in the modern sense of a complete and coherent statement of the law; and though they were in form a statute, it is unlikely that in substance they departed much from the traditional customary law. Such at least are the conclusions which it seems reasonable to draw from what evidence we have, but there is a great deal of uncertainty and conjecture in any assessment of the Twelve Tables, since our knowledge of their content is fragmentary and derives from a much later date. The original tablets are said to have perished when the Gauls burned Rome in 390 B.C., and certainly there was no official text at the end of the Republic, though there must have been many private copies. (Cicero records that in his youth boys learned them by heart at school.) We cannot be sure what proportion of the whole is represented by the surviving fragments, but their scale suggests that only the more salient rules were expressed, the main framework of the customary law being taken for granted. Procedure seems to have been dealt with in more detail than the substantive law, no doubt because it was here that the unskilled litigant was most likely to be tripped up. In spite of the story of the mission to Greece, nearly all of what survives seems to be of indigenous origin, and this accords with the remainder of the traditional account, which pictures the Plebeians as seeking not the reform of the law but its publication. However this may be, we can at least form an idea of the style of the Twelve Tables. The quotations give us a collection of very brief and abrupt imperatives. The opening passage apparently ran thus: 'If a man is summoned to court and does not go, let witnesses be called, and then let the plaintiff seize him. If he resists or runs away, let the plaintiff lay hands on him. If he is ill or aged, let the plaintiff provide an animal to carry him. If he refuses this, the plaintiff need not provide a covered carriage.'[1] Other passages run thus: 'If a man is mad, let the agnates and gentiles have control of him and his property'; 'If a man commits theft by night and is killed, let the killing be lawful.'[2]

Although *lex* was thus in a sense the foundation of the law, it played, as we have said, only a small part in its development. In the four centuries between the Twelve Tables and the end of the Republic we know of only some thirty statutes affecting the private law. The *lex Aquilia* was of fundamental importance in the law of delict, and others, especially the *lex Aebutia*, effected important reforms in the law of actions and procedure, but the remainder are for the most part significant only for the detail of the law.

Senatusconsulta.[3] We have seen that in the Republican constitution the Senate had in form no legislative power. Its resolutions (*senatusconsulta*) were merely advice to magistrates, and though this advice was unlikely to be ignored, it had no legal effect until it had been embodied either in a resolution of the assembly or

---

[1] It is impossible to express in intelligible English the abruptness of the original, which runs thus: 'Si in ius vocat, ni it, antestamino; igitur em capito. Si calvitur pedemve struit manum endo iacito. Si morbus aevitasve vitium escit, iumentum dato. Si nolet, arceram ne sternito.' That this was the opening passage is inferred from Cicero's remark that 'we learned the *si in ius vocat* as children', but the remainder of the arrangement habitually adopted in modern editions, though it is convenient for purposes of citation, is almost entirely conjectural.

[2] For another passage, see below, p. 247.

[3] Cf. above, pp. 5 and 10.

in a magisterial edict. The advent of the Principate brought no immediate change. *Senatusconsulta* continued for some time to take effect only through the medium of a magistrate's edict, but they increased in importance as the assembly withered away. It became plain that they had for practical purposes replaced the old forms of legislation, and constitutional theory accommodated itself to the new facts. Thus Gaius[1] records that in his time (the middle of the second century A.D.) *senatusconsulta* were acknowledged to have the force of *lex*, though this had been disputed in the past. When the dispute ended is uncertain: the earliest *senatusconsultum* which beyond doubt directly created law dates from the reign of Hadrian (A.D. 117–38), but the transition may have occurred much earlier.

But the life of the Senate as a substantial source of law was short. By the end of the second century even the semblance of initiative has gone. The Senate merely confirms what the Emperor puts before it, and the jurists when they wish to refer to the measure thus passed speak of it simply as a speech (*oratio*) of the Emperor. The *senatusconsultum* has merged into direct legislation by the Emperor.

Constitutiones principis. Though the *senatusconsultum* can thus be seen as a bridge between the legislative forms of the Republican constitution and the undisguised imperial power of the later Empire, this power, which is expressed in the famous maxim 'quod principi placuit legis habet vigorem',[2] was in fact acknowledged very early. Gaius, though, as we have seen, he admits the earlier existence of hesitations as to the legislative force of *senatusconsulta*, makes the no doubt politic assertion that there had never been any doubt that the pronouncements of the Emperor (*constitutiones*) had the force of *lex*.

Constitutiones took several forms, and not all were statutes in the sense in which we have used the term. Many were more akin to what an English lawyer would call precedents. The closest to statutes were *Edicta*. The Emperor held magisterial powers and therefore, like all higher magistrates, could issue

---

[1] See below, pp. 34 ff.

[2] 'What the Emperor has determined has the force of a statute.' The maxim, attributed in the Digest to Ulpian, was included in the Institutes of Justinian, and was invoked in medieval and later Europe to justify the absolute power of the prince. See below, p. 49.

edicts setting out his orders or the policy he intended to follow in his sphere; and since the sphere of the Emperor was unlimited, his edicts covered a large variety of subjects. The most famous is the *constitutio Antoniniana* (*c.* A.D. 212), which gave Roman citizenship to the bulk of the free inhabitants of the Empire. *Mandata* also had a certain general character. They were in form administrative instructions to officials, especially provincial governors, but by accumulation they formed what amounted to standing orders. These were, however, of only minor and sporadic importance for the private law. On this the Emperor's influence was most vigorously and regularly exercised through his decisions in individual cases, and these provide the great majority of surviving *constitutiones*. They took two main forms —*decreta* and *rescripta*. *Decreta* were judicial decisions of the Emperor, who exercised jurisdiction either as a trial judge or on appeal. In general there was in Rome no idea of the binding or even persuasive force of precedents, but the unique authority of the Emperor gave to his decisions the character of authentic statements of the law. *Rescripta*, on the other hand, were not judgments but written answers to questions or petitions. Such questions or petitions might be submitted either by officials or public bodies or by private individuals. Many of them would have no bearing on the private law, but it was permissible for either a judge or a litigant to seek a decision on a point of law involved in a case. There was no judgment, since there was no investigation of the facts, but the imperial ruling would determine what the decision must be if the facts were as stated in the petition. This practice of submitting a preliminary issue of law to the Emperor became increasingly common from the reign of Hadrian onwards, and a great many rescripts from the time before Constantine are preserved, mainly in the *Codex* of Justinian.[1] They vary greatly in length and complexity, and also in the difficulty of the point of law involved. Indeed one is astonished at how elementary were the questions which were sometimes submitted to the imperial chancery.[2]

---

[1] See below, p. 42.

[2] The following are short and simple examples drawn from the *Codex* of Justinian (to which the citations in brackets refer): 'The Emperors Diocletian and Maximian to Aurelius. The opinion which has prevailed is that a partnership can validly be created in which one partner contributes money and the other labour' (C. 4.37.1). 'The Emperor Alexander to Aurelius Maro, soldier. If your father sold the house

2. EDICTS OF MAGISTRATES

The power of higher magistrates to issue edicts has already been mentioned. From the edicts of those magistrates whose sphere included jurisdiction, and above all from that of the Urban Praetor, there derived the *ius honorarium* or magisterial law. This stood side by side with, and either supplemented or qualified, the *ius civile*—i.e. the traditional common law as embodied in or modified by statute and the *interpretatio* of the jurists. It was the Urban Praetor's edict which, more than any other single factor, transformed the Roman law from the rigid narrow set of rules which we see in the fragments of the Twelve Tables into the flexible and comprehensive system which was to serve the needs of Europe through many changing centuries. And it achieved this work of transformation while leaving the *ius civile* ostensibly unaltered. It reconciled conservatism with the need for change. For the Praetor had no more than any other magistrate the power to make law: his power was only over the remedies, i.e. the means by which the law was enforced. But this power enabled him indirectly to alter the law. For an understanding of this central contradiction of the Roman law some further explanation of the functions of the Praetor is necessary.

We have seen[1] that the sphere of the Praetor is the administration of the private law between citizens. Within this sphere he can be said to have a particular and a general function. The particular function is the day-to-day control of litigation; the general function is the issuing of the Edict in which he sets out the circumstances and ways in which he will discharge his particular function during his year of office. It is the general function which gives him his importance as a source of law.

The general function of the Praetor. 'Ubi ius, ibi remedium' is the modern principle. The right, not the remedy, is the primary

under duress the transaction will not be upheld, since it was not carried out in good faith; for a purchase in bad faith is void. If therefore you bring an action in your own name the provincial governor will intervene, especially since you declare that you are ready to refund to the buyer the price that was paid' (C. 4.44.1). The date, expressed by reference to the consuls for the year, was added and is usually reproduced in the *Codex*. The dates of the rescripts quoted here are A.D. 293 and 222 respectively.

[1] Above, p. 4. What follows is concerned with the Urban Praetor; for the Peregrine Praetor, see below, p. 23.

concept. The law is made up of rights (and correlative duties), and remedies are merely the procedural clothing of these rights. But this was not the approach of the Roman lawyer. He thought in terms of remedies rather than of rights, of forms of action rather than of causes of action. A claim could only be pursued in a court of law if it could be expressed in a recognized form. In the same way it has been said that it was with writs and not with rights that the older English law was concerned. The difference is of course mainly one of emphasis, but it has the important practical consequence that the man who controls the granting of remedies controls also the development of the law. In Rome that man was the Praetor. By creating a new form of action or extending an old form to new facts he could in effect create new rights. In form there was merely a new remedy, in substance there was new law.

For the first two centuries of his existence, however, this power of the Praetor lay dormant. A claim could be initiated only in one or other of five ritual modes recognized by statute (*legis actiones*). The Praetor could, it seems, neither create new forms of action nor extend the existing *legis actiones* to claims not recognized by the law. He only began to make his influence felt when a new and more flexible system of actions—the formulary system—was introduced. This system, which was the framework of the Roman law throughout its classical period, is remarkable for its simplicity, economy, and adaptability. By the use of a very small number of typical 'parts' or elements, the essentials of any dispute could be concisely and clearly expressed.

The characteristics of this system were that for each cause of action there was an appropriate form of action, and that each action was expressed in a set of words or *formula*, which constituted the pleadings.[1] Thus, if there had been a contract of sale (*emptio venditio*) and the seller refused to deliver what he had sold, the buyer had an action on the purchase (*actio empti*), and conversely if the buyer refused to pay the price, the seller had an action on the sale (*actio venditi*); and each action had an appropriate *formula* in which the issue was defined. It was this principle that each cause of action should have its appropriate form of action which gave the Praetor his opportunity. For obviously if he could create new forms of action he

[1] See further below, pp. 23 ff.

could thereby in substance create new causes of action; and the structure of the *formula* was such that it could comfortably accommodate any new action which he might thus create.

Precisely how and when the formulary system was introduced is uncertain. The decisive step was evidently taken by statute—a *lex Aebutia*. What evidence there is suggests that this *lex* must have been passed in the first three-quarters of the second century B.C., and most probably towards the end of this period, but all that is certain is that in the last quarter of the second century the new system was in force, and with it the Praetor's free power to create new actions. Nor is it surprising that this crucial innovation should have occurred in the period when so much else in Roman life, and particularly in Roman economic and commercial life, was on the move. The rigid system of the *legis actiones* and the narrow *ius civile* which it enforced could never have met the needs of the emerging Roman Empire.

The principal instrument by which the work of adaptation was carried out was the Praetor's Edict. At the beginning of his year of office the Praetor issued an Edict which consisted of a series of statements of policy (themselves referred to as edicts). These individual edicts varied greatly in length and complexity and to some extent in grammatical structure, but the purpose of all was to define the circumstances in which the Praetor would exercise his power to grant new remedies.[1] In theory each Praetor's Edict was independent of his predecessor's and was valid only for his year of office, but obviously a system in which a substantial part of the law changed every year would be unworkable, and though in the earlier years there was no doubt a certain amount of experimentation, the main body of the Edict was carried over from year to year, successive Praetors making only such additions and deletions as seemed necessary.[2]

---

[1] The following are among the shorter edicts: 'If there is an allegation of fraud (*dolus malus*) and no other action will lie, then, if good cause is shown and not more than a year has elapsed since the plaintiff was in a position to sue I shall give an action.' 'If it is alleged that anyone has in bad faith harboured or incited another's slave, male or female, so as to diminish his or her value, I shall give an action against him for double damages.'

[2] The Edict which was thus carried over and made permanent was called *edictum tralaticium*. The term *edictum perpetuum* (continuous) was applied to the Edict which was issued at the beginning of the year and which was to be continuously in operation throughout the year, as opposed to edicts which might be issued for particular purposes in the course of the year.

In this way the Edict acquired the character, though not the form, of a legislative document, to be commented on and expounded by the jurists. It must also have been the jurists who were substantially responsible for its contents, since the Praetor would not usually be learned in the law and would therefore rely upon the advice of those who were.[1] This natural inclination must, moreover, have been reinforced by the Roman habit of consulting an informal council of advisers before making any important decision in public or private life.[2]

In addition to the statements of policy, the Edict contained pattern *formulae* for each of the remedies promised and also for those which already existed to enforce the traditional *ius civile*. Of these last there was no other mention in the Edict, since it was superfluous for the Praetor to declare that he would carry out his primary function, the enforcement of the *ius civile*.

The publication of the Edict did not exhaust the Praetor's power to innovate. He could at any time, if he thought fit, either on the facts of a particular case or on more general grounds, grant a new remedy. Such remedies would often presumably be made permanent in the next year's Edict.

The building of the Edict seems largely to have been completed by the end of the Republic. In the first century of the Empire the initiative in the development of the law was increasingly left to the interpretative activity of the jurists and to the various forms of imperial intervention. It was indeed inconsistent with the emerging constitution of the Empire that a magistrate should have what amounted to legislative power, and it was, once again, in the reign of Hadrian that the new facts were openly acknowledged and given permanent form. The great jurist Julian[3] was commissioned to make a final revision of the Edict, which thenceforth was not to be altered. The career of the Praetor as a source of law was thus terminated. The only way in which the *ius honorarium* could develop was by juristic interpretation of the words of this final Edict, or by the granting of new 'Praetorian' remedies by the Emperor.

---

[1] For example, Cicero tells us that his friend Aquilius Gallus, who was a distinguished jurist, 'produced the *formulae* concerning *dolus*', which had a profound effect on the law. Aquilius Gallus did hold the rank of Praetor (in 66 B.C.), but apparently not as either Urban or Peregrine Praetor. He presumably 'produced' them in his capacity as jurist.

[2] Cf. below, pp. 67 and 85.   [3] See below, pp. 29 f.

The Urban Praetor's Edict was not the only source of *ius honorarium*. The Peregrine Praetor also issued an Edict, and many of the features which we find in the Urban Praetor's Edict may well have originated in that of his colleague. For the Peregrine Praetor, since he did not work within the framework of the traditional law, must have built faster and more freely than the Urban Praetor. But any statement about the content of the Peregrine Edict must be conjectural, since no part of it survives and even indirect evidence is very slight. Our knowledge of the Urban Edict derives from the extracts from juristic commentaries on it which make up a substantial part of Justinian's Digest, and which often quote the actual words of the provision on which they are commenting. Of the commentaries on the Peregrine Edict, however, no fragments survive, and the reason for this must be that after the almost universal grant of citizenship in A.D. 212[1] it ceased to have any practical relevance.

We know equally little about the Edicts by which provincial governors extended the *ius honorarium* to the Roman citizens living in their provinces. Gaius wrote a commentary 'on the Provincial Edict', and from the use of the singular we must infer that there was at any rate a substantial part which was common to every Governor's Edict. The few fragments of this commentary which survive in the Digest do not suggest any marked divergence from the Urban Edict. Of the Curule Aediles' Edict, on the other hand, we are relatively fully informed, but its importance was confined to the contract of sale and to a special provision concerning liability for animals. For all these reasons it is convenient here to confine our attention to the *ius honorarium* which derived from the Urban Edict.

The particular function of the Praetor. The Praetor's day-to-day function was the granting of remedies in individual cases. In any system of litigation there must be something to correspond to what the English lawyer calls pleadings, some method of ensuring that the issues between the parties are clearly defined before the actual trial begins. In the formulary system the place of pleadings was taken by the *formula*. The proceedings in an action were divided (as they had also been under the system of *legis actiones*) into two stages. The first took place before the

[1] See above, p. 18.

Praetor (*in iure*) and was devoted to the drawing up of the *formula*, and the second took place before a *iudex* or lay arbitrator (*apud iudicem*) and was devoted to the trial of the issues set out in the *formula*. The Praetor's function was therefore not to try the action but to satisfy himself that it could be expressed in a *formula* included in his Edict, or, exceptionally, to grant a new *formula* to meet the facts of the case. The *formula* consisted essentially of a direction to the *iudex* to condemn the defendant if he found the plaintiff's case proved and to absolve him if he did not. An example will make this clearer.

Let us suppose that the plaintiff's claim is that the defendant promised by *stipulatio* (the principal formal contract of the *ius civile*)[1] to pay him 10,000 sesterces and that the defendant has not done so. The parties appear *in iure*, no doubt with their legal advisers. The plaintiff then asks for the grant of the appropriate action, the *condictio certae pecuniae*, the *formula* of which, as set out in the Edict, runs as follows: 'Let *X* be *iudex*. If it appears that the defendant ought to pay 10,000 sesterces to the plaintiff, let the *iudex* condemn the defendant to pay 10,000 sesterces to the plaintiff. If it does not so appear, let the *iudex* absolve him.'[2] If the defendant's answer is a simple denial that he owes the plaintiff the sum stated (either because he never made the *stipulatio* as alleged, or because he has already paid the debt, or for some other reason recognized by the *ius civile*) he will simply accept the *formula*, since his answer is contained in its last sentence: 'It does not appear.' He may, however, wish to allege a circumstance which, although it does not by the *ius civile* invalidate the *stipulatio*, does according to the Edict afford a ground for the grant of a Praetorian plea in bar of the action (*exceptio*). For example, he may wish to assert that the plaintiff subsequently agreed that he need not pay the debt. Such a bare

---

[1] See below, pp. 193 ff.

[2] This *formula* is the one exception to the principle stated above (p. 20), that each cause of action had its appropriate form of action. See further below, p. 229. It is chosen here for its simplicity. The *formulae* of other actions *in personam* (below, pp. 99 ff.), though in essential structure the same, are more elaborate and always state the cause or ground of the defendant's alleged duty to the plaintiff. For example, if the plaintiff's claim were that he had sold the defendant a slave and that the defendant had not paid the price, the *formula* would run: 'In so far as the plaintiff sold to the defendant the slave Stichus, whatever on that account the defendant ought to convey to or do for the plaintiff in accordance with good faith, to that extent let the *iudex* condemn', &c., as above.

agreement (*pactum*) had no effect under the *ius civile*:[1] the defendant should have secured a formal release (*acceptilatio*).[2] It was, however, a recurrent theme of Praetorian policy to give effect to the intention rather than the form of an act, and the Edict in circumstances such as these promised an *exceptio pacti* to bar the plaintiff's enforcement of his right. For this, therefore, the defendant will now ask, and the enlarged *formula* will run: 'If it appears that the defendant ought to pay 10,000 sesterces to the plaintiff, unless there was an agreement between the plaintiff and the defendant that the money should not be claimed, let the *iudex* condemn', &c., as above. Once again, if the plaintiff's reply to this *exceptio* is a simple denial, nothing further need be added to the *formula*; but if he in turn wishes to raise a countervailing plea recognized in the Edict, this will be inserted as a further conditional clause (*replicatio*) following on the *exceptio*, 'or unless . . .'. To this the defendant may add a still further reply, still in the same grammatical form, and so forth until each party's case is fully stated.[3] When the pleadings are thus completed the *iudex* is chosen by agreement between the parties from an official list of well-to-do laymen who undertake this function as a public duty. The whole *formula* is then put into writing and finally approved by the Praetor. This is the moment of joinder of issue (*litis contestatio*), i.e. the moment by reference to which the issues between the parties must be decided and after which there can be no alteration of the pleadings and no fresh action on the same issue.

At some time after *litis contestatio* the hearing of the case by the *iudex* took place. The parties were represented by advocates and adduced evidence, either documentary or oral, but there were no such strict rules of evidence or procedure as govern the trial of an English action. Within the limits of the *formula* the *iudex* had a wide discretion. He was judge of both fact and law, and took what advice he chose in arriving at a decision. Since he was not a jurist, he would be guided in matters of law by the opinions of those who were.[4] His decision was binding as between the parties, but since the Roman law knew no system of precedent, it had no wider significance.

---

[1] See below, pp. 191 ff. [2] See below, pp. 198 f.
[3] The pleading was simpler in *bonae fidei* actions. See below, p. 163.
[4] As to the binding character of the opinions of patented jurists, see below, p. 31.

Character of the ius honorarium. Papinian, in a famous definition preserved in the Digest, declares that the Praetorian law supports, supplements, and corrects the *ius civile*. It cannot directly alter or abrogate it, for the Praetor, as we have seen, has no legislative power. He supports the civil law[1] by giving on occasion a more effective remedy; he supplements it by giving a remedy in circumstances when the civil law is silent; most importantly he corrects it, and this he does either, as in the case which we have just considered, by merely granting an *exceptio* to bar the enforcement of a civil law right, or, more extensively, by both denying a remedy to a person who is entitled by the civil law and giving a remedy to a person who is not. In substance he has made law, but in form he has merely barred or created a remedy. The difference is primarily one of pleading and of the formulation of remedies. Thus, in the example we have just considered the Praetor has in substance declared that a right created by *stipulatio* is extinguished by a subsequent agreement not to sue, just as the civil law declares that it is extinguished by *acceptilatio*, but there is a difference in pleading. If the defendant wishes to allege an agreement not to sue he must plead it expressly by way of *exceptio*, whereas if he wishes to allege an *acceptilatio* he need not, since in that case there is no longer any debt. Similarly, where the Praetor gives an action to a person who has no right by the civil law, it has to be so formulated, often by the use of a fiction, as not to allege that the plaintiff has a right. These are technical matters, but in a system as dominated by its forms of action as the Roman they colour the whole formulation of the law and make it necessary to state both the civil law and the Praetorian modification of it, rather than simply their combined result. Moreover, on occasion the distinction between civil and Praetorian law has consequences which are more than merely technical. One such occasion may be mentioned here by way of example. By the civil law the ownership of a slave could only be transferred by a formal conveyance and not by a simple delivery.[2] If therefore A sold and delivered his slave to B but omitted the formal conveyance,

---

[1] The term 'civil law' is hereafter used, unless the context indicates otherwise, to denote *ius civile* as contrasted with *ius honorarium* (see below, p. 59). Modern Civil law (see above, p. 2) is indicated by the use of the capital letter.

[2] See below, pp. 105 f.

no ownership could pass, and by the civil law A could claim the slave from B or from anyone else into whose hands he might come. The Praetor, however, giving effect to intention rather than to form, would bar A's action against B and would also give B an action against A or anyone else who was in possession of the slave. In other words, B had the remedies of an owner and A had not. For most purposes, therefore, it is substantially correct to say that B is the owner; but not for all. If B were to manumit the slave, his act would have no effect by the civil law. For only an owner could manumit, and A was still the owner. The Praetor could indeed prevent B from going back on his act by asserting title to the slave, but he could not give to the slave the legal rights of a free man.[1]

Actions and procedure of the late law. When, with the consolidation of the Edict by Julian,[2] the general function of the Praetor lost its importance, the particular function none the less continued. But already there was growing up beside the formulary system another system of procedure more akin to those found in the modern world and more congenial to the increasingly bureaucratic character of the Empire. The characteristic features of the formulary procedure were that the trial was divided into two stages and that it was in form a voluntary submission to arbitration in which the only part played by the state was the approval of the *formula* and of the appointment of the *iudex*. There was no direct state enforcement of the appearance of the parties or of the execution of the judgment, and there were no professional judges. In the new, 'extraordinary', procedure (*cognitio extraordinaria*) all this was changed. The magistrate, either in person or through an official delegate (*iudex pedaneus*), heard the whole case and took steps for the enforcement of his decision. The *formula* gave place to an informal system of pleadings. This new procedure was introduced at first only for particular purposes. For example, when Augustus decided to give effect to informal testamentary trusts (*fideicommissa*)[3] he entrusted their enforcement to the consuls, and later a special *Praetor*

---

[1] See below, p. 74, n. 1. There is an obvious parallel between the Praetor's control of the *formula* and the early English Chancellor's control of writs, and to a more limited extent between the *ius honorarium* and English Equity. See Buckland and McNair, *Roman Law and Common Law* (2nd edn.), pp. 4–6.

[2] See above, p. 22. [3] See below, p. 267.

fideicommissarius was appointed. By the beginning of the Dominate, however, the formulary system had disappeared and the 'extraordinary' procedure alone survived. But the law had taken shape in the mould of the *formula* and of the contrast between the *ius honorarium* and the *ius civile*, and to recast it would have required a greater zeal and capacity for reform than were to be found in the late Empire. Justinian did indeed cut away much that was obsolete, but, as we shall see, the very method and purpose of his compilation was incompatible with any radical reform. Hence it is that just as the English lawyer still very largely thinks in terms of the forms of action which were abolished a century ago, so also the greater part of Justinian's law is intelligible only in terms that had lost their practical importance two hundred and fifty years before.

3. JURISTIC INTERPRETATION

All law requires interpretation. The need is most obvious where, as in a statute or Edict or a modern Code, the law is embodied in specific words, but it is none the less present where it is not. Moreover the function of interpretation will necessarily fall to those who are in some sense professional lawyers. In England it is discharged principally by the courts. In Rome, where, in the formative period of the law, there were, as we have seen, no professional judges and no regular courts, it was discharged until perhaps the end of the fourth century B.C. by the priestly 'college' of *pontifices*, but thereafter by lay jurists.

Interpretatio prudentium. The Roman jurists have no exact parallel in the modern world. In the formative years of the later Republic they were men from the leading families who undertook the interpretation of the law as part of their contribution to public life. They were not professional men in our sense: they received no remuneration and the law was only one facet of their public career; they were statesmen who were learned in the law. In the closing years of the Republic and thereafter there was some widening of the class from which they came and a few, even of the most eminent, seem to have taken no other part in public life than as jurists, but their essential character and cast of mind remained the same. They were men of affairs, interested in practical rather than theoretical questions, and yet not immersed like the modern professional lawyer in the details of daily practice. To English eyes they have some of the characteristics of both the academic and the practising lawyer. For on the one hand they built up a great legal literature and also undertook what legal teaching there was, and on the other hand they influenced the practice of the law at every point. They advised the Praetor in the formulation of his Edict and in the granting of remedies in individual cases; they advised the *iudex* in the hearing and decision of a case; and they advised private individuals in the drawing up of documents and the making of other legal acts, and also in the conduct of cases before the Praetor or the *iudex*. But they were advisers, not practitioners, and in particular they did not appear in court to argue cases. That was the province of the advocate; and though a distinguished advocate, such as Cicero, might have a very fair knowledge of the law, his main interest was in the art of persuasion rather than in the science of law.

The jurist as we have described him was a product of Republican political and social life, and he could not remain wholly unaffected as the forms of Republican government were cast aside and the new bureaucratic structure of the Empire emerged. He retained his eminence in public life, but was now more and more commonly to be found among the highest officials in the Emperor's service. Of this new type of imperial jurist, who begins to appear towards the end of the first century A.D., Javolenus[1] provides an example. As well as passing in the old way through the Republican magistracies to the consulship, he held command successively of two legions, was the leading judicial official in Britain, and became subsequently Governor of Upper Germany, Syria, and finally Africa. Thereafter he remained in Rome as a member of the Emperor's Council under Trajan. At the same time, following in the old tradition of the jurists, he wrote, advised, and taught. One of his pupils, even more distinguished than he, both in the law and in public life, was Julian, who has already been mentioned.[2] Born in what is now Tunisia, he held a great variety of official positions: he served on the official staff of Hadrian (and was, it is recorded, given double the usual salary because of his learning), was in

---

[1] L. Octavius Tidius Tossianus Javolenus Priscus.
[2] Salvius Iulianus; see above, p. 22.

charge of the state treasury and of the military treasury, was Praetor and Consul (148), and subsequently governor of Lower Germany, Nearer Spain, and Africa. He was a member of the Imperial Council in the reigns of Hadrian, Antoninus Pius, and Marcus Aurelius and Lucius Verus.

The great jurists of the early third century A.D., to whom we owe most of the surviving legal literature, were even closer to the centre of imperial authority. Papinian,[1] often considered the greatest of the Roman jurists, is first heard of as head of the department of the imperial chancery which dealt with petitions by individuals, and from A.D. 203 until A.D. 212, when he was put to death by Caracalla, he held the most powerful appointment in the Empire, that of Prefect of the Praetorian Guard.[2] The careers of Paul and Ulpian[3] were similar. Both held the Prefectship of the Praetorian Guard under Alexander Severus (222–35), Ulpian being murdered by his own troops in 223.

Not long after this the long line of jurists ends. For half a century the very existence of the Empire is at stake, and when from this period the Dominate emerges, there is no room for individual *interpretatio*, even by jurists as identified with the Emperor's service as were Papinian, Ulpian, and Paul. The sole source of law is now the Emperor, and the place of the jurist is taken by the anonymous civil servant in the imperial chancery. The life has gone out of the Roman law.

We have mentioned only a handful of the greatest names. There were of course others, but the number is not large. In the two and a half centuries between the advent of the Principate and the disappearance of the last of the jurists we hear of only some seventy, and for nearly half of these there is little that survives but a name. Indeed the circle of jurists of the type we have been describing must always have been small. In their writings they continually refer to each other's opinions, and it is unlikely that many have escaped this network of mutual citation. On the other hand, so small a number engaged for the most part

---

[1] Aemilius Papinianus.

[2] The Prefect was very much more than the commander of the household troops: he was the Emperor's chief of staff and as such had wide powers and, in particular, a wide jurisdiction. Papinian is said to have been put to death for refusing to compose a justification of Caracalla's murder of his brother and co-Emperor, Geta, declaring, so the story goes, that 'it is easier to commit murder than to justify it'.

[3] Julius Paulus, Domitius Ulpianus.

so fully in public life can have supplied only a small part of the legal advice which was needed in so large a city as imperial Rome. There must have been many lesser lawyers, the attorneys and notaries of the ancient world, who did not aspire to the authoritative and creative position of a jurist, but earned a living in the daily practice of law both in Rome and in the provinces. We are thus faced with the question whether there was any formal distinction between the jurist as we have described him and these lesser practitioners.

Ius respondendi. We have seen that one of the functions of the jurists was to give opinions on questions of law submitted to them. How far were such opinions (*responsa*) authoritative? How far were they binding on a *iudex*? This is one of the unsolved problems of Roman law. Certainly in the Republic the matter was unregulated: a *iudex* was free to make his own assessment of the weight to be given to a *responsum*, though in doing so he would no doubt take account of the reputation of the jurist who gave it. In a passage preserved in the Digest,[1] however, Pomponius, a jurist of the reign of Hadrian, tells us that Augustus, in order to give greater authority to the law, conferred on some jurists the privilege of giving *responsa* with the Emperor's authority, and that this practice was continued by his successors. It is the nature of this *ius respondendi* which is in doubt. Pomponius does not tell us what the effect of Augustus' innovation was. It is inconceivable that Augustus, reluctant in so many other respects to make an open break with the past, should have made these *responsa* formally binding. It is more likely that he wished to mark out certain jurists as peculiarly eminent, knowing that a *iudex* would not lightly disregard this sign of imperial favour. It is even possible that only such authoritative *responsa* could be cited in court, in somewhat the same way as in an English court, at least according to the traditional rule, only the writings of dead authors may be cited. From an obscure passage of Gaius it seems that by the second century this *de facto* authority was no longer confined to *responsa* given for the particular case, but had extended to all writings of patented jurists, living or dead. This would present the scrupulous *iudex* with a difficult problem when, as would be increasingly likely, there was a

[1] See below, pp. 40 ff.

conflict of juristic opinion. Hadrian, apparently, had little sympathy with such scruples: Gaius refers to a rescript of his which declared that if juristic opinion was unanimous it had the force of *lex*, but that otherwise the *iudex* was free to choose. This must have been cold comfort to the inquirer, since the most difficult questions in law are precisely those over which learned opinion is likely to differ.

We are ignorant not only of the legal effect of the *ius respondendi*, but also of the names of the jurists who enjoyed the privilege, and how long its grant continued. One might expect it to be the mark of a particular jurist's authority, and yet it is never mentioned as such in all the surviving literature, and we are directly informed of its grant to only one jurist, Sabinus.[1] Nor can we certainly say that it continued to be granted after the reign of Hadrian. It is perhaps safest to assume that it was never more than one factor in determining the authority of a jurist, and that as the leading jurists were drawn into the direct service of the Emperor it lost what importance it originally had.

The Sabinian and Proculian schools. In the Republic there was no formal legal education. A young man learned his law by, as we should say, 'reading in chambers'. He attached himself to a jurist and, by accompanying him in his daily practice and by discussing with him the problems which emerged, he worked himself into a practical knowledge of the law. This practical oral tradition remained a feature of the Roman law, but in the Empire there emerge two 'schools' to which most if not all of the leading jurists of the first two centuries of the Empire seem to have belonged. They were founded, we are told, by two leading jurists of the reign of Augustus, Capito and Labeo, but took their names from two subsequent heads, Massurius Sabinus, already mentioned, and Proculus. They seem to have been more than merely schools of thought, but of their organization and functions we know nothing. We learn of a large number of points of law on which the two schools differed, and many of the other disputes of which we hear are probably also attributable to this conflict between the schools, but, in spite of many attempts, no convincing doctrinal basis for these differences of opinion has been found. We are driven to the conclusion that the doctrines of each school must have been an accumulation of the opinions

[1] Massurius Sabinus (see immediately below).

of successive heads of the school on different problems, preserved by tradition and adhered to out of loyalty and conservatism. The schools seem to have died out in the course of the second century, for there is no sign that the great jurists of the third century belonged to either.

Forms of legal literature. In the perspective of history the most important function of the jurists was to write, and their literature was vast and varied. We owe almost all that survives to the Digest,[1] and that, large as it is, contains only a fraction even of what still survived in Justinian's day. This literature took many forms and had many names, but it can be very broadly classified under four headings: the expository textbook, introductory or more advanced, the commentary, the problematic work, and the monograph. Only of the textbook do we possess a virtually complete example, the Institutes of Gaius.[2] The rest are preserved only in fragments, though often very substantial fragments, in the Digest and in a few small intervening compilations. The largest category in point of surviving bulk is that of the commentary. In addition to commentaries on the Edict, which contribute more than a third of the Digest, there were commentaries on individual *leges* and *senastusconsulta* and, more especially, commentaries on the works of earlier jurists. Pomponius, Paul, and Ulpian, for example, all wrote works *ad Sabinum*—commentaries on Sabinus' textbook on the *ius civile*—and works of other jurists were treated similarly. Even in such commentaries dogmatic exposition is freely interspersed with illustrations and problems, but the casuistic approach of the Roman jurist is best seen in the problematic literature, which makes up some third of the Digest. In works of this category we find loosely strung together an immense number of problems, sometimes with a citation and discussion of the opinions of other jurists, sometimes simply with the writer's own conclusion. It is this problematic literature which gives Roman law its extraordinary richness of detail. It provides the case law of the Roman system. But whereas the development of the Common law has largely depended on the appearance of problems in the actual practice of the courts, the Roman lawyer elaborated his system with the aid often of hypothetical problems. For though some

---

[1] See below, pp. 34 f. and 40 ff.   [2] See below, p. 35.

of the problems discussed arose in actual practice and were submitted to the jurist for his *responsum*, others arose in discussion with pupils, and others again were simply the product of the writer's own speculations. Some of these problems appear far-fetched, but we should remember that it is often the extreme and improbable case which reveals the limits of a principle.

An idea of the possible scope and extent of the writings of a leading jurist can be gained from the list of the known works of Paul (who seems however to have been the most voluminous of all). The list runs to some eighty works (of many of which little or nothing but the title survives) in some two hundred and seventy-five 'books'.[1] The most substantial are a commentary on the Edict in eighty books, two problematic works (*Quaestiones* and *Responsa* in twenty-six and twenty-three books respectively) and four commentaries on the works of earlier jurists in alto-gether forty-one books. The remainder consists of a short text-book, collections of imperial decisions, a dozen commentaries on individual *leges* and *senatusconsulta*, and more than fifty mono-graphs.

The 'classical period'. The great formative period of Roman law fell in the last one hundred and fifty years B.C. Growth thereafter was less rapid, and was largely completed in the work of Julian, who both by his consolidation of the Edict and by his writings summed up the developments of the preceding centuries. The work of the great jurists who followed him was one of elabora-tion and exposition. Accordingly, the period from Julian to the middle of the third century or, more widely, the period of the Principate, is commonly called the classical period of Roman law. It is from the classical period in the narrower sense that more than nine-tenths of the surviving juristic literature comes, and it is about this period therefore that we might expect to be most fully informed. This expectation, however, is disap-pointed because the literature is, with one exception, of uncertain reliability. The exception is the Institutes of Gaius.

The Institutes of Gaius. Justinian's purpose in compiling the Digest[2] was to select and preserve the best of the classical literature, but

---

[1] One 'book' would probably have occupied between thirty and fifty pages of a printed book such as this.   [2] See further below, pp. 40 ff.

in order to ensure the unquestioned authority of his compilation once it was completed, he forbade any further recourse to the original texts. These have therefore almost entirely perished. Moreover he directed his compilers to alter the texts which they used so as to make them represent the law of his own time. What we have is therefore not only fragmentary, but does not necessarily represent what the author originally wrote. An exiguous literature survived in the Western parts of the Empire, but this consisted only of post-classical compilations, altered and simplified for a civilization in which legal science was in eclipse.[1]

So it was that until 1816 no classical work was known to have survived in its original form. In that year the German scholar Niebuhr detected underneath a text of St. Jerome in the cathedral library at Verona an earlier juristic text[2] which proved to be that of the Institutes of Gaius, a student's textbook which was known to have formed the basis of Justinian's Institutes but which hitherto had been represented only by a few fragments in the Digest and elsewhere, and by an abridgement in the *lex Romana Visigothorum*.[3] Three sheets of the Veronese manuscript are missing and a number of passages remain illegible, but probably not more than a tenth is lost. And though it dates only from the fifth or sixth century it is widely held to give the text substantially as Gaius left it. This view was on the whole confirmed by the discovery in Egypt in 1933 of some pages of a manuscript of the late fourth or early fifth century. For though the new manuscript yielded a passage which had been altogether omitted from the Veronese text and another which probably occurred on one of the missing sheets, it showed no significant differences where the two manuscripts coincided. The Institutes of Gaius are therefore of unique importance because they provide the only evidence for the classical law which we can with reasonable certainty believe to be free from alteration either by post-classical editors or by Justinian's compilers. In particular, they give us a great deal of information about the *legis actiones* and the formulary system which was omitted as obsolete from post-classical work and from Justinian's compilation.

[1] See below, pp. 36 ff.
[2] As a measure of economy parchment was often re-used—sometimes more than once—by scraping or washing off an unwanted text and writing over it a new one. Such a manuscript is called a palimpsest.
[3] See below, p. 36.

The personality of Gaius remains a mystery. His prestige was great in post-classical times; his Institutes were a prescribed textbook in the law schools of the Eastern Empire; and extracts from eighteen of his works appear in the Digest. And yet we know nothing of him except what emerges from his writings. He is never mentioned by any classical writer, in spite of the jurists' liking for citing each other's opinions. Even his full name is unknown ('Gaius' is only a first name). Internal evidence suggests that he completed the Institutes soon after the death of Antoninus Pius (A.D. 161) and that he was a Roman citizen. Since he refers to the leaders of the Sabinian school as 'our teachers' he had presumably studied at Rome, and he was presumably himself a teacher. It has been suggested that he was a provincial, but all that we can reliably infer is that he was not accepted as a member of the select group of leading jurists. We have seen that there must have been many lesser lawyers outside this group; Gaius was probably one of these, rescued from oblivion by the simplicity and clarity of his exposition in the Institutes.

The post-classical period. We have seen that the day of the independent jurist ended in the upheavals of the middle of the third century. Something of the old quality could still be found in the rescripts issued from Diocletian's chancery, but the decline had already set in. It was hastened by the growth of what is called the 'vulgar law'.

By the *constitutio Antoniniana* (c. A.D. 212) the peregrine population of the Empire was accorded Roman citizenship and was therefore required to conduct its affairs according to a system of law of which it knew little or nothing. In the result, the law which was in fact applied in the provinces was a mixture of debased Roman law and local practice, varying from area to area but far removed from the refinement and elaboration of the classical law. Something of this vulgar law can be seen in the codes promulgated for their Roman subjects by the Germanic rulers in the West after the downfall of the Western Empire. Of these the most important is the *lex Romana Visigothorum*, promulgated in 506 by Alaric II, King of the Visigoths (and sometimes therefore called the Breviary of Alaric). It consists of some imperial constitutions, an abridgement of Gaius' Institutes, a selection from a post-classical and much edited anthology of the writings of Paul (the *Sententiae*), and one *responsum* of Papinian, all, except the abridgement of Gaius, accompanied by a commentary or paraphrase. The result is but a thin, distorted echo of the Roman law.

The metropolitan lawyers of the East, trained in the law schools of Beirut and Constantinople, maintained a greater continuity with the classical law, but even they were unable to manipulate the vast mass of juristic literature.[1] Doubts arose as to the authenticity and authority of different works, and these doubts eventually called forth the famous Law of Citations of A.D. 426. This singled out as authoritative the writings of Papinian, Paul, Ulpian, Modestinus, and Gaius. Where there was a conflict, the majority opinion was to be followed; if numbers were equal, Papinian's view was to prevail; only if numbers were equal and Papinian silent was the judge to decide for himself. Such a rule, if deplorably mechanical, is at least clear, but, as it is preserved, the constitution also allows quotation from any author referred to by the five principal authorities, provided that such quotation is confirmed by a comparison of manuscripts (presumably because copies of their works were scarce and of uncertain authenticity). And these secondary authorities were to be included in the calculation of majority opinion. The jurists were, as we have seen, much given to citation, and this system, if it was ever applied, must have produced entirely haphazard results, depending on the chance of how many relevant quotations could be tracked down.

The probability, however, is that the ordinary lawyer had recourse to only a very limited literature of anthologies and abridgements of classical works. A few such compilations have survived, almost all, however, from the West. The *Sententiae* of Paul have already been mentioned. The *Fragmenta Vaticana* (so called because they were found in the Vatican Library in 1821) provide the best example. These are fragments of a large fourth-

---

[1] In the constitution establishing the Theodosian Code (see below, p. 38) the Emperors lament, in the elaborate language of the time, that 'Our Clemency has often been perplexed to know the reason why, in spite of the great rewards that have been provided to nourish art and learning, so few have emerged, and so infrequently, who were fully endowed with a knowledge of the civil law, and why the gloomy pallor of their night-long labours has brought scarcely one or two to the completeness of perfected learning.'

century anthology drawn from the works of Papinian, Paul, and Ulpian, and from imperial constitutions.

The typical post-classical literary forms are thus the abridgement and the anonymous anthology. Such initiative as there was found expression in the imperial constitutions, and the ever-increasing bulk of these presented two difficulties. The first was that of reconciling the conflicts which inevitably occurred, particularly when so many constitutions were rescripts directed to individuals and concerned with particular cases. From the time of Constantine onwards there is a series of attempts to prevent the use of rescripts as precedents and to confine legislative validity to 'general' constitutions, but in a system in which the Emperor was the sole and absolute authority it was inevitable that his will, however expressed, should be regarded as law.

The second difficulty was that of obtaining access to so diffuse a mass of material. Surprising as it may seem, there had been in classical times no system of permanently accessible publication, it being presumably the function of the jurists to keep professional opinion informed. But now that such jurists had disappeared other means were necessary. The first attempt to meet the need was the publication, probably under Diocletian, of two private collections, the *Codex Gregorianus* and the *Codex Hermogenianus*. Neither survives, but constitutions are quoted from them in later collections, and the compilers of Justinian's *Codex* drew on them. It was not however until 438 that, under the auspices of Theodosius II, an official compilation was made, the *Codex Theodosianus*. This was indeed more than a compilation, since the commission entrusted with the work was directed to make alterations and amendments in the interests of clarity and consistency. It was superseded in the East by Justinian's *Codex* but it continued to be used in the West and a substantial part has been recovered from various manuscripts and from other sources, especially the *lex Romana Visigothorum*.

III. THE WORK OF JUSTINIAN

In 518 there came to the throne an elderly soldier, Justin. Born of a peasant family in what is now Yugoslavia, he had risen from the ranks despite his complete lack of education. For his relatives, however, he provided what he lacked himself: younger members of the family, and in particular the nephew and adopted son whom we know as Justinian, received the best education that Constantinople could offer.

When Justin came to the throne Justinian was thirty-six, and by his conspicuous abilities he soon acquired great influence. Already in his adoptive father's reign he must have formed his ambition of restoring the greatness of the Roman Empire. For on his accession in 527 he lost no time in embarking on his great projects. His short-lived military conquests have already been mentioned.[1] His great church of the Holy Wisdom in Constantinople still stands as a reminder of his interest in religion. What concerns us here is his codification, which was later to be called the *Corpus Iuris Civilis*.

The Corpus Iuris Civilis. Justinian's first project was the relatively modest one of doing again for his own time the work which, ninety years before, Theodosius II had done for his. In February 528 he appointed a commission of ten, including Tribonian, then head of the imperial chancery, to make a new collection of constitutions. They were to omit all that was obsolete and were to make such consolidations, deletions, and alterations as were necessary to remove contradictions. The work was quickly completed and the Code[2] was promulgated in April 529. It remained in force, as we shall see, only until 534 and has not survived.

Justinian then turned his attention to the juristic law. Theodosius himself had intended to make a collection of juristic writings but had abandoned the project. Justinian seems at first to have envisaged only the settling of outstanding controversies and the formal abolition of obsolete institutions. The constitutions by which these reforms were enacted are referred to as the Fifty Decisions, but as such they have not come down to us, though many must be contained in the second Code.[3]

---

[1] Above, p. 14.

[2] This English rendering of the word 'codex', though habitual, can be misleading. 'Codex' means in general simply a book, but acquired the special meaning of a collection of *constitutiones*, as in the *Codex Theodosianus* and the *Codex Justinianus*. In modern usage, however, 'code' has acquired a third meaning—that of a systematic enactment of an entire body of law, e.g. the Napoleonic Code. In this sense the entire *Corpus Iuris Civilis* can be called a Code (though it is far from systematic).

[3] See below, p. 42.

It was apparently at this point that Justinian conceived the far more ambitious project of a compilation, the Digest or Pandects, which would both preserve the best of the classical literature and provide a statement of the law in force in his own time. This task was entrusted, on 15 December 530, to Tribonian, who by this time was, in modern terms, Minister of Justice, and who was to choose a commission to help him. He chose sixteen men—one great officer of state, eleven practitioners, and four professors, two from Constantinople and two from Beirut. They were to read and make excerpts from the old literature, and these excerpts were to be collected into fifty books, divided into titles (chapters) according to subject-matter. Moreover they were to abridge and alter as much as was necessary to ensure that the work contained no repetitions, no contradictions, and nothing that was obsolete.[1] At the same time, they were to record the provenance of each excerpt, giving the name of the author, the title of the work, and the number of the book. (This is called the 'inscription', e.g. 'Ulpian, first book *ad Sabinum*'.)

Even to envisage such an undertaking was remarkable, and supports the view, for which there is some other evidence, that there had been a revival of classical learning in the law schools of Constantinople and Beirut. Tribonian was to be the central figure and his may well have been the inspiration. Certainly Justinian records, in the constitution promulgating the Digest, that a large part of the books used came from Tribonian's library and that many of them were unknown even to the most learned. The scale of the undertaking was heroic. Justinian declares that nearly 2,000 'books'[2] were read, containing 3,000,000 lines, and that they were reduced to 150,000 lines. And even these 150,000 lines give us a work one and a half times the size of the Bible. The excerpts are taken from thirty-nine authors, ranging from Q. Mucius Scaevola, who died in 82 B.C., to two otherwise unknown jurists who probably wrote early in the fourth century A.D., but the great bulk (95 per cent.) of the work is taken from authors of the period between A.D. 100 and 250. Even in this period a few predominate. Ulpian contributes

---

[1] These alterations are now referred to as 'interpolations'. The term is misleading, since it includes not merely the insertion of new matter but any alteration even if only by abridgement or omission.

[2] See above, p. 34, n. 1.

well over a third, and Paul more than a sixth, of the whole. Nevertheless the frequent citations by these later classical authors of their predecessors in the early Principate give us a much wider picture than these figures would suggest.

The time allotted for the work was ten years, but it was completed within three. It was promulgated by Justinian on 16 December 533, and came into force fourteen days later. To many it has seemed astonishing that so vast a work should have been completed in so short a time, particularly since Justinian says the alterations made were 'many and very great'. It has therefore been suggested that the compilers must have had recourse to pre-existing compilations used in the law schools. This involves, however, convicting Justinian of a lie when he speaks of the 2,000 books which have been read, a lie which would have been obvious to any lawyer. And the achievement is less astonishing than it seems at first sight. As we shall see, the compilers appear to have split up into three committees for the preparatory work, and there may well have been a still further division of labour within each committee. And the work was very imperfectly done.

Meanwhile Tribonian and two of the professors (Theophilus from Constantinople and Dorotheus from Beirut) had been entrusted also with the task of producing an official elementary textbook for students, the Institutes. This too was promulgated in December 533, and was even given legislative force. No more than the Digest, however, is it an original work. It is a patchwork of passages of classical institutional works, filled out, where a change of law or some other reason makes this necessary, with pieces of the compilers' own composition. In this respect it differs from the Digest only in that the provenance of the individual passages is not indicated. This is often, however, discoverable. For a large part of the Institutes is borrowed from the Institutes of Gaius, and a fair number of other passages are reproduced in the Digest. This patchwork character accounts for the rather disjointed and occasionally contradictory appearance of the text.

The Institutes are indebted to those of Gaius not only for a large part of their substance but also, to an even greater extent, for their arrangement, and especially for the division of the law into three main parts, concerning Persons, Things, and Actions.

This division, which will be discussed later,[1] exercised a great influence on subsequent legal thinking.

By this time the enactment not only of the Fifty Decisions but also of a great many other reforming constitutions had made the Code of 529 obsolete, and Tribonian was accordingly commissioned, with Dorotheus and three of the practitioners from the Digest commission, to prepare a new edition. Once again the commissioners were given wide powers of alteration, rearrangement, and deletion. The work was published on 16 November 534, and came into force on 29 December of the same year. It is this second Code (*Codex repetitae praelectionis*) which survives, though its manuscript tradition leaves a great deal to be desired. It is about half the size of the Digest and contains some 5,000 constitutions dating from the reign of Hadrian onwards.

The work of codification was now complete, but the flow of constitutions continued. Justinian had envisaged an official collection of these new constitutions (*novellae constitutiones*—hence their modern name, 'Novels') but the project was never carried out, and the collection which appears as the final part of the *Corpus Iuris* in modern editions is derived from three unofficial or semi-official collections. The Novels are for the most part concerned with public law or ecclesiastical affairs, but they include also a number of important reforms of the private law, particularly in matters of family law and succession.

Character of the Digest. The Digest is not only the largest but also by far the most important part of the *Corpus Iuris*, and something more must be said of its character. Justinian describes its compilation as 'a most difficult, indeed an impossible undertaking'. This was written in a spirit of hyperbole but was in a sense the truth. For Justinian had two incompatible objectives, to preserve the best of the classical literature and yet to reform and set out the law of his own day. In seeking to achieve both he failed fully to achieve either, and the failure was only accentuated by the haste in which the work was done.

The authority of the Digest derived from Justinian alone, and recourse to any literature outside it was expressly forbidden. And yet each fragment states in full its provenance, and the whole abounds in the citation and discussion of the views of

[1] See below, pp. 60 f., 98 f., 158 f.

named authors. Again, the original works from which it derived were written over a period of some three and a half centuries and therefore contained not only the conflicts of opinion which are inevitable in any living system of law but also the differences which derive from historical development. Justinian did indeed order the compilers to alter the texts, and confidently asserted that no contradictions would be found which an acute mind could not reconcile, but there were in truth innumerable contradictions. For not only did the compilers fail to expunge many of those which already existed in the classical materials, but they also added others of their own by altering some texts to state the law of their own time while leaving others untouched. In later centuries many acute minds were to labour to reconcile these contradictions, but to the lawyer of his own time the task must have seemed impossible, and, as we shall see, the Digest was quickly laid aside.

Nor was the lawyer's task made easier by the arrangement of the work. The order of books and 'titles', each 'title' being devoted to one topic, is that of the Edict. Unlike the order of the Institutes, this was only in its broadest divisions systematic, but it was no doubt familiar and adequate, especially as the ancients, classics as well as Byzantines, set less store than we do by scientific arrangement. But within each title the order of fragments appears to be arbitrary. There is the further hazard that fragments in one title may well have a bearing on the subject-matter of another, quite different, title, and there are no cross-references. The order of the fragments remained a mystery until 1818 when a young German, Bluhme, unravelled it. By a study of the 'inscriptions' of the fragments he showed that there are three main groups, or 'masses', of works, the extracts from each of which come regularly together in each title; and he showed further that, though the order of the masses varies, the order within each mass is usually the same. From this he inferred that the compilers were divided into three committees, each responsible for making excerpts from one mass, and that the full commission met only to do the final work of editing the whole.

The spirit of the Digest is thus as remote as it well could be from that of a modern code, such as that of Napoleon. But it was the spirit of the age, an age which was in most spheres almost obsessively unoriginal. Justinian himself declares that 'the man who amends what is imperfectly done deserves more praise than the original author'. Only in an age when this could be said could a work as contradictory in its purposes as the Digest have been undertaken. In seeking to preserve the greatness of the past Justinian failed to produce a practical codification which his own subjects could use, and in seeking to present the law of his own day he distorted what he was trying to preserve.

And yet he was to succeed in a time and place and in a manner of which he could not have dreamed, and these very defects were to be one of the sources of this unforeseen success. He declared that he had given the best of laws not only for his own age but for the ages to come. Centuries later these words would be heard again, and the work of Justinian the legislator would become the common law of the continent of Europe. Later still, and in our own time, the historian of law would find in the work of Justinian the preserver a rich record of the greatest achievement of the Roman mind.

In the history of law Justinian marks the ending of the ancient world. In his reign the Roman law enjoyed a brief second summer before the onset of the winter of the next five hundred years. And the Roman law which emerged from that winter was a medieval law, a law of the book. Once the legislator's hand had been laid upon it the character of the Roman law was changed: its authority now lay not in the balance of the free debate between the jurists but in the words of the book in which the debate was preserved. This result must follow on any codification; it was only the more marked because of the habits of mind of the Middle Ages.

Justinian's importance lies in his having succeeded, at a moment when the ancient world was dissolving, in collecting together, in a form which could survive, the literature of the Roman law. And in the survival of this literature even his conquests can be seen as playing a part. For his conquest of Italy made possible the promulgation there of his codification, and it was probably in Italy, and within half a century of Justinian's death, that the manuscript was written to which we owe the survival of the Digest.[1] How it was preserved we do not know,

[1] This manuscript, which we know as the Florentine, has been in the Laurentian

but we may remember that it was soon after Justinian came to the throne that in Italy, at Monte Cassino, St. Benedict founded his first monastery. In the dissolution of the ancient world the medieval world was taking shape.

IV. THE SECOND LIFE OF ROMAN LAW

Survival in the East. In the Eastern Empire the history of Roman law continued unbroken until the fall of Constantinople to the Turks in 1453, but it was a history of decline, and Byzantine law in its last form is a very remote descendant of the classical law. Justinian, with the codifier's habitual belief in the perfection of his work and in the possibility of preventing the growth of fresh controversies, had forbidden all commentaries. He made exceptions, however, for literal translations into Greek and for *indices* and *paratitla*. The latter are usually taken to be brief summaries and references to parallel passages. If this is so, the exceptions were, even in Justinian's lifetime, liberally construed and the ban was later altogether ignored. This was inevitable. The language of the Eastern Empire was Greek, and even the Institutes must to many have been inaccessible. (An expanded Greek paraphrase, attributed to Theophilus, survives.) But the Digest presented the additional difficulties that it was vast, complex, and ill-arranged, and that it embodied institutions and concepts which were not in practice understood or applied. The need for summaries and commentaries was compelling. This Greek literature is best seen in the *Basilica* ('Imperial Law') promulgated by the Emperor Leo the Wise (886–911). This was compiled from earlier materials, and consists of drastically abridged and simplified Greek versions of the Digest, Code, and Novels, put together to form a single work. To these was later added an extensive apparatus of marginal comments or *scholia*, written mainly in the sixth or seventh centuries. In works such as this a form of Roman law survived until 1453, and indeed longer. For a manual in six books (the *Hexabiblos*), compiled in about 1345 by Harmenopoulos, a judge at Salonica, remained, in theory at least, the basis of the law of Greece until the coming into force of the Civil Code in 1946.

library in Florence since 1406. It was brought there from Pisa, where it had been at least since the twelfth century. From it all other manuscripts ultimately derive.

Survival and revival in the West. Even in the West the Roman law never wholly died out. The Roman subjects of the 'barbarian' rulers in southern France, Spain, and Italy continued to live by the 'vulgar law'[1] to be found in compilations such as the *lex Romana Visigothorum*. In Italy, it is true, Justinian's codification had been promulgated in 554, and some fragmentary knowledge of the Institutes, Code, and Novels survived, but the Digest was entirely forgotten. And in northern Europe almost all trace of Roman law disappeared.

The great influence of Roman law derives, however, not from this attenuated survival, but from the revival which began, as part of a wider renaissance of learning, at the end of the eleventh century. The Digest was rediscovered and for the first time thoroughly mastered. The first and greatest figure in this revival was Irnerius (*c.* 1055–*c.* 1130) who taught at Bologna. He and his successors at Bologna set themselves the task of elucidating, harmonizing, and expounding the *Corpus Iuris* text by text. The main literary form which this work took was the note or gloss written in the margin or between the lines of the text to explain its meaning and to provide the cross-references and reconciliations without which the work was unusable. For this reason Irnerius and his successors are called the Glossators, but their writings took also other forms, both systematic and controversial.

Enthusiasm for the new learning was immense. Students came to Bologna from all western Europe, and by the middle of the twelfth century their number had reached 10,000. Moreover, from Bologna the study of Roman law spread to other nascent universities in Italy and far beyond. In the middle of the twelfth century, for example, Vacarius was teaching it at Oxford. The main impulse continued, however, to come from Italy, and after little more than a century the work of the Glossators was done. It was summed up and completed by Accursius (d. 1260), who combined all the glosses into one great gloss. This *glossa ordinaria* thereafter held the field alone, both in the manuscript versions of the *Corpus Iuris* and in the early printed editions.

This revival of Roman law was an academic revival, both in the sense that it originated in the universities and in the sense

[1] See above, p. 36.

that it was unconcerned with the law which was applied in the courts. In the former sense its academic character was never lost—and has to a large extent been transmitted to the modern civil law—but the practical law could not long remain uninfluenced by the ferment in the universities. And there was a corresponding change in the direction of academic interest. The successors of Accursius turned to the practical application of Roman law to the problems of their own time. For this purpose the method of the gloss was inadequate, and its place was taken by more systematic and extensive commentaries, the authors of which are therefore commonly called the Commentators (or Post-glossators). By applying, as occasion demanded, a restrictive or liberal interpretation, and by the use of fine distinctions, they adapted the ancient law to medieval needs. The material on which they worked was more often the gloss than the texts themselves, and the law which emerged was thus Roman law at third hand, but it was practical law and in this lay its strength. The greatest of the Commentators were Bartolus (1314–57) and his pupil, Baldus (1327–1400), whose authority was such that only the foolhardy would argue against it. *Nemo iurista nisi Bartolista* ran the maxim.

For the Glossators the attraction of the *Corpus Iuris* must have lain principally in the intellectual satisfaction to be derived from eliciting the underlying rational harmony of the texts. That the harmony was not always there to be elicited was inconceivable: both for them and for the Commentators the *Corpus Iuris* was not the final product of an historical process but a single authoritative expression of right order. And yet what made their work fruitful was precisely that the harmony had to be sought for and—though they did not see it in this way—imposed. The defects in Justinian's work now became virtues. Had it been a simple, systematic, closely coherent statement of sixth-century law, it could not have been so successfully adapted to the evolving needs of medieval society (and still less to those of later centuries). But, as it was, it provided an almost inexhaustible fund of solutions to practical problems which, while they presupposed a broadly consistent framework of principles, yet contained sufficient divergences and conflicts to enable the jurist to choose the solution best fitted to current needs. And so though he was in fact making a choice he could appear to be merely interpreting the authoritative text, merely proving that Justinian was right when he said that his work contained no conflicts which a subtle mind could not reconcile. For the lawyer in any system, be he judge or jurist, is in the dilemma that he sees—and wishes to see—the law as something which has its own life, which exists independently of himself and is merely applied by him, and yet he must on occasion in practice make law, either by laying down a rule for a case which has never previously arisen or by altering a rule which has become unjust or inconvenient. The medieval lawyer was fortunate in that, on the one hand, he could, in the spirit of his age, accord intrinsic value to a written text, and, on the other, could find within that ultimate authority more than one solution to many problems. In our eyes he made a choice, in his own he 'distinguished' the unique authoritative solution from those which were, on a proper interpretation, concerned with a slightly different problem. Where different solutions were given by different texts to apparently identical problems, it could be presumed, for example, that in one case some additional, unmentioned fact was to be taken into account.

The Reception of Roman law. The text had the authority of its own intellectual force, but it had also the authority of its imperial origin. For the imperial idea, imperfectly realized in the Holy Roman Empire, was still a force in men's minds. Both intellectual and imperial authority played a part in the process which accompanied the work of the Glossators and, still more, of the Commentators, and which we call the Reception of Roman Law—the process by which it became the common law of western Europe. But the course of this Reception was very different in different parts of the Continent. In the south—in Italy, Spain, and southern France—the Roman law had, as we have seen, never wholly died out, and therefore the gloss and the doctrines of the Commentators could be accepted as simply an enlargement of the law which had been preserved in the *lex Romana Visigothorum* and other compilations. There was here no catastrophic reception of a new system of law but rather a gradual revival and rediscovery of an old. In northern Europe, however, customary law alone survived, varying from place to place. The acceptance of Roman law was therefore much longer delayed and, when it came, much more sudden. The hostility to the new learning came partly from the local lay courts, jealous of their customary law, and partly sometimes, as in France, from the Crown. For outside the Holy Roman Empire it was precisely the imperial origin of the *Corpus Iuris* that was an obstacle to its acceptance, until it was seen that the King or Prince could, by presenting himself as Emperor within his own territory, apply to himself all the texts which propounded the absolute power of the Emperor.[1]

As the Middle Ages drew to a close the inconvenience and inadequacy of the innumerable local customs and the incompetence of the local courts made the claims of Roman law, and of the lawyers who had been educated in it, irresistible. The resulting Reception was most sweeping in Germany and the Netherlands. In the later fifteenth century new courts with wider jurisdiction and composed of judges trained in the Roman law appeared, and in the course of the sixteenth century the Reception was completed. Much local custom survived, particularly in matters of family law and inheritance, but the structure of the law and the lawyer's ways of thought and terminology were derived from the Roman law. The rules of customary law were a local variant intruding upon a universal system.

In northern France (the *pays des coutumes*, as opposed to the *pays de droit écrit* in the south) the Reception began earlier than in Germany and was both more gradual and less sweeping. The customs were codified in the sixteenth century and were thus better able to withstand the infiltration of Roman law, but nevertheless its influence on the methods and 'grammar' of legal thought was inescapable.[2]

In England, on the other hand, though the Roman law was early known and taught, it never obtained a foothold in the

---

[1] 'Rex Franciae est imperator in regno suo' ran the maxim or, more generally, 'Princeps imperator in regno suo'.

[2] One reason for this must have been the absence of any teaching of customary law at the universities. The first chair of French law was not established until 1679 (in Paris). It is true that the first chair of English law in England was not created until even later (1758, at Oxford), but the early strength of the Inns of Court and the early evolution of the Common law in the hands of the courts gave to English law a centre and a source which was quite independent of the universities. For this reason English law has never been academic in origin in the way that the continental Civil law to a large extent even now still is.

practice of the ordinary courts. The reason for this lay partly in the early establishment of the central power of the King which made it possible to replace the local customary laws by the common custom of the King's courts which we call the Common law; and it lay partly also in the existence of the Inns of Court, strong professional bodies situated near the King's courts but away from the universities, and having a common interest with the courts in the exclusion of Roman law.[1]

The Humanist revival. The culmination of the Reception was accompanied, however, by a reaction against the methods and purposes of the Commentators. The Humanist revival of classical learning produced scholars to whom the Commentators' bad Latin, their total lack of historical sense, and their neglect of the original texts were deplorable. 'Back to the texts' was now the call. And the revival of interest in the text was accompanied by an emphasis on the historical character of the *Corpus Iuris*, a desire to rediscover the Roman law as it was in Roman times. This in turn led for the first time to an attempt to detect the interpolations[2] in the *Corpus Iuris* and thereby to uncover the true classical law. This Humanist movement was particularly strong in France, where its principal representatives were Jacques Cujas (Cujacius, 1520 or 1522–90), Hugues Doneau (Donellus, 1527–91), and Antoine Favre (Faber, 1557–1624). The revival of interest in the Roman law as such led also to the recovery of some of the post-classical works which had survived independently of Justinian, and to a renewal of interest in the Theodosian Code, of which Jacques Godefroy (Jacobus Gothofredus, 1587–1652) published a great edition with commentary to which reference is still made.

Natural law. In the seventeenth and eighteenth centuries the antiquarian interests of the Humanists gave place to the new rationalism of the school of natural law. Believing that the law for any society could by the use of reason be derived from principles inherent in the nature of man and society, the

---

[1] Scots law occupies an intermediate position. It underwent a form of Reception in the sixteenth and seventeenth centuries, but in more recent times it has been much affected by English law.   [2] See above, p. 40, n. 1.

adherents of this school rejected the unquestioned authority which the medieval Commentators had accorded to the *Corpus Iuris*, and yet found in the Roman law, with its doctrine of the *ius gentium* and the *ius naturale*,[1] a great deal which they could accept as being the embodiment of natural reason. The first of the great exponents of the new doctrine was the Dutchman Grotius (Hugo de Groot, 1583–1645), who applied it especially to the formation of a body of international law.[2] It was indeed in this field that the school of natural law was most influential, but it encouraged also the elimination from the modern Roman law of the irrational, and therefore peculiarly Roman, features which the Humanists had emphasized, and insisted, even to excess, on the place of logic in law.

Codification and the modern Civil law. Natural law ideas led also to a call for codification. The ideal of a logically consistent set of principles and rules could best be realized and preserved in a written code. The call was partially answered in Bavaria (1756) and Prussia (1794), but incomparably the most important event in the history of modern European law was the enactment of Napoleon's *Code Civil* in 1804. Its importance lay not so much in the fact that France, for the first time in her history, had a single system of law, as in the fact that the Code was adopted or copied by many other countries. Sometimes its adoption was the result of conquest by Napoleon, but its attraction continued long after his final defeat and is attributable partly to the clarity and simplicity of the Code itself, and partly to the prestige of France in the nineteenth century. Codes more or less closely copying the French were adopted in Holland, Spain, Italy, Belgium, Louisiana, Quebec, Egypt, and in many parts of South America.

In Germany, too, a French code might have been adopted at the end of the Napoleonic wars but for the influence of the great jurist Savigny (1779–1861). He argued that the time was not yet ripe: a far more profound study of the Roman law than had been achieved by the medieval lawyers or the school of natural law was necessary before a satisfactory code could be achieved.

---

[1] See below, pp. 54 ff.
[2] He also wrote an *Introduction to the Jurisprudence of Holland* which exercised a great influence on Roman-Dutch law.

Thus began the last great period of the practical application of Roman law. In the hands of Savigny and his successors the *Corpus Iuris* was made to yield a highly systematic, closely analysed, and remarkably elaborate body of law (*Pandektenrecht*) for nineteenth-century Germany. It was not until the establishment of the German Empire that, on the foundations thus laid, the work of codification was begun, and not until 1900 that the German Civil Code finally came into force. More systematic and more elaborate than the French, it too has been copied elsewhere, by Japan and Brazil, for example, and its influence can be seen in the Swiss Code, which in its turn has been adopted by Turkey.

The movement for codification brought the second life of Roman law in one sense to an end. Except in South Africa and Ceylon, where the pre-Napoleonic Roman-Dutch law survives, the *Corpus Iuris* has ceased to be a direct source of law. Nowhere else can it be cited as authoritative, except on occasion where a code is silent or ambiguous. And yet in another sense codification gave Roman law a new life and extended it to territories into which it could never otherwise have entered. Uncodified systems are unsuitable for export, and by modern standards the Roman law is an uncodified system. The uncodified Common law has indeed spread over the globe, but it has followed the flag. It has only taken root where British rule, and with it lawyers trained in the Common law, have gone. Codes, on the other hand, as we have just seen, travel easily. But we must beware of exaggerating the extent to which the modern codes embody Roman law. The German, and still more the French, Civil Codes contain much that is entirely un-Roman, and even the Roman elements have often been transformed in the course of centuries; but in their structure, their ways of thought, and their essential terminology the Civil Codes have a strong family resemblance which, at least in the eyes of the Common lawyer, is more significant than their differences of detail. And this family resemblance derives from their common inheritance of Roman law. There is a danger, however, that we simply attribute to Roman law and the Roman jurists all the habits of mind which distinguish the modern Civilian from the Common lawyer, forgetting that the *Corpus Iuris* stands between the classical jurist and his Civilian successor, that the Civil law, whether codified or not, is a law of the book as the classical Roman law never was.

The modern historical study of Roman law. As the preparatory work for the German Civil Code began, the direction of Roman law studies changed. Roman law, it has been said, was handed over to the historians. At first in Germany, and later in Italy and elsewhere, scholars turned to the work, begun by the Humanists three centuries before, of rediscovering the classical law. And once again the defects of the *Corpus Iuris* appeared as virtues. The 'inscriptions' of the fragments in the Digest[1] made it possible partially to reconstruct some of the main works of the later classical jurists; and from the reconstruction of the commentaries on the Edict it was possible to recover the order and in part the substance of the Edict itself. Similarly, from the constitutions in the Code some developments of the post-classical law could be traced. But over all stood the problem of interpolations. Some of the more obvious had been noted by the Humanists, but now the work began in earnest, with all the equipment and ingenuity of modern scholarship. The methods used were sometimes simple. Very occasionally a text in the Digest has also survived independently—in the Institutes of Gaius for example; or the same text occurs twice in the Digest itself, in different versions. More commonly we can tell that the law stated in a particular text is not classical because it represents an innovation made by a surviving constitution of a later date, or because the law is stated otherwise by Gaius or another classical source. Where these criteria are lacking, more complex and less reliable methods have to be used. The language, the grammar, or the logical structure of a passage may reveal the hand of the compiler, or the same author may be credited with incompatible views in different fragments drawn from the same work. Methods such as these—and there are many variants—are obviously capable of abuse, and certainly in the third and fourth decades of this century the hunt for interpolations led to many exaggerated claims, but a great deal which is of indisputable validity remains,[2] and our knowledge of the classical law has been transformed. Indeed it has become plain that we know in many ways less about the law of Justinian and of the post-classical

[1] See above, p. 40.   [2] For examples, see below, p. 139, n. 1.

period than we do about the classical law. For whereas previously it had been assumed that the texts reached the compilers substantially unaltered, and therefore that if the interpolations could be detected we should know both the classical law and the law of Justinian, it is now realized that the truth must be a great deal more complex. On the one hand it has become clear that the texts (other than the Institutes of Gaius) which survive independently of Justinian were edited and altered in post-classical times, and that it is therefore likely that at least some of the texts which reached Justinian's compilers had been treated similarly. The search for these pre-Justinianean interpolations has begun. On the other hand, the divergence between the 'vulgar law' and the imperial law has been to some extent detected and described. There remains the further problem, as yet little investigated, of the extent to which the law of Justinian, in so far as we can see it in his constitutions and in those interpolations which can be attributed to his compilers, represents the law which was actually applied in the practice of his own time.

V. *IUS NATURALE, IUS GENTIUM*

Gaius begins his Institutes with these words:

Every people that is governed by statutes and customs applies partly its own peculiar law and partly law which is common to all mankind. For the law which each people establishes for itself is peculiar to it and is called *ius civile* as being the special law of that state (*civitas*); but the law which natural reason establishes among all mankind is observed equally by every people and is called *ius gentium* as being the law applied by all nations (*gentes*). And so the Roman people applies partly its own peculiar law and partly that which is common to all mankind.

Aristotle had made substantially the same distinction—between man-made law, which is peculiar to one state, and natural law, which is universal. The one has no intrinsic moral value and derives its validity from its adoption by the state (the rule of the road would be a modern example), while the other is universally valid, whether it is adopted or not. The one, it has been said, is right because it is law, the other is law because it is right. This idea, which is older than Aristotle, of natural law as an ideal and universally valid set of precepts, deriving from the principle of order which is manifest in the physical universe and which is represented in man by his reason, became a philosophical and rhetorical commonplace, particularly among the Stoics, who preached the doctrine of a 'life according to nature'. In surviving Roman literature it appears first—and frequently—in Cicero, who treats it, as Gaius also does in the passage quoted above, as synonymous with *ius gentium*. In this sense the two terms represent two aspects of the same idea. The term *ius naturale* looks to the origin of this law in natural reason (which Cicero identifies with divine reason), and the term *ius gentium* to its universal application. Gaius expresses this compendiously when he says that 'the law which natural reason establishes among all mankind is observed equally by every people'. To our way of thinking there is here an illogicality. *Ius naturale* is law which ought to be observed by all mankind, whereas *ius gentium* is law which is in fact observed by all mankind; and one cannot logically proceed either from the fact that a rule is observed to the proposition that it ought to be observed, or vice versa. The Romans, however, never made this clear distinction between positive law (i.e. law which is actually applied) and law as it ought to be. And similarly they never developed what may be called the revolutionary aspect of natural law as a higher law capable of invalidating the positive law.[1] Only in one respect did the jurists occasionally draw a distinction between *ius naturale* and *ius gentium*. For they adhered to the Stoic teaching (against that of Aristotle) that man was by nature free and that slavery was therefore contrary to the natural law; but clearly it was an institution of the *ius gentium*. But this is simply recorded as a fact. The jurists were not social reformers.

A quite different definition of *ius naturale*, attributed to Ulpian, deserves mention only because it appears prominently near the beginning of both Justinian's Institutes and the Digest, and therefore had a considerable, and distorting, influence on subsequent thought. 'Natural law', the text declares, 'is that which nature has taught all animals. For it is not peculiar to the human

---

[1] This is not to say that the ancients were unaware of the possibility of conflict in the conscience of the individual between the positive law and the moral law. This is the theme of the *Antigone* of Sophocles and the *Apologia* of Socrates, to take but two famous examples.

race but belongs to all animals. From this law comes the union of male and female, which we call marriage, and the begetting and education of children. For we see that all other animals are likewise governed by a knowledge of this law.' This idea, which seems to derive from the Pythagoreans, confuses the promptings of instinct with the precepts of law. It is the same confusion which sometimes results in English from the use of the word 'law' not only in the lawyer's sense, as in 'the law of contract', but also in the natural scientist's sense, as in 'the law of gravity'. The former is a statement of what in given circumstances ought to happen, the latter a statement of what in given circumstances does happen, or to be precise, of what, as far as we can tell, will happen. The former is a rule of conduct, the latter a prediction. The confusion is plain in the illustration given in the text. Roman marriage, little regulated by law though it was,[1] was not simply the union of male and female. The function of the law of marriage was, and is, to regulate the instinct which man shares with all animals.[2]

Neither the term *ius naturale* nor the term *ius gentium* occurs in legal literature until Gaius,[3] two centuries after Cicero. Too little, however, of the juristic writings of these two centuries survives[4] for us to be able to determine whether this silence is significant. Certainly the jurists, as men of culture and education, must have been acquainted with current philosophical ideas, and yet, severely practical as they were in their attitude to law, they may well in their writings have ignored the philosopher's *ius naturale* or *ius gentium* as mere speculation. Even where—in Gaius and the great jurists of the late classical period—the idea of 'nature' or 'natural reason' does appear, it is either, as in the passages quoted above, purely ornamental, or else it bears a meaning which varies according to the context but has little connexion with the philosophical idea. In common language we ourselves use 'nature' in a similarly imprecise way.

But imprecise though it was, 'nature' provided a device of

---

[1] See below, pp. 80 ff.
[2] Apart from this one text, the Institutes give to *ius naturale* the same meaning as Gaius. On the 'patchwork' character of the Institutes, see above, p. 41.
[3] Pomponius, a jurist of the time of Hadrian, uses the term *ius gentium* in what has come, since the seventeenth century, to be its usual modern sense, i.e. the rules governing relations between states (public international law).
[4] See above, p. 34.

some importance for the interpretation and classification of the law. The 'nature' of a thing or legal institution was commonly its intrinsic character, and the jurists sought to derive their rules from this character. It is the nature of some animals to be wild, and therefore we can only own them so long as we have physical control of them; it is the nature of the sea to be open to all and therefore it is not susceptible of private ownership, and so forth. In a similar way it was held that certain methods of acquiring ownership were natural, or derived from natural law or natural reason, because they seemed to follow inevitably from the facts involved. If, for example, I wish to make you owner of a thing, the 'natural' way of doing so is to hand it over to you. Or if a house is built with my materials on your land, it follows from the nature of this merger, or so the jurists thought, that the whole must belong to you. (Such methods of acquisition, being natural, were of course held to be universal and therefore to be of the *ius gentium*.) In other contexts 'nature' or 'natural reason' is equivalent to 'justice', or 'common sense', or 'good order'. And still other meanings can be found.

We have seen that the term *ius naturale* looks to the supposed origin or basis of a rule or institution, while the term *ius gentium* looks to its universal application. But the statement that a given institution is universal is of no practical significance for the lawyer. It has been called 'a piece of superficial comparative jurisprudence'—superficial because it can be true, if it is true at all, only in a very loose sense. The contract of sale (*emptio venditio*), for example, like most contracts, is of the *ius gentium*, but it is universal only in the sense that other systems have institutions which serve the same purpose. The Roman jurist did not suppose that the detailed rules of the Greek contract of sale were the same as those of *emptio venditio*.

Ius gentium had a second sense, however, which was of considerable practical importance. In this sense it was that part of Roman law which was applied both to citizens and to peregrines. Ancient law was in principle 'personal': the law by which a man lived depended not on where he was, but on who he was—on his nationality. Roman law applied to Roman citizens, Athenian law to Athenian citizens. Such a principle presents obvious problems. What law was to be applied to a foreigner living within the Roman jurisdiction? One solution would have been to apply his own law, and to some extent this was done, particularly in the field of family law and succession. But what law was to govern his relations with Roman citizens or with peregrines of other nationalities? To apply the principle of personality here would have called for a set of rules of what we call 'conflict of laws' to determine which system should apply in each individual case. What in fact emerged was something quite different—a body of law, Roman in character but without the formality and technicality of the old *ius civile*, which could be applied to citizen and non-citizen alike. How this law grew up remains a matter of conjecture. Its main features were already fixed in the last century B.C., and our knowledge of the period before then is very slight. The Peregrine Praetor, whose province it was to administer just such a law, must have played a large part, as also perhaps did the provincial governors, who were faced with the same problem, but we lack the evidence to go farther than this. Moreover, as we know it, this body of law applied not only to transactions involving peregrines, but even to transactions wholly between citizens. If therefore it originated in the Edict of the Peregrine Praetor, it had in some way been 'received' into the province of the Urban Praetor. And there must have been some 'reception' in the reverse direction also. For in the law as we know it a few institutions which were part of the old, strictly Roman, *ius civile* were nevertheless applicable also to peregrines, notably the contract of *stipulatio*[1] in all but one of its forms. But here again we lack the evidence to tell how this development occurred. Nor, as we have seen, can we know how early the term *ius gentium* was applied to this body of law, or what influence the philosophical idea had upon its development. All that is certain is that in Gaius the term is used both in the philosophical or theoretical sense discussed above and in this practical sense, and that in either sense it embraces the greater part of the law outside the law of persons and the law of succession. Without it the Roman law would never have held the place in history that it does, and yet we know next to nothing of its origin or growth.

The two senses of *ius gentium* are often indistinguishable. Most of the *ius gentium* in the practical sense is informal and simple and therefore 'universal'. But while all institutions of the *ius*

[1] See below, p. 193.

gentium in the theoretical sense were necessarily part of the *ius gentium* in the practical sense, the converse was not always so. The *stipulatio*, already mentioned, makes this plain. It existed in no system except the Roman, but it was open to citizens and peregrines alike.

The distinction emerges also in the use of the term *ius civile*. Like our term 'common law', *ius civile* derives its meaning from its context. By contrast with *ius gentium* in the theoretical sense it denotes the law peculiar to a particular state; by contrast with *ius gentium* in the practical sense it denotes that part of Roman law which is confined to Roman citizens. In the first sense *stipulatio* is of the *ius civile*, in the second it is not. There is, moreover, a third sense of *ius civile* which must be borne in mind. By contrast with *ius honorarium* it denotes—and it is principally in this sense that we shall use it[1]—that part of Roman law which derives from *lex* and *interpretatio*.

[1] See above, p. 26, n. 1.

II

LAW OF PERSONS

INTRODUCTORY

The arrangement of the Institutes. Justinian's Institutes declare that
'the whole of our law relates either to persons or to things or
to actions'. This classification, which has coloured all subsequent legal thinking, is repeated from the Institutes of Gaius,
and even there was perhaps already traditional. The modern
lawyer, for whom the 'elements' of which the law is composed
are rights and duties, sees the classification in those terms.
From this point of view 'persons' are those entities, whether
human or artificial (such as corporations), which are capable of
rights and duties; 'things' are the rights and duties themselves;
and 'actions' are the remedies by which the rights and duties
are enforced. To put it in another way, every rule of law has
three aspects—the persons affected, the subject-matter concerned, and the remedies. It is unlikely, however, that Gaius
saw the division in so precise and abstract a way. What emerges
from his book is something much more rough and ready. With
the meaning of 'things' we shall be concerned later, but here
something more must be said of 'persons'.[1]

The Romans never evolved a coherent theory of legal personality. For the modern lawyer, as has been said above, the
word 'person' means any entity capable of rights and duties, but
for the Roman lawyer the word *persona* had no such technical
meaning. It meant simply, as 'person' does in ordinary speech
today, a human being, whether capable of rights and duties or
not. And so a slave was a *persona*, but he was not a person in
the modern legal sense. The Romans had in fact no term to
differentiate those *personae* who were capable of rights and duties
from those who were not. But they had less need for such a
term than we do. For we admit the possibility that a legal

---

[1] 'Actions' will not be treated separately. Something has been said of them
already (above, pp. 19–28), and since their importance for the modern reader lies
primarily in their influence on the substantive law they are here treated in con-
junction with it.

person may not be a human person—may not be a *persona* in the
Roman sense at all. In modern law a group of individuals, small
or large, may constitute a legal person distinct from and additional to its members (e.g. a limited company), but for the
Roman lawyer such a group was, it seems, no more than a
certain number of individuals in a certain relationship to each
other. Only human beings could have rights; legal persons
were necessarily also natural persons. Admittedly natural persons were not always legal persons, but no doubt it seemed self-
evident that a slave could have no rights, and so no one was
likely to be misled by the lack of a clear terminology.

Moreover the slave might become free and was therefore at
least a potential subject of rights and duties. This is perhaps the
key to the content of the law of persons. For this part of the law
is in fact concerned with the different categories of legal person
and the ways in which a man may enter and leave each category.
More precisely, since the category of the normal man of full
capacity is taken for granted, it can be said to be concerned
with the different categories of 'status'—in the modern sense
of a condition in which a man's rights and duties differ from
the normal, that difference not having been created simply, or
at all, by his own consent. (In a modern system young children
and lunatics provide obvious examples.) Even this is too wide for
Gaius, who deals only with the ways in which each status can
be created and terminated, leaving the capacities and the in-
capacities which result from it to be mentioned, if at all, in the
later parts of his Institutes. In this respect, however, we shall not
follow his example.

Formalism. Primitive systems are given to the use of forms. Legal
consequences do not follow from a mere agreement or from a
simple expression of intention. If rights are to be created or
transferred, some particular act must be performed or some
particular words must be uttered. The act or the words (or
both) are the form, and it is the form which produces the legal
consequences. If the form is not observed, or not fully observed,
no consequences follow, and conversely if the form is observed
but there is a defect of intention (mistake or fraud) the legal
consequences nevertheless still follow. The form is both essential
and sufficient.

The Roman's attachment to forms was not confined to the private law, and the Englishman may well sympathize with it when he considers the extent to which, particularly in public affairs, he himself adheres to forms even when they have lost their original significance. Moreover there are sound practical reasons for requiring formality in some parts of the private law. Forms give certainty and clarity to an act—they serve not only to make precise the character of what is done and to mark the moment of its completion, but also to make the parties stop on the brink of the act and thereby to ensure that they know that the decisive moment has come. On the other hand forms have the disadvantage of inflexibility and often of inconvenience. In modern law, on the whole, contracts are informal but acts concerning the conveyance of land or the passing of property on death are formal, though the form is usually simple.

Roman law differs from most other systems both in what has been called its 'economy of forms' and in the simplicity of the forms themselves. It makes a very small number of forms serve a wide variety of purposes, and the forms contain little that is not necessary for defining and making evident the inner purpose of the act. The forms of Germanic law, by contrast, were much more diverse and had much that was merely picturesque or dramatic.

There were four main forms. One of these, the *stipulatio*, an oral question and answer, was used only in the law of contract. The others appear in slightly different guises and in different combinations in different parts of the law, and are prominent in the law of persons. They can therefore most conveniently be treated together at the beginning.

(a) *Act before the comitia curiata.* This, the least important of the three forms, was ostensibly a legislative act—a 'private bill'—and was used for one kind of adoption and for the earliest form of will. The *comitia curiata* which 'passed the bill' was the oldest of the Roman assemblies,[1] but in historical times it had no substantial existence as a legislative body, the thirty *curiae* of which it was composed being represented by the thirty lictors who were in attendance on the presiding magistrate. The substance of the proceedings was therefore the magistrate's approval of a private act.

[1] See above, p. 6.

(*b*) *Mancipatio*. This was in form a conveyance on sale. In the presence of five witnesses and of a sixth person (*libripens*) who held a pair of bronze scales, the transferee grasped the object to be conveyed in one hand and a piece of bronze in the other and said (in the case, for example, of a slave), 'I declare that this slave is mine by Quiritary right,[1] and be he purchased to me with this piece of bronze and these bronze scales.' He then struck the scales with the bronze, which he gave to the transferor. All the participants had to be Roman citizens.

Mancipatio is thus in appearance a cash sale, and one which derives from a period before the existence of coined money. But the weighing out and transfer of the bronze seems to have been merely symbolical even in the time of the Twelve Tables, i.e. perhaps a century and a half before the (surprisingly late) introduction of coined money in Rome, and in historical times *mancipatio* had no necessary connexion with sale at all. It was merely a conveyance, and the sale, if there was one, was a separate transaction. *Mancipatio* could be used for the conveyance only of free persons *in potestate*, slaves, and certain other things (*res mancipi*),[2] and for the conveyance of these it, or *in iure cessio* (below), was essential. The mere handing over of a slave, for example, even in pursuance of a valid sale, would not transfer ownership according to the civil law.

(*c*) *In iure cessio*. As another method of conveyance, applicable to any property,[3] the Romans used what appears to be a collusive version of the action asserting ownership (*vindicatio*) as it appeared in the *legis actio* procedure. The parties go before the Praetor (*in iure*) and there the transferee, grasping the thing to be transferred, utters the opening words of the old *vindicatio* (which are identical with the first clause of the formula of the *mancipatio*). The magistrate then asks the transferor whether he makes an opposing claim (*an contra vindicet*); the transferor either remains silent or says 'no', and the magistrate then 'adjudges' the thing to the transferee. In this form *in iure cessio*

---

[1] i.e. by the ancient civil law.   [2] See below, p. 105.

[3] But in practice used only for the creation of *iura in re aliena* (below, pp. 140 ff.), for which purpose it alone was usually apt. For, as Gaius says, what is the point of going to the trouble of an appearance before the Praetor if one can achieve the same object in private with the help of one's friends (i.e. by *mancipatio*)? And the argument would apply with even greater force where mere delivery (*traditio*) sufficed.

is collusive only in a special sense. For the magistrate is necessarily a party to the collusion, since in an ordinary *vindicatio* if the defendant made no defence the plaintiff merely took the thing claimed, without any 'adjudging' by the Praetor. Moreover, it has the effects of a conveyance rather than a judgment (e.g. the transferee becomes owner only from the moment of 'adjudgment' whereas a judgment would declare him to be already owner). The explanation is probably that it began as a collusive proceeding and, once established, acquired many of the features of a conveyance. A closely similar proceeding was used to manumit a slave.

In these acts, as in nearly all the formalities of Roman law, there is an insistence on the use of formal words. It is not sufficient, for example, to utter merely the substance of the transferee's assertion. The solemn words alone are capable of producing the legal result intended.

I. MAIN FEATURES OF THE LAW

Citizens and non-citizens. The 'normal man' referred to above[1] is, of course, a citizen. From the ordinary ancient principle that law was 'personal'[2] it followed that a non-citizen, a foreigner (*peregrinus*), had no rights under the specifically Roman *ius civile*. The development of the *ius gentium* did indeed considerably mitigate this disability, but a significant part of Roman law remained closed to the *peregrinus*.

Very early, however, the Romans found it convenient to accord limited rights under the *ius civile* to their immediate neighbours, the Latins, and a similar status was later allowed to the growing number of colonies which the Romans established as their rule spread. This status, between that of citizen and peregrine, continued to be called 'Latinity' though by the end of the Republic it had long ceased to have any geographical or ethnical significance. Nor were the privileges it conferred always the same. One must distinguish here three different rights. *Commercium* (or *ius commercii*) was the right to be a party to a *mancipatio* and perhaps to use some other specifically Roman methods of acquiring property and making contracts; *conubium* (*ius conubii*) was the right to contract with a Roman citizen

---

[1] See above, p. 61. [2] See above, p. 57.

a marriage recognized by the civil law; *testamenti factio* was the right to make, and take under, a Roman will. All Latins had *commercium*, some at least had *testamenti factio*, few had *conubium*.

Latinity was not, however, the most that the non-Roman could aspire to. Although grants of citizenship were rare until the last years of the Republic, the Romans then relented. By the end of the Republic the citizenship had been extended to all Italy, and grants were frequently made by the Emperors either to whole communities or to individuals. Moreover the slave population provided a never-failing source of new citizens. For, with rather surprising generosity, the Romans conceded to their manumitted slaves the privilege which as late as 91 B.C. at the cost of a bitter war they refused to their Italian allies.[1]

A new class was created by a *lex Junia* (? A.D. 19), which accorded Latinity, but without *conubium* or *testamenti factio*, to imperfectly manumitted slaves (Junian Latins).[2] In the early years of the Empire the promise of citizenship was increasingly used as an instrument of policy to attract these and other Latins into activities in the public interest—the building of houses, the shipping of grain to Rome, service in the fire brigade (a matter of great importance in so crowded and inflammable a city as ancient Rome), the bearing of children, and so forth. In the result, any enterprising Latin must have been able to raise himself to the citizenship.

The importance of the distinction between citizen and non-citizen largely disappeared after the grant of the citizenship in A.D. 212 to the bulk of the population of the Roman world, though Junian Latins seem to have been excluded from this grant.

The Roman family—patria potestas. In the early law, and to a considerable extent throughout Roman history, the family is the legal unit. Its head, the *paterfamilias*, is the only full person known to the law. His children, of whatever age, though they are citizens and therefore have rights in public law, are subject to his unfettered power of life and death. Again, only he can own property, and anything which his children acquire belongs to him alone. This *patria potestas* was thought by the

---

[1] See above, p. 9.　　　　　　　　[2] See below, pp. 74 f.

Romans to be peculiar to themselves. The powers of a Greek father served only a protective purpose, like those of a guardian, and ended when the child came of age.

Patria potestas could, as we shall see,[1] be artificially created and terminated, but normally a Roman citizen was in the *potestas* of his oldest living male ancestor, and as such was called a *filiusfamilias*. He became himself a *paterfamilias*, with *potestas* over his descendants, if any, on the death of his last surviving male ancestor. Thus a man whose father and grandfather were both living was in the *potestas* of his grandfather. On his grandfather's death he would be in the *potestas* of his father, and on his father's death he would himself be a *paterfamilias*.

The family was thus based on the agnatic relationship, i.e. one traced exclusively through the male line. For example, a man is agnatically related to his sister, but not to his sister's children, to his brother and his brother's children, but not to the children of his brother's daughter. (The English system of surnames is agnatic, except for the rule that a wife takes her husband's name.) The daughter of a *paterfamilias* is therefore in his *potestas*, but her children are in the *potestas* of their father or his *paterfamilias*. To put it in another way, a man's agnates are those persons, male or female, who are in the same *potestas* as himself or who would be in the same *potestas* if their common ancestor were alive. His cognates, on the other hand, are simply his blood relatives, whether agnatic or not. The agnatic relationship was for most purposes the only one recognized by the civil law, but by the end of the Republic old ideas had given place to new and the Praetor was increasingly replacing the agnatic by the cognatic tie.[2]

In early law there was evidently little difference between son and slave, both being regarded as the property of the *paterfamilias* to be disposed of as he wished. Thus the formalities for the emancipation and adoption of sons were in essentials the same as those used for the conveyance of property,[3] and in early law a *paterfamilias* could as freely sell his sons as his slaves. In regard to the public law, however, sons did differ fundamentally from slaves. They could vote, and could hold any public office. And, of course, the status of a slave, unlike that of a son, was not affected by the death of the *paterfamilias*.

---

[1] Below, pp. 76 ff.   [2] See below, pp. 248 ff., 260.   [3] See below, pp. 76 ff.

In the exercise of the power of life and death (*ius vitae necisque*), as in the making of all important decisions, the Roman was in the habit of consulting an informal 'council' of advisers, who constituted what amounted to a domestic tribunal. This was, however, only a matter of custom, not of law. The Censors might take notice of any gross abuse, but otherwise the exercise of the *ius vitae necisque* could not be questioned. We know, for example, that one of those who took part in the Catilinarian conspiracy (63 B.C.) was put to death simply by his father's order. It is not until the beginning of the second century A.D. that we hear of any attempt at restriction, and then it is only by 'extraordinary' imperial intervention in particular cases, more akin to the old Censorial supervision of morals than to the establishment of a rule of law. Thus Hadrian banished a man who had killed his son for committing adultery with his stepmother—but the killing had been done while out hunting, not 'judicially'. But social habits were changing, and the over-indulgent parent was replacing the stern father of an earlier day,[1] so that by the end of the classical period the power of life and death was probably obsolete—except for the practice, common in the ancient world, of exposing new-born babies; this was made criminal in A.D. 374, but it evidently still survived in Justinian's day.

If a father could kill his child he could also sell him. If sold abroad ('across the Tiber') the child became a slave, but such sales were very early obsolete. If the sale was made within Roman territory the child did not become a slave, but had a quasi-servile status (*in mancipio*), which differed from slavery in a number of minor ways but mainly in that his rights as a free man were only in suspense and therefore revived if he were manumitted.[2] In the classical law such sales, though they survived among the formalities of emancipation and adoption, had substantial use only in noxal surrender.[3] In the later Empire we do indeed hear of the sale of new-born children, but the father always retained the right to redeem any child whom he had sold.

---

[1] See the examples in J. Carcopino, *Daily Life in Ancient Rome* (Penguin Books edn.), pp. 82 ff.

[2] For the status of the manumitted slave, see below, pp. 75 f.

[3] See below, p. 223.

The *paterfamilias* was said to be *sui iuris* (in his own power); those in his power (whether children, slaves, or persons *in mancipio*) were *alieni iuris* (in the power of another).

Proprietary incapacity of filiusfamilias. The civil law rule was that a *filiusfamilias* could own nothing, anything that he acquired belonging automatically to the *paterfamilias*. This rule was obviously inconvenient, and it became customary for the *paterfamilias* to allow his son the free use of some property (his *peculium*), and in particular of such property as he acquired by his own exertions. In law this *peculium* remained the property of the *paterfamilias*: he could take it away at any time and on his death it reverted to his estate. But the practice was very different from the law, and the *peculium* was evidently treated in fact as the private property of the son: the father would not usually interfere with it, and would so draft his will as to take account of its existence. Even so, such a compromise between practice and law is always unsatisfactory. At best it leads to circuity (and so actions in respect of the *peculium* had to be brought by and against the father) and at worst to injustice (as happened, for example, when no will was made or the will failed).

This merely socially recognized *peculium*[1] (to which the commentators have given the name *peculium profecticium*) was particularly unsatisfactory for the *filiusfamilias* who was a soldier, serving perhaps for long periods away from Rome, and Augustus accordingly allowed him a legal title to what he acquired on service. In its developed form this *peculium castrense* was owned by the son for all purposes except that if he died intestate it reverted to his father. Under Constantine and subsequent Emperors the principle was extended to earnings in various other branches of the public service (*peculium quasi-castrense*). In the same period the son was allowed a limited interest in other property (*bona adventicia*)—at first in what he received from his mother or her relations, and finally in anything which he did not derive from his father. But this was not a *peculium*: the son had no right to enjoyment of the property during the father's life but became fully entitled on the father's death. If the son was emancipated, the father retained a life-interest (usufruct) in half, the other half going immediately to the son.

[1] It did however have some indirect legal consequences: see below, pp. 201 f.

In this piecemeal way the *filiusfamilias* eventually acquired considerable property rights, even though in the case of *bona adventicia* they were only reversionary rights. In modern French and German law, though little else remains of the Roman *patria potestas* but the name and a certain patriarchal attitude, the father still has the right to the enjoyment of his child's property, though only until the child comes of age and subject to a duty to maintain and educate him. In English law, by contrast, the father has no right at all to the enjoyment of his child's property.

It must also be remembered that although *patria potestas* was in principle life-long, emancipation was in fact fairly common.

Position of slaves, in law and in fact. In law the slave was a thing. Being endowed with reason and often indeed well-educated, he was inevitably a peculiar thing and could, for example, acquire rights for his master. But he himself had no rights: he was merely an object of rights, like an animal. It was not until the first and second centuries A.D. that any attempt was made to regulate the master's treatment of his slave, and such regulation as there was took the same form as our legislation for the protection of animals. The master might be punished criminally for abuse of his powers, but the slave could not himself invoke the protection of the law. For example, the master was, early in the Empire, forbidden to send his slave to fight wild beasts in the arena without the approval of a magistrate, and later any killing of his slaves without good reason was made criminal. And there were many other more particular instances of imperial intervention, especially by Hadrian and Antoninus Pius. The latter even allowed the slave to take the initiative for his own protection. If a slave took refuge from the 'intolerable cruelty' of his master at a statue of the Emperor,[1] the master would be compelled to sell him. To this limited extent the slave may be said to have become the subject of a right. Finally, under Justinian, the master was allowed no more than reasonable chastisement.

[1] This form of asylum, which derived from Greece, has, it seems, a curious counterpart in the present-day sheikhdoms of the Trucial Coast. 'The right of manumission of slaves is still exercised by the British Political Agent, after a slave is seen clutching the Union Jack flag pole and after he or she has stated a reasonable cause for manumission'. *The Times*, 11 March 1957.

This was the law, but the slave's position in fact naturally varied greatly according to the abilities, and therefore the value, of the individual slave, and the character of his master. Large-scale ownership of slaves, as of other forms of capital, only began with the extension of Roman conquests to the Eastern Mediterranean in the second century B.C.[1] Until then slaves were few in number and usually of the same race as their masters, and lived in close proximity to them. By the end of the Republic, however, they had come in vast numbers from all corners of the known world. Caesar on a single occasion in Gaul sold 63,000 captives, and the Younger Pliny records, admittedly as worthy of note, that a man who had himself been freed from slavery had amassed at his death 4,116 slaves. The growth of the large estates was made possible by large gangs of labouring slaves, drawn mainly from the ruder and hardier races of the north. Their condition was as hard and inhuman as it well could be. Slaves such as these were the machines of the ancient world. Varro indeed speaks of a slave as a 'speaking tool',[2] and Cato could argue coldly that it was more economical to work a slave to death and then replace him than to treat him properly. Nor was the condition of house-slaves necessarily better. It was the traditional practice, for example, to keep the door-keeper slave chained to his post, and Juvenal no doubt draws from the life his picture of the lady's maid mercilessly flogged by her petulant mistress. At the other end of the scale, some slaves were highly educated men, usually from Greece and the Near East, who, even on Cato's principle, would deserve to be treated well. They might be doctors or teachers or private secretaries, and were treated like free men. Indeed they were often made free by their masters as a reward for faithful service. Many also were engaged in commerce or as managers of their masters' estates. It is the existence of slaves like these that differentiates Roman slavery from any that the modern world has known, and which explains the bulk and complexity of the Roman law governing the consequences of their transactions. The labourer on the plantation provides little scope for the private law. It is quite otherwise with the manager of a large business.

The independent activity of slaves was made possible largely by the *peculium*. This was identical with the *peculium profecticium*

---

[1] See above, p. 8.   [2] Aristotle had similarly called him an 'animated tool'.

of the son. It was owned legally by the master but 'socially' by the slave. How firmly established was the slave's claim to his *peculium* can be seen from the common practice whereby the master made him a gift of freedom in his will provided he paid a sum of money to the heir. The only source from which he could draw this sum was his *peculium*, and yet by law this was already the property of the heir as successor of the master. In the same way, we hear of slaves having business dealings with their masters as if they were independent persons. It must moreover be remembered that the *peculium* was not just a sum of money, but might include any form of property, even other slaves. It might, for example, be an entire business conducted by the slave at his own discretion; and, if the business prospered, he might offer to 'buy' his freedom with the money he had saved. Yet in law it all belonged to the master. For the law was the same for slaves as for sons: any property they acquired belonged automatically to the master. In the same way, a slave could alienate nothing without his master's authority, but a general authority was normally assumed to accompany the grant of the *peculium*, and a slave could therefore in practice, so far as property rights were concerned, act as if he were an independent person. His contracts, however, presented greater difficulties. Contractual rights, like property rights, passed to his master, but few contracts create only rights, and the law held that a man could incur no duties under a contract entered into by someone else, even his own slave. This strict rule would have deprived slaves of much of their commercial usefulness had not the Praetor intervened to modify it.[1]

2. CREATION AND TERMINATION OF SLAVERY

How slavery arises. The two normal sources of slavery were birth and capture in war. Both were of the *ius gentium*, and from this two main consequences followed. The rule of enslavement by capture applied as much to Romans who fell into the hands of the enemy[2] as vice versa; and the status of a child at birth

---

[1] See below, pp. 201 f.

[2] To answer the problems raised by the return of a Roman from captivity the notion of *postliminium* was evolved. The prisoner's rights were in suspense so long as he lived. If he returned they revived automatically and retrospectively; if he died in captivity his death was deemed to have occurred at the moment of his

was in general decided, according to the rule of the *ius gentium*, by the status of the mother. The child of a slave woman and a free man was therefore a slave, but the child of a free woman and a slave man was free. To this rule the classical law added the gloss, in favour of freedom, that if the mother had been free at any time between conception and birth the child was free.

There were also a few cases of enslavement under the *ius civile*. Condemnation in a criminal proceeding sometimes involved slavery, and under Claudius it was enacted that a woman who persisted in cohabiting with a slave after warning by his master should herself become a slave. The practice in the later Empire of selling new-born children into slavery has already been mentioned.[1]

How slavery ends—manumission. The Roman slave could always hope for manumission, and in the earlier Empire this hope must for many of them have been well-founded. It has been estimated that over eighty per cent. of the population of Rome were then either freedmen or descended, immediately or remotely, from freedmen.

The old civil law recognized three methods of manumission. All these of course were formal, but other, informal, methods developed later.

(*a*) *Manumissio vindicta.* Like *in iure cessio*[2] this appears to be a collusive action. If a man who was held as a slave wished to assert that he was free, he obviously could not bring an action himself, since it was precisely his capacity to do so which was in issue. A 'prisoner's friend' (*adsertor libertatis*) therefore brought the action, which was a variant of the action asserting ownership, the *adsertor* claiming not that the man belonged to him but that he was free. Obviously, if a collusive version of the ordinary *vindicatio* could, in the form of *in iure cessio*, be made to serve the purpose of a conveyance, a collusive version of a claim of liberty could equally be used to give freedom to a slave. This is at least

---

capture. This principle applied to rights, but not to 'facts', i.e. to legal relationships which required for their existence some physical manifestation. Such relationships did not revive automatically, but had to be physically resumed. Thus possession (below, p. 115) ended on capture and if resumed on return was a new possession dating from that moment; similarly the captive's marriage came to an end and did not revive unless and until a married relationship was by agreement resumed.

[1] Above, p. 67.   [2] See above, pp. 63 f.

the probable origin of *manumissio vindicta*—the owner acquiesced in the claim of the *adsertor* and the Praetor adjudged the slave to be free—but in the form in which it survives in the classical law it has, like *in iure cessio*, lost many of the characteristics of an action. In particular, just as *in iure cessio* had the effect of a conveyance and not of a judgment, so here freedom dated only from the manumission, whereas in the true claim of liberty the supposed slave was necessarily declared not to have been a slave at all. And the process of degeneration, if such it was, had gone even further than in *in iure cessio*. For there the proceedings must still, like those of an ordinary action, take place *in iure*, whereas *manumissio vindicta* could be performed anywhere, even, Gaius tells us, when the Praetor was on his way to the theatre or the baths; and the part of *adsertor* was played by one of the Praetor's escort of lictors. It was a very threadbare form indeed.

There was one further difference between the *in iure cessio* and the *manumissio*, and that gave the *manumissio* its name. The *adsertor*, when making his claim, touched the slave with a wand —*vindicta*—and so did the manumitting master. This laying on of the wand, apparently as a symbol of ownership, occurred in the ordinary *vindicatio* of the *legis actio* procedure, but not, it seems, in *in iure cessio*.

(*b*) *Manumissio censu*. With the consent of his master a slave might be added to the list of citizens by the Censors,[1] but since the census was taken only every four or five years and was not taken regularly at all after the end of the Republic (the last was apparently in A.D. 74) this method cannot have been of much importance.

(*c*) *Manumissio testamento*. The most common form of manumission, which already existed in the time of the Twelve Tables, was by will. By a provision in his will in appropriate formal words a master could direct that on his death one or more of his slaves should be free, either immediately or subject to some condition (e.g. that the slave should pay so much to the heir). This method of manumission enabled a master to be generous without inconvenience to himself, and at the same time to satisfy the common Roman desire for a grateful cortege at his funeral. So popular indeed had this practice become by the end of the Republic that limits had to be set to it by legislation.[2]

---

[1] See above, pp. 4 f.   [2] See below, p. 76.

(*d*) *Informal manumission.* The Praetor, pursuing his usual policy of looking at the substance of a transaction rather than its form, gave a limited recognition to informal expressions of intention to manumit. We hear of two customary methods of expressing such an intention—by letter (*per epistulam*) and before witnesses (*inter amicos*)—but the Praetor probably recognized any properly evidenced act. By the civil law of course such a manumission was void, and since the Praetor could not make law he could not simply declare the man free. As usual he had to proceed indirectly, by barring any action brought by the master to assert his ownership. In this way the slave was protected in the *de facto* enjoyment of his freedom, but otherwise he remained a slave. He could bring no actions himself; he could own no property (any that he might in fact enjoy was held as a *peculium* from his master, to whom it therefore reverted on death); and, of course, his children were slaves. He was said to be at liberty under the protection of the Praetor (*in libertate tuitione Praetoris*).[1]

The *lex Junia*[2] replaced this unsatisfactory twilight condition by Latinity. The slave now became free, but not a citizen (a Junian Latin). He had *commercium* but neither *conubium* nor *testamenti factio*,[3] the latter disability being reinforced by a provision that his whole property should pass on his death to his former master. (The master's right of succession to a fully manumitted freedman was much more limited, and was altogether excluded if the freedman had children.) It was presumably this advantage to the master (and perhaps the avoiding of the 5 per cent. tax on full manumissions), rather than reluctance to go to the trouble of a formal manumission, which provided the usual motive for informal manumissions; for the formalities of *manumissio vindicta* were hardly very burdensome. On the other hand it is not so easy to see why the Junian Latin should have been denied also the other aspect of *testamenti factio*, namely the power to take under a will. But this disability was in any case circumvented.

The Junian Latin, though not a citizen, was not debarred

---

[1] The Praetor gave the same protection in one other case, mentioned above, pp. 26 ff., namely that of a manumission, whether formal or informal, by a bonitary owner (see below, pp. 125 ff.).

[2] See above, p. 65.

[3] See above, pp. 64 f.

from obtaining citizenship. His master could at any time make the manumission fully effective by repeating it in one of the three recognized forms (*iteratio*), and we have seen[1] that there were various ways in which he could achieve the same end by his own efforts.

With the advent of Christianity a new informal method of manumission appeared, or rather a variant of the old *manumissio inter amicos*: the master made his declaration before the congregation in church. By the time of Justinian, however, the status of Junian Latin had become rare, and he therefore provided that all manumissions, whether formal or informal, should confer citizenship.

Consequences of manumission. Latin has two terms for 'freedman'. One (*libertinus*) indicates his relationship to society at large, the other (*libertus*) his relationship to his former master (his *patronus*).

As a *libertinus* he was free and either a citizen or a Junian Latin. Even as a citizen he was under some political disabilities (mainly exclusion from magistracies and from the Senate), though in the early years of the Empire freedmen achieved positions of immense power as members of the Emperor's personal civil service, and many in this way or in commerce made large fortunes.

As a *libertus* his status was an echo of his former subjection. He owed his patron the duty of *obsequium*—respect. This was largely a social matter but it had incidental legal consequences, especially that he might not bring an action against his patron without the Praetor's permission. There was, moreover, a reciprocal duty of support in case of need, and it was also usual to exact from the slave before manumission an undertaking on oath to render certain services (*operae*), the extent and nature of which were precisely defined by law.

This relationship of patron and freedman must be seen in its context. Until the Empire the patron could exercise over his freedman a power of life and death, just as he could over his son. Moreover manumission would often make very little difference to the freedman's position in fact—he would often continue to live in his patron's household and even to perform the same

---

[1] Above, p. 65.

functions as he did as a slave. Again, the relationship of patron and freedman was only one aspect of a much wider relationship of patron and 'client' which spread all through Roman society and of which we have a vivid picture in the satires of Juvenal. It has been said that 'however high a man might climb in the Roman hierarchy, there was always someone to claim his homage. There was in fact no one in Rome, save the Emperor alone, who recognised no one greater than himself.'[1]

The children of a freedman were normal citizens, subject to none of these disabilities.

Public control of manumission. A surprising feature of the law of the Republic is that although manumission conferred the much-prized privileges of citizenship, including the right to the corn-dole, there was, *manumissio censu* apart, no effective public control. It was not until the time of Augustus that any steps were taken in this direction. The *lex Fufia Caninia* of 2 B.C. limited manumissions by will (in which irresponsibility was obviously most likely) to a fixed proportion of the total owned by the testator (e.g. of a total of 10 not more than 5, of 100 not more than 25 could be manumitted, and in no circumstances more than 100). The *lex Aelia Sentia* of A.D. 4 required the approval of a special council for manumissions of any kind made by a master under 20 or of a slave under 30. It also provided that slaves whose bad character was evidenced by their having been subjected to serious punishment by their masters could become only *dediticii*—incapable of ever becoming citizens and forbidden to live within 100 miles of Rome.

Justinian repealed the *lex Fufia Caninia*, partly out of *favor libertatis* and partly no doubt because the decline in wealth in general and in the ownership of slaves in particular had largely removed the problem with which the *lex* had been intended to deal. He retained, however, in a modified form, the restrictions of the *lex Aelia Sentia*.

3. CREATION AND TERMINATION OF *PATRIA POTESTAS*

How patria potestas arises. Patria potestas was normally, of course, created by birth out of a Roman marriage (*iustae nuptiae*). This will be considered below. It could also, however, be artificially

[1] J. Carcopino, *Daily Life in Ancient Rome* (Penguin Books edn.), p. 175.

created by adoption. This took two forms, both of great antiquity—*adrogatio* of a person who was already *sui iuris*, and *adoptio* (in the strict sense) of a person who was in the *patria potestas* of someone else. The original motive for adoption must have been the desire of a childless man to ensure the continuance of the family cult (*sacra*), though it is possible that in very early times it also served as a crude substitute for a will. When the religious motive had lost its force, there remained the common desire to perpetuate the family, and the survival of many Roman families through the centuries was made possible only by adoptions.

(*a*) *Adrogatio.* This was achieved by an act of the *comitia curiata*, preceded by an investigation by the *pontifex maximus.*[1] The reason for the legislative form and for the investigation was that *adrogatio* made possible the continuation of one family and its *sacra* only at the cost of the extinction of another. The *pontifex* must be satisfied on religious grounds, and the *comitia* had an interest in the political consequences of the merger of two powerful families. In historical times, as has been said, the *comitia curiata* had no longer any substance as a legislative body, but the investigation by the *pontifex* was maintained, and certain principles which guided his discretion were evolved. In particular, since the justification for *adrogatio* was the desire to continue the family, the person adrogating must have no children, either natural or adoptive, and must either be over the age of 60 or for some reason have no prospect of begetting children. And the person to be adrogated must not be older than the person adrogating.

Since the *comitia curiata* met only at Rome, *adrogatio* could take place only there until, certainly under Diocletian and probably before, a new form of *adrogatio*, by imperial rescript, was introduced. This was a change of form rather than of substance: the official approval was merely manifested in a different, and less formal, way. The old form thereafter disappears.

(*b*) *Adoptio.* The transfer of a person from one *potestas* to another involved first his release from the old *potestas* and then his subjection to the new. The Twelve Tables recognized no method of release from *potestas*, but there was a clause, intended apparently to put a limit to misuse by a father of his right to sell his children, which provided that if a father sold his son three

[1] The head of the priestly 'college' of pontifices (cf. above, p. 28).

times the son would be free. This was turned to advantage in a characteristic way by pontifical *interpretatio* to achieve both emancipation and adoption, the two ceremonies differing only in their final stages. For the purpose of adoption the ceremony runs as follows. In the presence of the usual five witnesses and *libripens* the father mancipates the child to be adopted (*adoptandus*) to the adopter. The *adoptandus* is as a result *in mancipio*[1] to the adopter, who then manumits him *vindicta* (i.e. the parties go to the Praetor and the father claims that the *adoptandus* is free, and the adopter acquiesces). The son is then free, but once more in the *potestas* of the father. A second mancipation and a second manumission follow, producing of course the same result. The father then mancipates the son a third time to the adopter. By the Twelve Tables rule the *adoptandus* is then out of the *potestas* of the father, but is *in mancipio* to the adopter. The adopter therefore mancipates him back to the father, and the final stage is once more before the Praetor—the adopter makes a collusive claim that the *adoptandus* is his son (*in iure cessio*).[2]

By a characteristic piece of well-intentioned but illogical pedantry the pontifical lawyers held that as the Twelve Tables referred only to sons, only one mancipation was necessary to break *potestas* over a daughter or a grandchild. Justinian at last swept away the whole of this cumbersome ritual and left only the essential—a declaration before a magistrate, entered on the court records.

The effect of both *adoptio* and *adrogatio* was to place the adopted person for all legal purposes in the same position as if he had been a natural child in the *potestas* of the adopter. The adopted son took his adoptive father's name, and was agnatically related to his adoptive father's agnates. In consequence he acquired rights of succession on death (which by civil law depended on the agnatic relationship) in his new family and lost all such rights that he previously had. Moreover 'adoption

---

[1] See above, p. 67.

[2] The number of stages in this complicated proceeding could be reduced by one if an extra person, a man of straw, were introduced. The three mancipations and two manumissions would then take place not between the father and the adopter but between the father and the man of straw. The *adoptandus* would then after the third mancipation be *in mancipio* to the man of straw, from whom the adopter could collusively claim him. Gaius says that the former method is more convenient, presumably because the *dramatis personae* are fewer by one.

imitates nature', and therefore an adoptive relationship was, for example, as much a bar to marriage as a natural one. *Adrogatio* had of course the additional consequences that the property of the person adrogated passed to his adoptive father, and that any children in his *potestas* passed into the *potestas* of the adoptive father.

Adoptio was a possible source of injustice in that the adopted son might subsequently be emancipated by his adoptive father and, since emancipation destroyed all existing agnatic ties, would then have lost all rights of succession not only in his natural family but also in his adoptive family.[1] Justinian therefore made a radical alteration in the law. In the ordinary case *adoptio* was to be no more than a grant of rights of succession in the new family (*adoptio minus plena*). For all other purposes, including the retention of existing rights of succession, the *adoptandus* remained in his natural family—he merely now had rights of succession in two families. *Adoptio* was to have its full effect (*adoptio plena*) only if the adopter was a natural ascendant of the *adoptandus* (e.g. his maternal grandfather), and was therefore less likely to indulge in capricious emancipation.

The Roman ideas of adoption, but without the distinction between *adrogatio* and *adoptio* or between *adoptio plena* and *minus plena*, have passed into modern Civil law, but the Common law knew nothing of such an institution. It was not until 1926 that adoption was introduced (by statute) into England, and then it created little more than a special kind of guardianship: it was confined to children under 21, conferred no rights of succession, and created no relationship which would be a bar to marriage. In the last two respects English law was brought much nearer to Roman ideas in 1949, but adoption of adults, common in Rome, and still practised in, for example, Germany, remains unknown.

How patria potestas ends. Patria potestas is terminated, as we have seen, by *adoptio*, or by *adrogatio* of a *paterfamilias* who has children in his *potestas*, but also of course by death, and by the loss of liberty or citizenship, and in various other minor ways. The

---

[1] It is true that the Praetor restored to him his rights of succession to his natural father (see below, p. 249), but this might be cold comfort: his natural father might have died before the emancipation took place.

most important artificial method of terminating *patria potestas* was, however, emancipation. As was said above, the form here was closely similar to that of *adoptio*. There were three mancipations and two manumissions, which left the son out of the *potestas* of the father but *in mancipio* to the man of straw. The son could then be made free simply by a manumission by the man of straw.[1] It was in this final stage that the only difference from *adoptio* occurred: the collusive claim was that the son was free, rather than that he was in the *potestas* of the claimant.

Emancipation not only freed the son from *patria potestas*, but also deprived him of all rights of succession. We must not therefore think of it as necessarily the conferring of a benefit; it might equally well in earlier times be a punishment, casting the son out into the world without property and without hope of inheriting any from his father. The Praetor, however, gave rights of succession on intestacy to emancipated children,[2] and in the classical law they could no more be cut out of their father's will without good cause than could their unemancipated brothers and sisters.[3]

4. MARRIAGE

Main characteristics. There are few Roman institutions which differ so fundamentally from their modern counterparts as marriage. From the legal point of view marriage is to us a status, the creation and termination of which are closely regulated by law, and which not only founds a number of rights and duties between the parties but also to some extent affects the relationship of the parties to the rest of the world. A Roman marriage, on the other hand, was very largely a social fact, about the creation and termination of which the law had very little to say, and which had almost no effect on the legal condition of the parties.

In modern English law a marriage is only valid if the parties, being capable of marrying (i.e. being sane, not within the prohibited degrees of relationship, and not below the permitted

---

[1] This had, however, one disadvantage: the rights of succession which belonged to anyone who manumitted a person *in mancipio* or a slave, and also, if the son were *impubes*, the right of *tutela* (see below, pp. 90 ff.), would accrue to the man of straw. It was therefore usual for the man of straw to mancipate the son back to the father who would then himself make the manumission.

[2] See below, p. 249.   [3] See below, pp. 261 ff.

age), go through certain formalities. Roman law imposed similar conditions as to capacity to marry (to which were added the specifically Roman requirements of *conubium* and, if either of the parties, no matter what his age, were in *patria potestas*, of paternal consent), but subject to these conditions all that was required for a valid marriage was a manifestation of a common intention to be married. And what constituted an intention to be married, as opposed to an intention merely to live together, was a question of fact, of social convention. Similarly, the intention must be manifested in some act, but what this act must be, except that it need not be consummation, was again left to be settled as a question of fact. There were, of course, social ceremonies which customarily accompanied a marriage, and which would in the normal case leave no doubt as to the existence of the requisite intention, but none of these ceremonies was legally necessary. Divorce was equally free: a marriage was terminated by any manifested intention by either party no longer to be married. The resulting uncertainty in some cases as to whether a union was (or was still) a marriage would seem to us intolerable, but would be of much less importance in Rome where the legal consequences of marriage were, as we shall see, very few.

In modern English law, though the old rule that husband and wife were in law one person has been almost entirely swept away, marriage still produces a number of legal consequences, especially the 'conjugal rights' of cohabitation, the husband's duty of support, an almost complete mutual immunity from suit in tort, and in some circumstances the husband's liability on his wife's contracts, but Roman law knew none of these. In particular, 'conjugal rights' could mean nothing in a system which admitted an unrestricted right of unilateral divorce. It is significant that marriage finds a place in Gaius' arrangement only as a source of *patria potestas*. The validity or invalidity of a marriage was relevant primarily, as we shall see, to the status of the children, though it was relevant for some other purposes also. Thus, if a union were not a marriage, any property contributed by the woman could not be subject to the rules governing dowry (*dos*),[1] and conversely the rule forbidding gifts between husband and wife[2] could have no application. Again, the existence of a

---

[1] See below, pp. 87 ff.   [2] See below, p. 90.

marriage would be relevant to the husband's right to prosecute the wife for adultery. But such a list only serves to emphasize the gulf between the Roman and the modern conceptions of marriage. In particular, the Roman law, unlike the old Common law, gave to the husband no rights over the wife's property (apart from *dos*) and no rights over her person. If she were *sui iuris* she retained her independence and her property, if she were *alieni iuris* she remained in the *potestas* of her father. In neither case, according to the agnatic principles of the civil law, was she related to her husband's family, nor even to her children.[1]

Manus. The free consensual union described above was the normal marriage under the Empire, but until the end of the Republic, and to a dwindling extent thereafter, marriage might result in a very different relationship. The wife was said to be in the hand (*manus*) of her husband. *Manus* was closely similar to *patria potestas.* The wife was in the position of a daughter to her husband and consequently if he were *alieni iuris* she was a grand-daughter to his father. The effects of the creation of *manus* were in general the same as those of *adrogatio* if she were *sui iuris*, or of *adoptio* if she were not. Her property, if any, vested in her husband or his *paterfamilias*, and she had the same rights of succession to him as did her children.

Manus came into existence in three ways. The usual method of creating it was *coemptio*, a form of *mancipatio* of the woman to her husband, differing from an ordinary *mancipatio* in that she was thereby placed in his *manus* and not *in mancipio*. It is presumably a survival of the marriage by purchase which is commonly found among primitive peoples. *Confarreatio* was a religious ceremony, necessary for and probably confined to the members of certain priesthoods. Finally, *manus* could arise by prescription (*usus*). We shall see[2] that if a slave or other *res mancipi* were handed over without *mancipatio* the resulting lack of ownership in the recipient would be made good by the continuance of possession for one year (or two for land). In the same way, if a woman were married without *coemptio* the resulting lack of *manus* would be made good by one year's cohabitation.

---

[1] For the consequences of this in the law of succession, see below, pp. 247 ff.
[2] Below, pp. 122 ff.

Indeed the possibility of 'free' marriage was only preserved by a provision of the Twelve Tables that a wife could prevent the establishment of *manus* by absenting herself for three nights in each year. But the whole institution was obsolete in Gaius' day. *Manus* could then only be created expressly by *coemptio*, and was probably even so very rare.

Usus makes clear the nature of *manus* as something added on to marriage: the wife is married for a year before she passes into *manus*. In the same way, at least in the mature law, the marriage itself could be broken by repudiation by the wife, but she would still be *in manu* until her husband emancipated her, though she could require him to do so.

Iustae nuptiae and non-Roman marriage. Marriage in Rome, as throughout the ancient world, was a matter of personal law, and therefore a Roman marriage (*iustae nuptiae*) could exist only if both parties were citizens or at least peregrines with *conubium*. Whether a union was *iustae nuptiae* or not was important primarily because it determined the status of the children. And this it did in two ways. First, as we have seen, children born from *iustae nuptiae* were in the *potestas* of the father (except when he was a peregrine, for although he had *conubium* he was still incapable of *patria potestas*); and, secondly, their status as citizens or not was determined by the civil law rule, that they took the status of their father, and not by the rule of the *ius gentium*, that they took the status of their mother. Thus, children born from a marriage between a Roman citizen mother and a peregrine father with *conubium* would themselves be peregrines with *conubium* and would be governed by the personal law of their father; whereas if the father had not had *conubium*, the rule of the *ius gentium* would have made them Roman citizens.[1]

Concubinage. Marriage differed from a merely casual or surreptitious liaison in the existence of an intent both to enter into a permanent union and to give to that union the social and legal consequences of marriage. Already in the Republic,

[1] This rather paradoxical result was, however, reversed by a *lex Minicia* (date unknown), which made the children in this case also peregrines. The law governing such unions between persons without *conubium*, and in particular the distinction between them and a merely casual union, presents difficulties which cannot be adequately discussed here.

however, there existed an intermediate type of union in which the former intent was present but not the latter. For example, a man might enter into a permanent union with his freedwoman without wishing to give her the social and legal recognition accorded to a wife. Such a union necessarily lacked even the limited legal consequences which followed from marriage, but was accepted as a social fact and was termed concubinage. (The morganatic marriage later served a similar purpose in the more limited society of the German princely families, but did have legal consequences.)

Concubinage acquired sharper outlines in the early Empire as an unintended consequence of legislation which forbade marriage between persons of widely differing rank (members of senatorial families with freedmen and freedwomen, any freeborn citizen with a woman of ill-repute). The only permanent union which was now possible between such persons was concubinage, socially accepted and in no way illegal, but not recognized by the law. This way of escape became more important when to the list of forbidden marriages were added those between provincial officials and women of their province, and when, astonishingly enough considering the length of service required of them, soldiers were, at any rate in some circumstances, forbidden to marry altogether. In other cases however, particularly in that of a union between a patron and his freedwoman, concubinage remained simply an alternative to marriage, freely chosen for social reasons. Nor was it always an alternative to marriage —a man might not have two wives, but there was no legal reason why he should not have a wife and a concubine or more than one concubine.

The later Empire however, under the influence of Christianity, was hostile to concubinage as an unregulated union, and tended to make of it a left-handed marriage, subject to some of the rules of a full marriage. In particular it became exclusively a monogamous alternative to marriage, permitted only within the same limits of age and relationship.

Legitimation. Out of concubinage there grew the historically important institution of legitimation. Until the time of Constantine the only way in which an illegitimate child could be brought into his father's *potestas* and otherwise legitimated was for the father to adrogate him, and this would not always be possible—for example, if the father had other (legitimate) children. Constantine, out of a desire to encourage those living in concubinage to marry, enacted that such a marriage should legitimate any children already born. This enactment dealt only with existing unions, however, and legitimation by subsequent marriage did not become a regular institution until shortly before the time of Justinian. Moreover it still applied only to children born in concubinage, and the parents must have been capable of a lawful marriage at the time of conception.

Canon law adopted the institution from the imperial law, but since it did not recognize concubinage it extended the benefit of legitimation by subsequent marriage to the children of any union which was not adulterous or incestuous. From the Canon law this passed into the systems of modern Europe, the English excepted. For legitimation, like adoption, was unknown to English law until introduced by statute in 1926.

Legitimation was also granted by imperial rescript in cases where legitimation by subsequent marriage had become impossible by, for example, the death of the mother. This prerogative power passed to the rulers of medieval and early modern Europe, and traces of it may still be found in some continental systems of law.

Divorce. Since Roman marriage depended for its existence merely on the parties' living together with the intention of being married, it could equally be brought to an end by the free will of either or both. And just as no formality was needed for the beginning of a marriage, so also none was needed for its termination. All that was necessary was some evidence of intention. We hear indeed of the uttering of customary words or the sending of a document, just as we hear of customary words and ceremonies at the beginning of a marriage, but none of these was legally necessary. (Augustus did however require, at any rate in some cases, a declaration in the presence of seven witnesses.)

Until the later years of the Republic this total freedom of divorce was kept in check by public opinion and by the Roman habit of consulting a family council before making any important decision. There was, moreover, the possibility of Censorial sanctions. Thus, in 307 B.C. a Senator was deprived of his dignities for divorcing his wife without consulting a family council. By the last century B.C., however, divorce had become a matter of course, at least among the upper classes, for whose habits alone we have any evidence. The respectable Cicero put away his wife after thirty years of marriage in favour of a young and wealthy bride, and Cato of Utica had no compunction in remarrying his divorced wife when she was left a wealthy widow by her intervening husband. Augustus himself had divorced his first wife before marrying Livia; and a famous inscription of the time (*Laudatio Turiae*), in praise of a wife who had died after forty-one years of marriage, records that such marriages, ending in death and not in divorce, were rare. Seneca, fifty years later, remarks that women reckon the years not by the names of the consuls, but by those of their husbands.[1]

So fundamental was this unfettered freedom of divorce that even an agreement not to divorce was void as being incompatible with the Roman idea of marriage. The only practical deterrent to divorce was provided by the rules governing the return or retention of the wife's dowry.[2] A man who thought nothing of divorce might still hesitate to lose the dowry, and conversely, if there were children, the husband's right to retain a proportion of the dowry might give the wife pause for thought. But such motives would have no force if there were a wealthier match in sight.

With the advent of Christianity as the official religion of the Empire, a radical change in the attitude to divorce might have been expected. Consent was indeed the foundation of Christian as of Roman marriage, but for the Christian the effect of consent was exhausted in the creation of the marriage, leaving no room for the Roman idea that what had been created by agreement could be dissolved by contrary agreement or by disagreement. Such was the Christian teaching, and the Empire was formally Christian, but it embraced within its borders a very heterogeneous population many of whom evidently did not live up to the new teaching (ecclesiastical penalties against remarried

---

[1] For further illustrations see J. Carcopino, *Daily Life in Ancient Rome* (Penguin Books edn.), pp. 100 ff.

[2] See below, pp. 88 f.

divorcees are common). Even the most forcefully Christian
Emperors did not venture wholly to uproot the old law, but
sought rather to restrict its application by imposing increasingly
severe penalties on divorce by either party unless for a reason
recognized by the legislator. And even unjustified divorce,
though penalized, was effective.[1] More important still, and more
surprising in a Christian context, divorce by mutual consent
remained quite untouched by the hand of the legislator until
542. In that year Justinian did forbid it, but the old ways
evidently died hard, for within five years of his death the prohibition had been repealed.

In this respect, however, Roman law died without issue. The
marriage law of western Europe was to be the Canon law, and
the Canon law, though in other ways it often thought in Roman
terms, inevitably rejected the Roman view of divorce. Nor is the
divorce of modern secular systems of law at all comparable. A
modern divorce is an act of the court and not, as in Roman law,
of the parties.

Matrimonial property. Marriage, and still more the termination of
marriage, raises problems concerning the property which each
party brings into the union, and the solutions to these problems
are usually deeply rooted in the customs of each community.
Hence it is that in countries such as Germany, or even France,
which achieved unity of law only fairly recently, the diverse
customary solutions, or 'régimes of matrimonial property', still
remain for the choice of the intending spouses or their families,
and make this part of the law extremely complicated. A recurrent feature is some form of joint ownership, coupled however
with the vesting of a wide power of administration in the husband. The rule of the old Common law, on the other hand, was
that husband and wife were one person and that the property of
the wife vested to a large extent in the husband.

Neither of these principles accorded with the classical Roman
idea of 'free marriage'.[2] In principle, as in present-day English
law, each party retained unfettered ownership of his or her
property, but this entire separation was considerably modified

---

[1] But for the peccant wife for whom Justinian decreed lifelong confinement in
a convent the distinction had little interest.

[2] Marriage with *manus* is here ignored, and it is assumed that neither husband
nor wife is in *patria potestas*.

by the institution of dowry (*dos*) and, in the later law, by the complementary practice of a gift by the husband to the wife (*donatio ante nuptias*).

Dos underwent considerable changes in the course of Roman history. In the early law the husband acquired full ownership of all dotal property, but by the time of Justinian, though he was in theory still owner, he had for practical purposes little more than a right to the income from it so long as the marriage lasted. This transformation of *dos* corresponded to the increased freedom of women and still more to the enormously increased frequency of divorce.

In the early law *dos* was merely a contribution from the wife's side to the expenses of the household, and so long as divorce was uncommon it was not intolerable that this contribution should become wholly and irrevocably the property of the husband, particularly as the children's rights of succession were to their father and not to their mother. Moreover the wife, or whoever provided the dowry, could stipulate expressly for the return of the dowry at the end of the marriage. With the increase in divorce in the late Republic, however, *dos* came to serve a second purpose, to provide for the wife in the event of the break-up of the marriage, and there accordingly developed an action (*actio rei uxoriae*) by which the wife could, without the need for any express provision, require the return of the dowry if the marriage terminated either by divorce or by the death of the husband. In this way the husband, though still owner of the *dos*, was required to account for his management of it, and conversely was entitled to retain fixed proportions of it in certain circumstances. In particular, if the divorce were due to the fault of the wife or her father he could retain one-sixth for each child up to three. The wife's right was, however, only *in personam*[1]—a right against the husband for the return of the value of the *dos* at the end of the marriage. In the meantime he could validly alienate any part of it, and the wife therefore took the risk of his eventual insolvency. Her position in this respect was, however, improved in two directions. Augustus forbade and declared void any alienation without the wife's consent of Italic land[2] forming part of the dowry, and any mortgaging of it even with such

---

[1] For the distinction between rights *in personam* and rights *in rem*, see below, pp. 99 ff.   [2] See below, p. 105, n. 4.

consent; and in the case of insolvency of the husband the wife was given priority over other unsecured creditors. She could thus in all circumstances be sure of the return of her Italic land, and in regard to other property ran the risk only of her husband's assets' being insufficient to meet the claims both of his secured creditors and herself.

Justinian, perhaps under the influence of Greek law which gave the ownership of the dowry to the wife, still further weakened the husband's rights. The rule as to the inalienability of Italic land was extended to land everywhere, and, further, alienation was no longer permitted even with the wife's consent. The husband's right to retain part of the dowry was abolished, and the whole reverted in all circumstances, including now the death of the wife, except that if the husband divorced the wife for good cause or the wife divorced the husband without cause the dowry might be forfeit. Moreover, the wife was now preferred even to secured creditors. For Justinian gave her a tacit hypothec (mortgage implied by law)[1] over all her husband's property, and this hypothec, though at first having priority only from the date of marriage, was later allowed to override even securities created before marriage. This has prompted the remark that Justinian having first ruined the credit of married men went on to ruin that of bachelors also.

In the legislation of the later Empire there appears the institution of *donatio ante nuptias*, complementary to *dos* but deriving from the practice of the Eastern provinces. This was a gift made by the husband in contemplation of marriage and intended to provide for the wife in the event of her being left a widow or being unjustifiably divorced. Under Justinian it became a symmetrical counterpart of *dos*: if there was a *dos* there must be a *donatio* of the same amount. And both *donatio* and *dos* could be either made or increased even after marriage, the former being therefore renamed *donatio propter nuptias*. Moreover the property was administered by the husband and there was therefore commonly not even a formal conveyance, but merely a promise of such conveyance on the termination of the marriage. The wife's right to the *donatio*, like her right to the return of her *dos*, was protected by a tacit hypothec over the husband's property, though without priority.

[1] See below, pp. 152 f.

Dos and *donatio propter nuptias*, when made or increased after marriage, were the principal inroads on the rule that gifts between husband and wife were void, a rule based on the same consideration as was invoked to justify a somewhat analogous rule in English law, 'lest they be kissed or cursed out of their money'.[1] In almost all other respects husband and wife were in their legal relationship to each other wholly independent persons.

Donatio propter nuptias had little subsequent history, but the essential Roman system of separation of property qualified by *dos* still survives in modern Europe, though less commonly than the various customary systems of community of property.

5. GUARDIANSHIP

Tutela impuberum. Children usually present two problems to a system of law. They must be prevented from squandering their property through inexperience; and, if either or both of their parents die, provision must be made for their upbringing and for the management of their property. In Roman law these are no more than two aspects of one problem, since it is only the child whose father has died (or has emancipated him) who is capable of owning property.

Tutela impuberum in the classical law corresponds broadly to the English guardianship of infants, but its original purpose was evidently very different. Modern guardianship is conceived exclusively in the interests of the ward, primitive *tutela* far more in the interests of the guardian (*tutor*). The history of *tutela* is best seen as a movement from one conception to the other, as the transformation of a privilege into a burden; but the transformation was never completed, and some of the characteristic features of the institution can be explained only in terms of the original conception.

(i) *Who is tutor?* The earliest rule was that the nearest male agnate was tutor. Here the primitive idea is plainly to be seen. For it was the nearest agnate who was entitled to succeed to the property of the ward (*pupillus*) if he died, and who was therefore personally interested in its preservation. This guardianship by the nearest male agnate was called *tutela legitima*, as deriving from the *lex* of the Twelve Tables, but it must have been established in the customary law long before, and, subject to what

[1] Buckland, *Textbook of Roman Law*, 2nd edn., p. 111.

follows, it remained in force until Justinian recast the law of succession on intestacy.[1]

Such was the original law, but already in the Twelve Tables the connexion between succession on death and *tutela* was broken. For the father could, and in fact usually did, appoint a *tutor* by will (*tutor testamentarius*). And in later times if there were neither a *tutor testamentarius* nor a *tutor legitimus* a magistrate would appoint one (*tutor dativus*). But there was no relaxation[2] of the primitive rule that no woman, not even the mother, could be *tutor*. This rule derived from the conception of *tutela* as being a continuation of *patria potestas* and therefore necessarily closed to women, and from the related fact that women were themselves subject to lifelong *tutela*.[3] In modern English law, by contrast, if either parent dies it is the survivor who is entitled to be guardian, either alone or jointly with a guardian appointed by the dead parent, and no difference is made in this respect between father and mother. Similar rules, though not always with such exact equality, are found in other modern systems.

(ii) *Duration of pupillage.* In most modern systems a child comes of age at 21, it being thought that at that age he should be capable of looking after his own affairs. In Roman law, however, he came of age at puberty, which was eventually deemed to occur at 14 for males and 12 for females. The reason for the difference lies in the different purposes of primitive *tutela* and modern guardianship. For at puberty the child became capable of having children of his own, and those children would be entitled to succeed to his property to the exclusion of the nearest agnate. The *raison d'être* of the *legitimus tutor* had disappeared and *tutela* therefore ceased. The introduction of the testamentary tutor, who might have no interest in the succession, and still more the later growth of the idea that *tutela* was a duty undertaken in the interest of the child, would have led a less conservative system to raise the age at which *tutela* ended, but

---

[1] See below, pp. 247 ff. A *pupillus* was not of an age to make a will, and therefore succession on intestacy was alone in question. There were two other cases of *tutela legitima* which show the same connexion between the right to be *tutor* and the right to succeed on death: if a slave were manumitted under age it was his patron who was both his tutor and his heir; and the same was true, if the right steps were taken, of the father of an emancipated son (see above, p. 80, n. 1).

[2] Until A.D. 390, when imperial legislation allowed the magistrate in certain circumstances to appoint the mother.

[3] See below, pp. 95 f.

the Romans left the old rule unaltered, and developed instead the parallel institution of *cura minorum*[1] to protect young persons over the age of puberty from the consequences of their own lack of judgment.

(iii) *Accountability of tutor.* Unlike the modern guardian, the tutor was concerned primarily, and in later law exclusively, with the property of the child. Custody and upbringing were usually entrusted to the mother or some other close relative. It is in the extent to which the tutor could be called to account for his conduct that the change in the nature of *tutela* can most clearly be seen. Under the early law a tutor could only be made liable for fraudulent misappropriation of the property, but in the late Republic there appeared a remedy (*actio tutelae*) by which the *pupillus* could, on reaching puberty, call the tutor to account for his management of the property according to the principles of good faith, and out of this remedy grew a body of rules which so regulated the conduct of the tutor that *tutela* became, like modern guardianship, a duty to be conscientiously discharged in the interests of the *pupillus*. This transformation of *tutela* from a privilege to a burden is marked by the development of an elaborate list of grounds on which a *tutor testamentarius* or *dativus* might claim to be excused from undertaking the office. The *tutor legitimus* was allowed no excuse.

(iv) *Functions of tutor.* We must now examine more fully the extent of the incapacity of the *pupillus* and the ways in which the tutor discharged his function of managing the property.

The tutor could act in two ways, either directly, by administering the property himself, or indirectly, by validating the acts of the *pupillus*. If he chose the former method, however, he was hampered by one of the most notable shortcomings of Roman law—its lack of a concept of agency.[2] It never accepted the principle, which is a commonplace of modern systems, that one man (the agent) acting on behalf of another (the principal) could create both rights and duties in that other and incur neither himself. Consequently nothing that the tutor did could either bind or entitle the *pupillus*, and he must take the risk that the *pupillus* might repudiate his acts at the end of the *tutela*. By the end of the classical period the worst drawbacks of this lack of agency had by various devices been removed, but it remained

---

[1] See below, pp. 93 ff.   [2] See below, pp. 201 ff.

true that the only way in which the *pupillus* could directly incur rights and duties was by his own act. And here the law required that some acts be validated by the tutor. This requirement needs further examination.

The period in a child's life before puberty fell into two parts. So long as he was incapable of reason (strictly, of speech—*infans*) he could perform no legal act at all. The ending of infancy was originally a question of fact, but the late law fixed it at the age of seven. During infancy the tutor had of necessity to administer the property himself. Thereafter the *pupillus* was capable of acting, but if the act was one which might make his position worse it required the express oral approval (*auctoritas*) of the tutor. In other words, without such *auctoritas* the *pupillus* could acquire rights but he could not alienate them nor could he incur duties. He could, for example, receive a gift, but could not make one; and he could enter into a contract which conferred only rights upon him (e.g. a *stipulatio* by which the other party promised to pay him money, but not vice versa). Most transactions, however, create reciprocal rights and duties, and such transactions, even if on balance advantageous (e.g. a sale at a profit), required *auctoritas*. Without it there could only be, in the language of the commentators, a 'limping transaction' (*negotium claudicans*)—the *pupillus* was not bound, but the other party was, though the *pupillus* could not require him to perform unless he for his part was prepared to do likewise. For example, if a *pupillus* had without *auctoritas* agreed to sell goods, he acquired a right to the price but could not enforce that right unless he delivered the goods; and this delivery would itself require *auctoritas*. Similarly, if he had already delivered the goods without *auctoritas* he could reclaim them. The buyer, on the other hand, could never take the initiative to enforce the contract.

Cura minorum. In the later Republic it became obvious that puberty was not an age at which a young man could be left to his own devices in the management of his property. The problem was met, characteristically, not by extending the period of *tutela*, but by gradually evolving another institution. The first step was taken about 200 B.C. A *Lex Plaetoria* (or perhaps *Laetoria*) imposed a penalty on anyone who fraudulently took advantage of the inexperience of a person under the age of twenty-five (*minor XXV annis*, here referred to as a minor). The transaction by which the minor was overreached was, however, though penalized, none the less valid, and it was left to the Praetor to give fuller effect to the policy of the *lex*. He intervened in two ways. If the transaction had not yet been carried out and the other party sued, the minor was allowed a defence in bar of the action. If, on the other hand, the transaction had already been carried out he would cause it to be rescinded by granting *restitutio in integrum*. The grant of this remedy lay in the discretion of the Praetor, but certain principles emerged. There need not have been fraud: it was sufficient that the minor had through inexperience made a bad bargain. There need not even have been another party to the transaction: to enter on an inheritance, for example, might be unwise since it involved liability in full for the debts of the dead man,[1] and in such a case the Praetor would give relief. On the other hand, if the transaction was at the time reasonable it was of no avail for the minor to plead that it had subsequently turned out badly (e.g. a healthy slave, bought for a fair price, suddenly dies).

The effect of the Praetor's intervention was obviously to make the ordinary man reluctant to deal with a minor at all, for fear that he would later allege that he had been overreached. To guard against this there grew up a practice of calling in an independent adult to approve the transaction. For a long time this curator, as he came to be called, had no formal legal recognition, being merely someone called in as necessary for each transaction. In the second century A.D., however, he had become so normal and permanent a feature of a minor's existence that the Praetor would make an appointment on the application of the minor.

The resemblance between the curator of a minor and the tutor of an *impubes* was at this stage no more than superficial. In particular, the effect of the curator's approval of a transaction was in principle quite different from that of a tutor's *auctoritas*. *Auctoritas* was, within the limits stated above, both legally necessary and legally sufficient—without it the act, even if on balance profitable, was ineffective; with it the act, even if wholly disadvantageous, was valid (though the tutor might have to account to his ward for his misconduct in authorizing it). The

[1] See below, pp. 235 ff.

consent of the curator, on the other hand, was neither necessary nor in itself sufficient. It was merely one kind of evidence, though no doubt the best kind, that the transaction was in the minor's interest. Accordingly, if there were no curator's consent, the minor still had to satisfy the Praetor that the transaction should be set aside, and, conversely, even if there were consent this was not conclusive against the minor's claim—he could, for example, adduce evidence that the curator had been negligent or fraudulent.

In the later law there was a progressive blurring of the distinction between tutor and curator, and nothing but the usual reluctance of Justinian's compilers to make a clean sweep can explain their failure to complete the process. Certainly it is the rules of *tutela* rather than of *cura* which have survived into, for example, German law. Of course some features which even in Roman times had lost their justification have disappeared. The age of full capacity, for example, is no longer puberty; and the modern *filiusfamilias* can own property, and therefore the rules apply equally to all persons under age, the father having in this respect the functions of the Roman tutor. The rules themselves, however, are recognizably Roman.

Other forms of guardianship. As we have seen, the original reason for the ending of *tutela* at puberty must have been that the possibility of the ward's having children of his own to succeed to his property destroyed the interest on which the *tutela* of the nearest agnate rested. But this was true only of males. A woman's children, not being agnatically related to her, could have no rights of succession to her property.[1] The nearest agnate therefore retained a lifelong interest, and to protect that interest the woman was subjected to a lifelong *tutela*. The same developments which destroyed the justification for the ending of *tutela* over males at puberty destroyed also the justification for its indefinite prolongation over females, but in both cases conservatism prevailed over logic. Indeed a new reason was found for the lifelong *tutela* of women—that they were incapable of looking after their own affairs. Gaius has the generosity to admit that this is a specious reason, and in fact in his day *tutela* of women had become for the most part an empty form. The

[1] See below, pp. 248 ff.

tutor's only function was the giving of *auctoritas*, and even this could in most cases be compelled. Devices had moreover been developed which made it more easy for a woman to change her tutor, and Augustus, in his zeal for raising the birth-rate, allowed the birth of three children (four for freedwomen) to terminate *tutela* altogether. The whole institution had disappeared before the time of Justinian.

Any system must make provision for the care of the person and the property of lunatics. The Twelve Tables, following the same principle as in *tutela*, had directed that the guardian (*curator*) of a *furiosus* should be the nearest agnate or the *gens*— i.e. those entitled on intestacy. If there was no one so entitled, a curator was appointed by the Praetor.

The same care for the family property is found in the institution, also deriving from the Twelve Tables, of the guardianship of the spendthrift (*cura prodigi*). A person who wasted his property could be debarred by magisterial interdict from the management of that property and placed under the supervision of the nearest agnate or the *gens*. This interdiction of spendthrifts survives in many Civil law systems of the modern world, but is quite foreign to English law, which accords to the adult of sound mind full freedom to dissipate his property as he will while he lives, just as until 1939 it allowed him completely to disinherit his dependants on his death.[1]

6. *CAPITIS DEMINUTIO*

Three elements may be seen in a man's status in Roman law —liberty, citizenship, and family rights—and changes of status may be analysed accordingly. The Romans speak in this connexion of *capitis deminutio*, or deterioration of status. *Capitis deminutio maxima* is the loss of all three elements, i.e. enslavement; *capitis deminutio media* is the loss of citizenship and family rights, usually as a punishment; and *capitis deminutio minima*, the most common, is the loss merely of family rights by either adoption, adrogation, marriage with *manus*, or emancipation. Some of these hardly seem to us to constitute a deterioration of status. For example, a *filiusfamilias* who is adopted from one family into another undergoes no change of status, and one who is emancipated achieves a higher status. But in each case there is a

[1] See below, pp. 263 f.

breaking of agnatic family ties and a loss of rights. The adopted son ceases to be a member of his original family and loses his civil law rights of succession in that family, though he acquires corresponding rights in his new family. The emancipated son loses his rights in his original family without acquiring any others, since he becomes the first head of a new family; he is a new person and can have no agnatic relatives except such children as are later born to him. On the other hand, a son who becomes *sui iuris* by the death of his father undergoes no *capitis deminutio* and retains his agnatic rights of succession.

The idea that a new person had taken the place of the old produced other consequences also. Life interests (usufruct and *usus*) were terminated, though Justinian restricted this result to *capitis deminutio maxima* and *media*, where the analogy with death was more obvious. A will previously made was no longer valid. Contractual obligations were dissolved, but the possibilities of injustice and fraud in this were obvious, and various forms of relief were devised.

III

LAW OF PROPERTY

INTRODUCTORY

The law of things. In the classification of the Institutes the second part of the law—and by far the largest—relates to things (*res*). *Res*, like 'thing', is an elusive word, and the Roman lawyers, as is their habit, leave its meaning to emerge from its use. In its simplest sense it denotes merely a physical object—a table, a house, a piece of land—but for the lawyer there are also abstract things, things which exist only in the mind's eye, such as a debt, a right of way, and many others. The common factor between these two kinds of thing is that both are assets of economic value, and it is in this wide sense that Gaius and Justinian speak of the law of things. It is that part of the law which governs the creation, transfer, and enjoyment of economic assets—of property in the widest sense. To use the language of rights, the law of things includes all those rights which are capable of being evaluated in money terms. It therefore excludes those rights which emerge from the law of persons, such as the rights of a father over his children or the right of freedom itself, since these are usually incapable of money valuation. In this sense, however, the law of things embraces so large a part of the private law that a further division is inevitable. The division which is discernible in Gaius is a threefold one, into the law of property (or things in a narrow sense), the law of succession, and the law of obligations. This division, preserved by Justinian, remains one of the most characteristic features of the Civil law,[1] but it presents a number of difficulties and it has been variously modified in modern codes. One difficulty stands out. Superficially at least this is a division into incomparables. Property and obligations are two types of asset, whereas succession is not a third type (the division into property and obligations is in fact exhaustive) but a method of acquiring the other two, as, for example, when an heir succeeds to the assets of a dead man.

---

[1] In the mouth of a Common lawyer it is a conscious Romanism.

Whether or not this criticism is wholly justified,[1] it provides a reason for abandoning here at least the order of the Institutes and dealing with property and obligations before going on to succession.

I. FUNDAMENTAL DISTINCTIONS

Property and obligations—actions and rights in rem and in personam. A man's assets are either property or obligations. The difference between the two is the difference between owning and being owed something. Thus a man's assets may be his house and his furniture, which he owns, his bank balance which, however much one may speak of 'having money in the bank', is a debt owed by the bank, and his right to his unpaid salary, which is likewise a debt. His assets will often, of course, be more complicated than this, but they will still fall into one of the two categories. For example, if he is a shopkeeper he will own, we may suppose, his shop and his stock-in-trade; he may have ordered, but not received, further supplies from a wholesaler, and these will, from the Roman point of view, be still owned by the wholesalers but will be owed to him (and if he has not yet paid for them he will correspondingly owe the price); he will have supplied goods on credit to his customers, and here again there is obviously a debt. He may have acquired the goodwill of the business of a former competitor, and this constitutes once more a debt—the debtor's duty being not, as in the previous cases, to pay a sum of money or to supply goods, but to refrain from soliciting his former customers.

This difference between owning and being owed is expressed

---

[1] For Gaius, and therefore for Justinian, the sequence of thought which leads to the treatment of succession immediately after property is this: in both alike we are concerned with the methods of acquisition of things, the subject-matter of the law of property being the acquisition of single (i.e. individual) things, and that of the law of succession being the acquisition of a man's entire estate (acquisition *per universitatem*, see below, pp. 235 ff.); it is therefore appropriate to deal with the two types of acquisition together. There still remains, of course, the objection that acquisition *per universitatem* may include obligations, but the reasoning does point to a difference of emphasis between Gaius' method of exposition and that of a modern writer. Gaius, and to a lesser extent Justinian, is concerned far more with methods of acquisition and loss (of status in the law of persons, of the various types of things elsewhere) than with the nature and content of what is being acquired and lost (cf. above, p. 61). The order of treatment is therefore much less forced than it would be in a book which places the emphasis differently. Cf. F. H. Lawson, *A Common Lawyer Looks at the Civil Law*, pp. 96 ff.

by the Roman lawyer in the distinction between actions *in rem* and actions *in personam*. Any claim is either *in rem* or *in personam*, and there is an unbridgeable division between them. An action *in rem* asserts a relationship between a person and a thing, an action *in personam* a relationship between persons. Thus the typical action *in rem* (*rei vindicatio*) asserts that a physical thing belongs to the plaintiff, and the simplest action *in personam* (*condictio*) asserts that the defendant owes a sum of money or a physical thing to the plaintiff. The Romans think in terms of actions not of rights, but in substance one action asserts a right over a thing, the other a right against a person, and hence comes the modern dichotomy between rights *in rem* and rights *in personam*. Obviously there cannot be a dispute between a person and a thing, and therefore even in an action *in rem* there must be a defendant, but he is there not because he is alleged to be under any duty to the plaintiff but because by some act he is denying the alleged right of the plaintiff. In a *rei vindicatio* he is denying the plaintiff's ownership by being in possession of the thing claimed. And so our hypothetical shopkeeper can assert his ownership of his stock-in-trade by bringing an action *in rem* against any person into whose hands it may come. For example, if it is stolen he can claim it from the thief or from anyone who subsequently acquires it, whether in good faith or not. On the other hand, his right to the further supplies which he has ordered, even supposing he can identify them, is *in personam* and can therefore be asserted against no one but the wholesaler. In this way a right *in rem* may be said to be a right available against persons generally, in contrast to a right *in personam* which is available against a particular person or persons.[1] Rights

---

[1] This is not of course the way a Roman would have put it, and it shows that once rights rather than actions have become the primary concept the strict Roman dichotomy becomes difficult to maintain. Ownership is the typical right *in rem*: it is protected by an action *in rem* (*rei vindicatio*) and is available against persons generally. And yet it may also be said to be protected by actions *in personam*. If my book comes into the hands of someone who denies my title I assert my ownership by an action *in rem*, but if someone negligently or wilfully damages it I bring an action *in personam* against him—he has committed a delict and is therefore under an obligation arising from that delict to make satisfaction to me (below, pp. 218 ff.). The Roman lawyer does not go beyond this, but the modern jurist pushes the inquiry one stage farther. He sees the law in terms of rights and duties, and the duty to make satisfaction for the damage done by breach of contract derives from the prior duty to carry out the contract. There must therefore, he says, be a duty

in rem are the subject-matter of the law of property, rights *in personam* of the law of obligations.

What is the practical importance of the distinction between actions *in rem* and actions *in personam*? One must begin by emphasizing that an action *in rem* is not, in form, one which compels the defendant to return the *res*. (This is the sense in which the Common law uses the term 'real action'.) Since the Roman process was essentially a voluntary recourse to arbitration, and since there was no machinery for the state enforcement of judgments, the result of a successful action, whether *in rem* or *in personam*, was simply an order to the defendant to pay to the plaintiff a sum of money, and it was for the plaintiff to enforce this order, if need be, by levying execution on the defendant's person or property. In such a system there is no place for decrees of specific restitution or specific performance. And yet, having said so much, one must then add that in most actions *in rem* the defendant would in fact be driven to restore the object claimed. This contrast between the formal and the substantial result of an action was achieved by a simple device. The *formula* of the action directed the judge, if he found for the plaintiff, to order the defendant to pay the value of the thing, but only if he failed to surrender it to the plaintiff.[1] On the face of it this gave the defendant simply an option, and put no pressure on him to take one course rather than the other. But the plaintiff had a further weapon: he was allowed to make his own assessment of the

on persons generally not to damage my property, and a correlative right in me against persons generally. And what is this right but one aspect of ownership? An action *in personam* therefore operates to protect a right *in rem*, and the Roman dichotomy is blurred. Similarly I have an action *in personam* if someone insults me (below, pp. 215 ff.). He has committed a delict and is under an obligation to make satisfaction to me. But this duty must derive from the breach of a prior duty not to insult others, and there must be a correlative right in those others not to be insulted —a right against persons generally. Should this not therefore be termed a right *in rem*? Or rather should not rights *in rem* be described as bundles of rights *in personam*? The Common lawyer is encouraged in this way of thinking by having (since the disappearance of the early writ of right) no action *in rem* in his own system. If a Common lawyer wishes to assert ownership of his book he must assert that the defendant is wrongfully detaining or converting it, in short that he is committing a tort. See further below, pp. 226 f.

[1] The complete *formula* of the *vindicatio* ran as follows: 'If it appears that the thing in question belongs to the plaintiff at civil law (*ex iure Quiritium*), then, unless at the direction of the judge the defendant restores the thing, let the judge condemn the defendant to pay the value of it to the plaintiff. If it does not so appear, let the judge absolve the defendant.'

value of the thing. This assessment was, it is true, made on oath, but the plaintiff would usually be able to achieve his purpose without straying over the line between optimism and perjury, and the judge, we are told, would in any case not be astute to draw that line. This feature does not, however, serve to differentiate actions *in rem* from actions *in personam*, since it is found in both, though only exceptionally in the latter.

The answer to our question[1] can perhaps best be found by contrasting two constructions which can be put upon a sale. If A agrees to buy B's book for a certain price, Roman law gives A an immediate right *in personam* to the delivery of the book (and B a concurrent right to the payment of the price), but gives A no right *in rem* until the book is actually delivered. Some other systems, however, give A both the right *in personam* and the right *in rem* as soon as the agreement is made.[2] The difference between these two constructions lies in their effect on third parties. There are two typical situations.

(i) B still has the book and merely refuses to deliver it. Here, leaving aside the question considered on the previous page, it will usually make no difference whether A proceeds *in rem* or *in personam*. In either case he will obtain the money value of the thing. But B may be insolvent, and then the distinction will be crucial. For if A's claim is only *in personam* it will take its place with the claims of all the other creditors against B's inadequate assets, whereas if it is *in rem* A will be able, as it were, to take the book out of B's bankruptcy and thus to satisfy his claim in full. For he is then not a creditor but an owner.

(ii) The book has passed out of the hands of B into those of C—B has, for example, persuaded A to pay the price in advance and has then sold and delivered the book to C (this, or some variant of it, is one of the commonest frauds), or C has stolen it or acquired it from a thief. In cases such as this the Roman construction gives A a remedy, if he has one at all, only against

---

[1] The Roman lawyer's own first answer might have been that the practical importance lay in the 'mesne process' (cf. Maitland, *The Forms of Action at Common Law*, pp. 76 f.), that is to say in the steps which the plaintiff took if the defendant failed to defend the action. In an action *in rem* he was authorized simply to take the thing, since it was against this that his claim lay, whereas in an action *in personam* he proceeded against the person or property of the defendant.

[2] This is in principle the position of English law, but it is so qualified by special rules that the practical result is nearly always the same as in Roman law (see Buckland and McNair, *Roman Law and Common Law*, 2nd edn., pp. 291 ff.).

B, while the other construction allows him to proceed against either B or C. Once again, of course, this difference will be of practical importance only if B is insolvent or has disappeared, but one eventuality or the other is not at all improbable. The man who sells to C in breach of his contract with A is not likely to await the bringing of an action, and even if he can be caught he is not likely to be still solvent. The problem which the law has to solve is the legal version of the eternal triangle. Which of two innocent parties is to suffer for the act of a dishonest third? There can be no solution which is both capable of practical application and ideally just. The law must choose the one which is most in the interest of the community at large.

Contract and conveyance. There is a further gulf set in Roman law between rights *in rem* and rights *in personam.* The ways in which they come into existence are kept distinct: the act which creates a right *in personam* does not create a right *in rem,* and vice versa. The most important application of this principle is in the distinction between contract and conveyance. A contract creates rights *in personam* but cannot create or transfer rights *in rem.* For this a conveyance is necessary, i.e. an act recognized by law as appropriate for the purpose. We have just seen that in a sale of a book ownership does not pass to the buyer by the making of the contract, but only by the actual delivery of the book. The delivery is the conveyance. If the object sold were not a book but a *res mancipi* such as land or a slave, a formal conveyance by *mancipatio* or *in iure cessio* would be necessary.[1] And a conveyance was likewise necessary for the creation or transfer of rights *in rem* other than ownership.[2]

This separation of contract and conveyance is rooted in the sound though inarticulate principle that rights *in rem,* since they potentially affect everyone, should not be secretly created or transferred, whereas there is no such objection to the secret creation of rights *in personam.* Hence it is that the Roman conveyance is essentially a visible and public act. *In iure cessio* takes

---

[1] See below, pp. 105 f.
[2] The principle was not, however, maintained inviolate even in the classical law (e.g. the creation of *hypotheca* by a simple agreement—below, p. 152) and in the law of Justinian, when the formal conveyances have disappeared, it has been largely forgotten (cf. below, pp. 119 f.).

place in open court.[1] *Mancipatio*,[2] though in form a private act, requires the presence of six Roman citizens in addition to the parties, and the reason for so large a number must have been the desire for publicity rather than the need for subsequent proof, since, by contrast, the formal contract of *stipulatio*, which created only rights *in personam*, could be validly made without any witnesses at all. Similarly, the informal conveyance by delivery (*traditio*) involved in principle the visible transfer of the object itself.

There is however a conflict, which any system of law has to face, between the interest of the community at large in the publicity of conveyances, and the desire of individuals to conduct their affairs in private. In Roman law the latter for the most part eventually prevailed. Both *in iure cessio* and *mancipatio* must in the classical law have been quite ineffective to ensure publicity. For *in iure cessio* was by then a very empty form, and the six participants in the *mancipatio*, though adequate enough for a small community, could constitute no hindrance to secrecy in so vast a society as imperial Rome. Even *traditio*, which increasingly replaced the formal conveyances, could eventually be performed without any visible transfer of the object, so that in the late Roman law, as in developed English law, a conveyance was often, like a contract, nothing more than a document drawn up between the parties.[3]

This blurring of the line between contract and conveyance is perhaps inevitable in a sophisticated society, and modern systems usually adopt other methods to ensure publicity for the creation and transfer of rights *in rem*. The only wholly effective method is registration—to require that all such creations and transfers shall be entered on a public register. This method is increasingly used in the modern world, but can obviously in practice only be applied to land (or to some exceptionally identifiable movables such as ships or motor-cars), and even so it cannot be initiated without an accurate survey and a body of skilled administrators. It was quite unknown to Roman law.[4] In regard to movables

[1] See above, p. 63. [2] See above, ibid.
[3] See below, pp. 119 f. There was a similar struggle to achieve secret conveyancing in English law, culminating early in the seventeenth century in the recognition of the device of a bargain and sale for a term followed by a release.
[4] There was something of the kind for land in Roman Egypt, but precisely what the effect of registration was is not clear.

there can be no simple solution. The Roman law, as we have seen, in principle required an actual delivery before ownership could pass. So long as this rule could be strictly maintained it was possible to say that no ownership could pass without the passing also of possession, but it could not also be said that no possession could pass without the passing also of ownership. This would have meant simply that the distinction between ownership and possession was obliterated. The thief would have owned what he had stolen. A less extreme rule might have excluded the thief by equating only the *bona fide* possessor (e.g. the man who innocently buys from the thief) with the owner, but this would have made a great inroad on the inviolability of ownership. And both the distinction between ownership and possession and the inviolable character of ownership were to the Roman lawyer fundamental.[1]

Classifications of res. The Roman law classifies 'things' in many different ways for different purposes, but only three of these classifications need be considered here.

(i) *Res mobiles, res immobiles.* Most, if not all, systems of law find it necessary to distinguish land, and the buildings which go with it, from all other property, both because of its intrinsic importance and because of the obvious fact that it is incapable of being moved. Roman law is no exception. The Twelve Tables laid down two years as the period for the prescriptive acquisition (*usucapio*)[2] of immovables, whereas one was sufficient for movables; and the distinction was relevant for some other purposes also. But it never acquired the central importance that, in the shape of the distinction between 'real' and 'personal' property,[3] it has in English law.

(ii) *Res mancipi, res nec mancipi.* A much more important distinction in the original civil law was the peculiarly Roman one between *res mancipi* and *res nec mancipi*. *Res mancipi* were slaves, beasts of draught and burden (oxen, horses, asses, mules), Italic land,[4] and rustic praedial servitudes (e.g. rights of way and of

---

[1] See below, pp. 107 ff., 129 f.   [2] See below, pp. 122 ff.
[3] The distinction is not identical with that between immovables and movables and is now less important than it used to be.
[4] Strictly, land capable of Roman ownership, and therefore originally only Roman land. As the Roman citizenship extended so also did the area of land capable

water) over such land. All other things were *res nec mancipi*. The practical importance of the distinction was that *res mancipi* could only be conveyed by *mancipatio* (hence the name) or *in iure cessio*; a mere delivery was ineffective to pass ownership. This was the rule of the civil law, but in the later Republic the Praetor gave to the recipient by delivery (the 'bonitary owner') almost all the substance of ownership,[1] and the distinction then took its place among the technical survivals which served to complicate the classical law. It survived in name until it was abolished by Justinian.

The origin of the distinction has been much debated.[2] Why should certain things be set apart as requiring a formal and public conveyance? If the question is framed in this way the obvious answer is that these must have been the most important things in early Rome, but it is not always easy to see why the particular things listed above, and no others, should have had this special importance. It may be, of course, that the original list was different, but at any rate in the later Republic the categories of *res mancipi* had become closed and arbitrary. For Gaius remarks that elephants and camels, though they were beasts of draught or burden, were nevertheless not *res mancipi*, because they were unknown when the list was settled.

(iii) *Res corporales, res incorporales.* As we have seen,[3] there is implicit in Gaius' threefold division of the law into persons, things, and actions, a distinction between physical things, such as a table or a house, and abstract things, such as a debt or a right of way. Gaius expresses the distinction in the terms *res corporales* and *res incorporales*. It is practically important for only one reason. Incorporeal things cannot be possessed, since possession requires essentially a physical holding, and they cannot therefore be acquired or transferred by any method which involves the transfer or acquisition of possession. In short, incorporeal things can neither be acquired by *usucapio* nor conveyed by *traditio*.

---

of Roman ownership until it included the whole of Italy. Thereafter, illogically, the extension ceased, except that the land of some privileged communities was, by the grant of the *ius italicum*, treated as if it were Italian.

[1] See below, pp. 125 ff.

[2] See the classical account in Maine, *Ancient Law*, ch. 8 (World's Classics edn., pp. 227 ff.), and, for a discussion of more recent views, Jolowicz, *Historical Introduction*, 2nd edn., pp. 139 ff. and 552 ff.   [3] See above, p. 98.

The distinction was primarily, however, an academic one, and as such was not generally used by the classical lawyers. But it was taken up by Justinian and has therefore become part of the legal language of Europe and, to some extent, of the Common law. It is a convenient distinction, and it certainly corresponds to the way we commonly speak—a man will say that he has bought one plot of land, a right of way over a second, and an option on a third—but on a strict examination it is illogical. It identifies ownership with the object owned. The strictly comparable statement to 'I have bought a right of way over a plot of land' is not 'I have bought a plot of land', but 'I have bought the ownership of a plot of land'. In each case I have acquired a right, the right of ownership being merely more extensive than the right of way. The Roman, however, preferred to think in terms of assets rather than of rights, and saw the land and the right of way as equally assets. He felt no need to make a clear distinction between ownership and its object, since for him only corporeal things could be owned, and *res corporalis* therefore changes its meaning according to its context. When the Roman says that only a *res corporalis* can be possessed, he is referring to the thing itself; when he speaks of the acquisition of a *res corporalis* he means the acquisition of ownership.

Ownership and possession. The most fundamental distinction of all in the law of property is that between ownership and possession. 'Ownership', says Ulpian, 'has nothing in common with possession.' And yet, for the most part, possession is the foundation of ownership. Thus, corporeal *res nec mancipi* are conveyed by *traditio*, a handing over of possession, and title by *usucapio* likewise depends on possession. We must now examine this apparent contradiction.

2. POSSESSION

There is an obvious distinction in ordinary language between having a thing and being entitled to have it. The thief is not entitled to what he has stolen but he nevertheless has it, and conversely the man who has pawned his ring is still entitled to it but the pawnbroker actually has it. This difference between being entitled to a thing and actually having it is at the root of the distinction which the Roman law, and less emphatically the English law, makes between ownership and possession, but the layman and the lawyer are nevertheless at cross-purposes when they speak of possession. There are three main reasons for this. In the first place, the English layman frequently speaks of 'possession' when he means 'ownership', no doubt because he usually owns what he possesses and possesses what he owns. In the same way he habitually speaks of what he owns as his 'possessions'. But the lawyer, here as elsewhere, has to be pedantically exact in his use of terms. Secondly, the Roman law, and to a very small extent the English, in some situations denies possession to the person who actually holds the thing and accords it to someone who does not. And thirdly, the difficulty of determining in particular cases what constitutes an actual holding gives rise in both systems to technical rules. For both these last reasons one cannot simply say that the man who has the thing has possession of it, but before going further into this question we should consider what is the practical significance of having possession in law.

Protection of possession. Possession by itself has in Roman law only the barest legal consequence—that it is protected. Subject to what is said below, the possessor has remedies by which he can restrain others from interfering with his possession and by which he can recover possession from anyone who dispossesses him. These remedies are known as possessory interdicts. Their procedure is, until the late law, complicated and archaic, but their operation is in essentials simple. For example, if A, who is in occupation of land, is evicted by B, he can compel B to restore the land to him provided he can satisfy two requirements: his occupation must have amounted to possession in law, as defined below; and that possession must not have been obtained *vi* (by force), *clam* (secretly), or *precario* (by grant at will) from B.

There are here three features which should be particularly noticed. (i) The remedy lies only against the dispossessor. If B is in turn dispossessed by C, or voluntarily delivers the land to him, A has no remedy against C unless he is also owner,[1] when

---

[1] In the classical law this was not necessarily so of movables. For in regard to them it was sufficient if A had had possession for longer in the previous year than C. The reason for this rule was presumably the ease and frequency with which movables may change hands. It had however disappeared by the time of Justinian.

he has a *vindicatio*. (ii) The title of either party is altogether irrelevant. The dispossessor may not even plead in defence that he is owner. What is in issue in a possessory interdict is possession, and to that in the Roman view ownership can have no relevance. This is the meaning of the Roman maxim: 'ownership has nothing in common with possession.' The Roman insistence on this rigid separation leads of course to circuity. If B is owner of the land of which he dispossesses A, the latter's victory in the possessory interdict will be short-lived, since B can immediately assert his ownership by a *vindicatio*. But this circuity was preferable to the blurring of the sharp outline of a basic concept, and it also had the practical advantage of discouraging self-help.[1] (iii) The possession which is in issue must not have been obtained *vi, clam,* or *precario* from the other party. This is not a matter of title, since, on the one hand, as we have just seen, it makes no difference that it is the owner who has obtained possession thus 'viciously', and, on the other hand, 'viciousness' is only relative —a possession which is 'vicious' as against one person will be good as against anyone else.[2] For it is irrelevant that the possessor has obtained possession 'viciously' from someone other than the dispossessor. In the example given above, where B is in turn dispossessed by C, B can bring an interdict against C, and C cannot object that B's possession was obtained *vi* from A. This objection is relevant only between A and B.

Importance of possession. The main advantage of the possessory remedy lies in the simplicity of proof. Because of its factual character possession is as easy to prove as ownership is difficult. Even, therefore, if A, who has been dispossessed by B, believes himself to be owner, he will, if he is wise, proceed by possessory interdict rather than by *vindicatio*, thereby leaving to B the burden of proving title in a subsequent *vindicatio*. As Gaius puts it, the possessory interdict serves to determine which party shall be defendant in a *vindicatio*.

Although possession by itself has only this one legal consequence that the possessor can assert or recover his possession in an interdict, it has much wider consequences when combined with other factors. In particular, as was said above, it lies at the

---

[1] Cf. the Assize of Novel Disseisin of the early Common law.

[2] 'Adversus extraneos etiam vitiosa possessio prodesse solet' (against third parties even a 'vicious' possession is effective).

root of the two most common methods of acquiring ownership, *traditio* and *usucapio*,[1] and therefore occupies a central place in the law of property.

Who has possession? There are, we have said, two reasons why the answer to this question cannot simply be that the man who has the thing has possession of it. The question in fact conceals two questions, which must be considered separately.

(i) *What categories of holder are in principle capable of having possession?* In English law the answer to this question is simple. Any holder is in principle a possessor except a servant or a person holding for a temporary and limited purpose, such as a railway porter. In Roman law it is quite otherwise. With a few exceptions, no one who holds in pursuance of a contract with the owner can possess, nor can anyone who holds in exercise of a right *in rem* less than ownership (in modern terms a *ius in re aliena*)[2]—for example the usufructuary, who has what is in effect ownership for life or for some shorter period. Of these two restrictions the former is the more important. It excludes from possession not only the borrower (*commodatarius*) and the depositee (*depositarius*) but also the hirer, including the lessee of land. Such holders have in consequence no remedy against third parties who interfere with their holding. They hold on behalf of the owner, who has possession through them. In the case of a lease, for example, the lessor can proceed by either *vindicatio* or possessory interdict against a third party who interferes with the lessee's occupation of the land, but the lessee can only proceed *in personam* against the lessor by an action on the contract. This may well be inconvenient if the lessor is, for example, absent or dilatory. The exclusion of beneficiaries of *iura in re aliena* is of less practical importance, because they could always assert their right by an action *in rem*, and because at any rate the usufructuary was eventually given a variant (*utilis*) form of the possessory interdicts and therefore had in this respect possession in all but name. There still remained, however, the important consequence that *iura in re aliena* could neither be conveyed by *traditio* nor acquired by *usucapio*.

---

[1] There are also other consequences, such as the right of the possessor in good faith to fruits (below, p. 139), and title by *occupatio* (below, pp. 130 f.).

[2] See below, pp. 140 ff.

The list of those who hold without in law possessing is so substantial that we should abandon the natural assumption that 'possession' has essentially the same meaning in Latin as in English, in Roman law as in English law. The Roman probably understood by 'possession' not simply the holding of a thing but rather the holding of a thing in the manner of an owner, the exclusive holding of a thing. It was therefore not a matter needing explanation, as it would be for us, that the borrower or the lessee had no possession. For this followed naturally from the meaning of the word.[1] The borrower does not hold in the manner of an owner. His holding acknowledges the superior right of the lender. Conversely if, in breach of contract, he ceases to acknowledge that right and attempts to hold adversely to the lender, he then acquires possession. For any wrongful holder, though he knows he is not owner, nevertheless intends to hold the thing as far as he physically can in the manner of an owner.

Again, the usufructuary, though he has for the time being all the enjoyment of an owner, acknowledges the superior right of the actual owner. There is indeed in the case of such *iura in re aliena* the simpler objection that they were incorporeal things and therefore were, as we have seen, incapable of being possessed. This is easy enough to understand in the case of the more limited rights, such as a right of way. For the person who is in 'possession' (i.e. in *de facto* enjoyment) of a right of way obviously does not purport to possess the land over which he walks, and in the Roman view there was nothing else which he could possess. There is more difficulty, however, with the usufructuary, who is for the time being in exclusive control of the land (or other thing) over which he has a usufruct. Why should he not therefore have possession, not indeed of the usufruct but of the land itself? The Romans themselves were evidently uncomfortable about the denial of possession in this case, and eventually, as has been said, compromised by granting interdicts in *utilis* form.

[1] It has been suggested that the etymology of the word bears this out. The latter part of 'pos-sessio' derives from the verb meaning to sit, and therefore corresponds to the German word 'Besitz' and the original English word 'seisin', both of which mean literally the mere 'sitting' on a thing. The derivation of the syllable 'pos-' is uncertain; but if it is related to 'posse' and 'potestas' the literal meaning of 'possessio' would be 'sitting in power'.

Even if one admits that the Roman 'possessio' had this stronger, more restricted meaning than the English 'possession', there remain several anomalous cases of possession which are probably to be explained either historically or on grounds of convenience.[1]

The Romans had no consistent single term to indicate a holding which did not amount in law to possession, but modern lawyers commonly use the word 'detention'. The Roman tenant, therefore, is a detentor and his landlord a possessor. This terminology is convenient provided that one bears in mind that 'detention', unlike the lawyer's usual technical words, indicates not the presence of legal consequences but their absence. To say that the lessee is a detentor is merely to emphasize that though he is physically in occupation of the land he has legally no relation to it.

(ii) *What amount of physical control is necessary for possession?* The answer we have given to the preceding question is not a Roman answer. The Romans offer no definition of possession. They take it for granted that the lessee, the borrower, &c., do not possess. What they are interested in is not the abstract question of the meaning of possession, but the practical question of how it is acquired and lost. This question offers peculiar scope to that evolution of principle from a multitude of hypothetical cases which is the delight and strength of the Roman lawyer, and his analysis and terminology have been adopted not merely by his civilian successors but also by the jurists of the common law.

In the Roman analysis the acquisition of possession has two aspects, mental and physical. 'One acquires possession', says Paul, 'by an act of the mind and an act of the body (*animo et corpore*); the act of the mind must be one's own, but the act of the body may be supplied by another.' The modern jurist, with his greater liking for abstract thought, transfers the analysis from the acquisition of possession to possession itself, and speaks

---

[1] The pledge-creditor (i.e. the person who is given something as security for a debt) and the *sequester* (i.e. the person with whom a thing is deposited to await the outcome of a dispute concerning it) both possess, and yet both hold in pursuance of a contract. The explanation is probably simply the demands of convenience: the purpose of their holding would be frustrated if they did not possess.

The explanation of the possession of the holder *precario* (by grant at will) and of the holder of public land lies probably in the history of these institutions. This is too large a question, however, to be adequately discussed here.

of *animus* and *corpus* as the two 'elements' of possession, but the difference is one of method, not of substance.[1]

We can consider here no more than the outlines of the Roman analysis. The *corpus* of possession (to adopt the modern way of speaking) requires the effective power of control, but what amounts to such an effective power must depend on the nature of the object. Thus a greater degree of physical control is necessary for the acquisition of possession of a book than of a pile of logs, of a horse than of a plot of land. Indeed the example of the land shows that it is impossible entirely to separate the *corpus* from the *animus*. If I wish to take possession of a farm, how else can I do so than by entering on some part of it with an intention to take control of the whole? Here indeed the physical element is whittled away to very little, but the Roman law nevertheless insisted on this minimum. I could not acquire possession by an act of intention alone (*animo solo*). But again, though this minimum is sufficient when possession is taken with the consent of the previous possessor (i.e. by a *traditio*), it will not be so where there is a rival claimant to possession—for example, if I am a squatter on your land or if both I and you are attempting to take possession of land which has hitherto been vacant.

The requisite *animus* is the intention to exercise the control which constitutes the *corpus*. Here again, of course, the two elements cannot be thus simply distinguished—an unintentional control is in the ordinary case a contradiction in terms, but a madman may exercise a very effective control and yet be incapable of forming an intention. And there are more difficult questions. Intention involves knowledge, but how detailed must my knowledge be? If, having bought a book from you, I ask

[1] The analysis was used by Savigny in his famous book on possession (1803) to provide an answer to the question, which we have just discussed, of the meaning of possession in Roman law. He found the differentiating factor between possession and detention in the *animus*, which he defined as *animus domini* (intention to be owner). The detentor had no possession because he had no *animus domini*. The cases of the pledge-creditor, *sequester*, holder *precario*, and holder of public land were explained as in the preceding note. Jhering (1889) rejected this emphasis on *animus* and declared that the *corpus* was the essential—that any conscious holding was in principle possession and that the cases of detention were exceptions for special reasons. The main objection to Savigny is that there is no evidence that the Romans saw the distinction between possession and detention in terms of *animus* and *corpus*, and to Jhering that his explanation of the non-possession of the detentors is very forced.

you to put it in my drawer and actually see you do it, clearly
I acquire possession at that moment, and, equally, if I have
neither asked you to put it there nor know that you have done
so, I cannot have possession. But what if I have asked you to
put it there but am not aware of the precise moment at which
you do so? Is such an anticipatory *animus* sufficient? (This
question becomes important if the book is taken from my
drawer before I know it is there. If my *animus* was sufficient
I shall have not merely the possessory but also the proprietary
remedies, and the action for theft, if any.) The related problem,
which has much agitated English lawyers, whether I possess
something which, unknown to me, is buried in my land or
hidden in my house, is answered in the negative—I have not
the necessary *animus*.

For obvious reasons of convenience the requirements of the
law are not so strict for the retention of possession as they are
for its acquisition. I do not lose possession of my house and its
contents merely by going away for a short time, nor do I lose
possession of a book which I have put in a cupboard and forgotten. This presumption of possession was taken even further
in the case of what was called retention *animo solo* (by mere
intention). The recurrent example is that of pastures used only
in winter or only in summer; a more likely modern case is that
of the seaside cottage. During the greater part of the year when
the cottage is left unoccupied, the *corpus* of possession is totally
lacking, but for convenience I am allowed to retain possession,
and this is explained as retention *animo solo*. But what if, unknown
to me, squatters have broken in and are in full occupation? They
have both the necessary *animus* and the necessary *corpus*, and therefore they and not I should possess, but the Romans eventually
preferred the specious argument that what is retained *animo* can
only be lost *animo*, and therefore I shall not lose possession until
I know of the intrusion of the squatters and fail to evict them.

Possession as a fact. The Romans often declare that possession is
a fact, and this has given rise to some debate among modern
jurists, who commonly prefer to see it as a right. There is,
however, a danger of being bemused by words unless one
inquires first what the Romans meant by possession as a fact.
And one should perhaps begin with what they did not mean.

The preceding pages show that possession was not a fact if by that one means that it was unregulated by law. In the case, for example, of my taking possession of a farm, whether I have entered on the land is indeed a question of fact, but whether such an entry, assuming it to have occurred, amounts to a taking of possession is a matter governed by legal rules. What the Romans did mean by possession as a fact can be seen by con-trasting possession with ownership, which is in this sense not a fact but a right. Ownership exists whether or not there is any material manifestation of it, whereas possession is dependent for its existence on such manifestation. If my handkerchief is picked out of my pocket I cease to possess it (I have lost possession *corpore*), but I still own it. Similarly, I can acquire ownership without knowing it, but not possession. To put it in another way, possession can be terminated by a wrongful act, whereas ownership cannot (unless, of course, the wrongful act destroys the object owned). If the facts on which possession rests cease, however wrongfully, possession ceases.

It was in this sense that the Romans declared that possession was a fact, but their desire to favour the retention of posses-sion led them eventually, as we have seen, to allow substantial inroads on this factual character. For possession is no longer a fact when I retain possession of my seaside cottage even though six strong men are in effective occupation of it. As between myself and the squatters this stretching of possession makes no difference: even if they had possession it would be as against me a 'vicious' possession and therefore I should succeed in the interdict. But as between the squatters and third parties (e.g. if they themselves are evicted) the difference is crucial. The squatters have no remedy, and the reason for this is in substance that their occupation is vicious as against me, or, in other words, that I have a better right than they; but this is a denial of the basic principle that title is irrelevant to possession. In short, the Romans were tending to treat possession as a right and were thereby blurring the line between possession and ownership which otherwise they so rigorously maintained.

3. MODES OF ACQUISITION OF CORPOREAL THINGS

Gaius and Justinian devote their main attention to the modes of acquisition of *res corporales*—the ways in which a thing may become mine. They classify these as belonging either to the civil or to the natural law in the sense explained above.[1] *Traditio*, for example, is a natural mode of acquisition, whereas *mancipatio* and *in iure cessio* are peculiarly Roman and are therefore civil modes. This classification is, however, difficult to justify in individual cases, and later commentators have usually adopted others, especially that into original and derivative modes. By a derivative mode one acquires from a previous owner, and therefore, in theory at least, one proves one's title by proving the title of one's predecessor.[2] By an original mode one acquires a title which is not dependent on any previous title. Either the thing has never before been owned (*occupatio* of a wild animal) or, if it has, the new ownership is proved without reference to the old. For example, if a cobbler soles my shoes, my title to the leather he has used depends not on his title to it (he may have stolen it), but on its having been incorporated in my shoe (*accessio*).[3] I prove my title by proving the incorporation.

We shall consider first the derivative modes and then the original, and within the latter we shall for convenience distinguish prescription, which in the form of *usucapio* is civil, from the other modes which are all natural.

4. DERIVATIVE MODES—CONVEYANCES

Mancipatio, in iure cessio. We have already examined these two conveyances of the civil law.[4] Both have disappeared from the law of Justinian, though neither was ever formally abolished. *In iure cessio* was in practice confined to the conveyance of incorporeal things, and had probably ceased to be used even for this purpose long before the time of Justinian. *Mancipatio* was deprived of any possible function in the law of property when Justinian abolished the distinction between *res mancipi* and

[1] p. 57.
[2] As to this *probatio diabolica*, see below, p. 155.
[3] Below, p. 133. The distinction between original and derivative modes is sometimes expressed differently, original modes being those by which property is acquired free from any 'burdens' which attached to it in the hands of the previous owner. Usucapion on this view is derivative, since the person usucapting takes the property subject to all existing servitudes. But even so the classification is hardly workable. *Occupatio* is the original mode *par excellence*, and, at any rate on the view which eventually prevailed, acquisition of abandoned things is by *occupatio*; yet the 'occupier' of abandoned land takes it subject to servitudes.
[4] Above, pp. 63 f.

res nec mancipi,[1] but this was probably no more than the recognition of existing practice. Even in the classical law it is a matter for speculation how far the actual use of scales and bronze survived. There are plenty of documents from this period which record, in words which are obviously common form, that a donee or a purchaser of a *res mancipi* 'received it by *mancipatio*', but we may wonder whether the parties were not often content to let the record do duty for the act. This was certainly what eventually happened in the West, where references to mancipation appear in documents even after the time of Justinian, but in a form which makes it clear that even the meaning of the word has been forgotten. The transferor simply declares that he 'hereby mancipates' the thing; and a century or two earlier the Epitome of Gaius which is partially preserved in the *lex Romana Visigothorum* explains that a *mancipatio* is a handing over. It is probable that in the Greek-speaking East it had lost even this shadow of life long before the time of Justinian.

Traditio. The only conveyance which survived in the law of Justinian was simple delivery, or rather delivery based on a valid ground or 'cause' (*iusta causa*) for the passing of ownership. For delivery is in law a colourless act. It derives its legal colour from the circumstances in which it is made. If I hand you my ring in pursuance of an agreement to sell it, I give you ownership; if I hand it to you as security for a debt (*pignus*), I give you possession; and if I hand it to you on hire I give you only detention. In technical language, the effect of a *traditio* depends on its 'cause', and 'cause' in this context means the parties' agreed purpose in making the *traditio*. In the case of my selling you my ring the 'cause' of the *traditio* is the fulfilment of the sale. Other 'causes' for the passing of ownership are the payment of a debt, the making of a *mutuum* (a loan, e.g. of money, in which it was not expected that the specific object would be returned), the making of a gift, &c. It was the agreement as to the purpose which mattered and not its fulfilment, and therefore if the agreed purpose was the fulfilment of a sale the *traditio* was

---

[1] He also swept away the old forms of emancipation and adoption (above, pp. 80 and 78), and the act *per aes et libram* therefore wholly disappeared. On the other hand *in iure cessio* was allowed to survive in its variant form of *manumissio vindicta*.

effective to pass ownership even though the sale was in law void and therefore incapable of fulfilment (e.g. because of a mistake). Again, it was not sufficient that the parties had a common intention to pass ownership if they had no common mind as to the 'cause' for their doing so; for example, if I delivered to you a sum of money with the intention of making a loan (*mutuum*), and you took it in the belief that it was a gift, we both indeed intended that ownership should pass, but we were not in agreement as to why, and therefore the *traditio* could pass only possession. This, elusive as it is, would seem to be the doctrine of the classical law, but the question is much debated. Certainly the law of Justinian was otherwise. The last-mentioned rule had been reversed and a common intention to pass ownership sufficed, the 'cause' being merely one way of evidencing that intent. In the language of the commentators, *traditio* was no longer a causal but an abstract conveyance. Its validity depended not on any 'cause' external to itself, but simply on there being a handing over with the intention to pass ownership. *Mancipatio* and *in iure cessio* were abstract in the same sense: it was sufficient that the formal act had been performed; the reason why was irrelevant.

Traditio requires in principle the acquisition of possession *animo et corpore* by the recipient, and it is the latter of these two elements which distinguishes *traditio* from a conveyance by mere consent and which therefore preserves the fundamental distinction between conveyance and contract. The classical lawyers therefore insisted on a certain minimum of physical transfer. In order to define that minimum they marked off certain typical situations in which the physical element, though attenuated, was sufficient, and the names which they or their successors gave to these typical situations have become part of the lingua franca of the Civil lawyer and to some extent even of the Common lawyer.

(*a*) *Traditio longa manu.* In the case of immovables or of bulky movables a physical transfer in any literal sense is obviously impossible. If I wish to give you possession of a pile of logs, it is sufficient if I point them out to you; to require that you should touch them would be simply pedantic. But it is not sufficient that I should simply tell you where they are: you cannot get possession until you are actually in sight of them. The traditional example of this 'long-handed delivery' is that of my giving you possession of land by taking you up a nearby tower and pointing it out to you.

A variant of this is what the commentators call 'symbolic *traditio*'. I wish to give you possession of the contents of my warehouse and therefore give you the keys. For the classical lawyers this is not symbolic at all, for they require that the keys be handed over at the warehouse, and this is as physical a delivery of the contents as is reasonably possible; but in Justinian's law it seems that the delivery of the keys might take place anywhere at all, and once this concession is made the keys become merely the symbol of what is delivered.

(*b*) *Traditio brevi manu.* I lend you a book and later agree to sell it to you. Must I take it back from you and then hand it over again? Clearly not, but the line between this and conveyance by consent is fine. Some lawyers simply conceded that this was a case of delivery *animo solo*, but it is better analysed as one in which *corpus* and *animus* are separated. The physical delivery precedes the intention.[1]

(*c*) *Constitutum possessorium.* This is the converse of *traditio brevi manu.* I sell you a book but we agree that I shall retain it on loan. Here too it was conceded that possession and therefore ownership[2] passed, but the line to be drawn is even finer, for there has been no physical transfer at all. But the argument is irresistible: if I buy your land of which X is tenant, I can acquire possession of the land by agreeing with X that he shall continue in occupation as my tenant; it can make no difference if you and X are the same person, i.e. if you are in occupation of the land yourself and I agree that you shall continue in occupation as my tenant. The difference between this and conveyance by consent, however, lies in the requirement that there must be some definite transaction, such as hire or loan or the grant of a usufruct, under which you remain in occupation on my behalf. It is not sufficient that we should merely agree that you remain. This is a very fine line indeed. If I sell you my book and we agree simply that I shall keep it until you want it, we achieve nothing, but if we agree that I shall keep it on loan, then possession and ownership pass. The way was open to con-

---

[1] Compare the lease and release of the older English law.

[2] In all these cases what is in issue is, strictly, the passing of possession. Whether ownership also passes is a question (*res mancipi* apart) of the *iusta causa*.

veyance by consent, and the practitioners of the later Empire evidently followed it. Documents of sale survive in which the seller reserves to himself a usufruct for a short time. Diocletian indeed protests that ownership passes by delivery and not by simple agreement, and Constantine requires a public announcement to the neighbours, but evidently to no purpose. The essential of a conveyance is now the agreement, and, since the agreement will usually be embodied in a document, the conveyance comes to be identified, as it is in modern English law, with the document. It is here that *mancipatio* and *traditio* meet and merge in a single documentary conveyance.

5. ORIGINAL CIVIL MODE—PRESCRIPTION

Introductory—limitation and prescription. In modern systems of law a man's legal position may be affected by lapse of time in two main ways, which are sometimes distinguished in English legal language as limitation and prescription, though the terminology is not fixed. Limitation applies to actions, prescription to rights. Under a system of limitation, if an action is available to me and I fail to bring it within a certain time, I am debarred from bringing it thereafter. But it is only the action which is barred; the right on which the action is based still survives. It is unenforceable or 'imperfect', but not void. The practical consequences of this distinction will differ in detail from system to system, but broadly they are two. The first is that if the right is *in rem*, I can assert it by action against anyone except the person against whom the barred action lay. For example, if you are in possession of my book without my consent, I can claim it from you; if I fail to do so within the period of limitation, my claim is barred but my ownership survives, and therefore if the book passes out of your hands into those of X, a new period of limitation will begin to run, and until it in its turn has expired I shall be able to claim the book from X, and so on. The second main consequence is that acts done in pursuance of the right are valid. To take an example of a right *in personam*, if you owe me money and I fail to claim it within the period of limitation, but you nevertheless subsequently pay me, you cannot reclaim the money as having been paid when it was not owing, since it was not my right to the payment which was extinguished by lapse of time, but only my action to enforce it.

By contrast, in a system of prescription the right itself is affected. There is, however, a further distinction between two possible forms of prescription, which may be called extinctive and acquisitive. Extinctive prescription merely extinguishes the right without giving any corresponding right to anyone else, whereas acquisitive prescription operates to create a new right.[1] The former is obviously the only sense in which prescription can ever apply to rights *in personam*—in the example just given of a debt owed by you to me, it would be meaningless to say that you had acquired my right to payment—but ownership can be subjected to either form of prescription. In any particular system, however, the legislator's choice will not be difficult. In a system such as the Roman in which there is no *tertium quid* between a possessory and a proprietary remedy, i.e. in which anyone who wishes to claim a thing must either show that he has been dispossessed by the defendant or that he is owner,[2] a system of extinctive prescription would be so inconvenient as to be unworkable. Ownership would in effect be *pro tanto* abolished. For at the end of the period the owner would lose his right, but the possessor would have no more than possession. If, for example, the thing were stolen from him by A and stolen from A by B, he could not claim the thing from B, and so on. On the other hand, in a system such as the English, which has no action corresponding to the *vindicatio* but which in principle gives to anyone who has lost possession without his consent an action not merely against the dispossessor but also against any third party who has no better title than he has, extinctive prescription is all that is needed.[3] In the example just given, the possessor will be able to sue not only B, but any subsequent holder, and since the only title superior to his has *ex hypothesi* been extinguished, he is for all practical purposes the owner.

---

[1] In the sense that the new right is proved without reference to the old (see above, p. 116). It is in this sense that prescription is classed as an original mode of acquisition; but see also ibid., n. 3.

[2] See further, below, p. 155.

[3] This is the current English system. The choice is in fact not between alternative systems of prescription, but between alternative methods of protecting ownership. If the Roman method is adopted there must be acquisitive prescription; if the English, extinctive. There are further consequential differences which must here be neglected.

It must be emphasized that terminology varies and that what is here called limitation is often called extinctive prescription.

The civil law had a system of acquisitive prescription (*usucapio*) with very short periods, but had in principle no limitation at all. Some Praetorian actions were barred after a year, but they were *in personam* and for the most part penal, and they need not concern us here. In the cases therefore in which *usucapio* did not apply,[1] an owner could assert his ownership no matter how long he and his predecessors in title had been out of possession. This was so throughout the classical law. Limitation did not become general until A.D. 424, when Theodosius established a period of thirty years for most actions. This seems excessively long to the English lawyer, accustomed to a normal period of six years (twelve for land), but it passed into the common law of Europe and is still commonly found in modern codes. It is supplemented, however, by a system of acquisitive prescription with shorter periods, and even this, as we shall see,[2] is much less important than at first sight it seems.

Usucapio. The Twelve Tables laid down a period of two years for the usucapion of land and one year for movables. These very short periods may seem surprising in a system which otherwise denies any effect to the lapse of time and gives unquestioning protection to vested rights, but usucapion requires much else besides just the lapse of time, and its scope is therefore very restricted. It serves, in fact, two main purposes, to cure a defect in the mode by which the thing was conveyed (*traditio* of a *res mancipi*),[3] and to cure a defect in the title of the person who conveyed it (e.g. sale by a non-owner). To achieve these purposes five requirements must be satisfied. The person claiming to usucapt must have had uninterrupted possession for the requisite period; the possession must have been acquired both *ex iusta causa* and in good faith; the thing must be capable of being owned (not, for example, a free man believed to be a slave); and it must not at any time have been stolen or taken by force.

The requirements of *iusta causa* (also referred to as *iustus titulus*) and *bona fides* are related. *Iusta causa*, which is similar to but not the same as the *iusta causa* of *traditio*, may be roughly

---

[1] See below.   [2] Below, pp. 129 f.

[3] It is convenient to include under this head cases in which possession was taken under an order of the Praetor and ripened into ownership if held for the requisite period, in particular the grant of *bonorum possessio* to the 'Praetorian heir' (below, pp. 243 ff.).

defined as some transaction by virtue of which the possessor would have become owner but for one or both of the defects already mentioned. For example, if you sell and deliver to me your slave, the 'cause' is the sale; if you give me a ring which unknown to either of us belongs to X, the 'cause' is the gift. In each case I would have been owner but for the defect—lack of *mancipatio* in the first case, lack of title in you in the second—which it is the function of usucapion to cure. Sale or gift are the commonest 'causes', but there are many others, such as legacy, dowry, or a promise by stipulation. The 'cause', unlike that of *traditio*, must be real. It was not enough that I thought there was a sale or a legacy if in fact there was none. Indeed if such a merely putative 'cause' had sufficed, it would have been hardly possible to distinguish the requirement of *iusta causa* from that of *bona fides*. Good faith is never easy to define, and this is no exception. In the case of the acquirer from a non-owner it would usually amount to a belief that he had become owner, i.e. that his taking of possession *ex iusta causa* had given him full title. In the case of the acquirer of a *res mancipi* by *traditio* it could hardly have any meaning at all, since he must know that he is not owner. In neither case, however, was proof of good faith either called for or indeed possible: it was for the person disputing usucapion to prove bad faith. And he would have to show not simply that the possessor was in bad faith at the time of the action, but that he was in bad faith at the moment when he acquired possession. For supervening bad faith was no bar to usucapion. If I bought from you a ring and neither of us then knew that it belonged to X, but immediately after I had taken possession of it I discovered the truth, I might nevertheless usucapt.

The most restrictive requirement, however, is the last. If a thing had once been stolen or taken by force it could never thereafter be usucapted[1] (unless either it had in the meantime returned to the hands of the owner or the owner had discovered its whereabouts and had neglected to claim it). And theft has a much wider meaning in Roman law than in English. It includes, in fact, any dishonest dealing with another man's movable

---

[1] This can, of course, have no application to the case of the bonitary owner who receives a *res mancipi* by *traditio*, since he has *ex hypothesi* received it from the owner, and there can therefore have been no theft.

property.[1] In the examples given above of the gift or sale of a ring, the reason why the donor or seller must be ignorant of the title of X is not that he is required to be in good faith, for he is not, but simply that if he is in bad faith the transaction will amount to theft. And even if he is himself in good faith it is almost certain, if the owner of the ring has been parted from it without his consent (as *ex hypothesi* he must have been), that there has been at some time a theft. Suppose that he lost it. The finder must then have been a thief, for he can hardly be heard to say that he thought it had been abandoned. Or suppose that he lent it and the borrower then sold it. Unless the borrower mistakenly thought that it was his own or that the owner had authorized him to sell it, he also is a thief. Hence it is that Gaius remarks that a *bona fide* possessor will rarely be able to usucapt a movable.[2] It may be otherwise, it is true, with land, for land cannot be stolen.[3] For example, if I squat on land which is for the moment unoccupied and then sell it to you, you will be able to usucapt it provided you are in good faith, and it will make no difference that I was in bad faith. But, though land cannot be stolen, it can be taken by force, and such a forcible taking will prevent the land from ever being usucapted, unless the owner has since either recovered it or acquiesced in its loss, as above.

We are driven to the conclusion that, apart from the curing of the formal defect in the title of the acquirer of a *res mancipi* by *traditio* and other similar holders, the rules of usucapion must usually have served to create not a definitive method of acquiring ownership, but a method of shifting the burden of proof. A person who had acquired possession *ex iusta causa* and had remained in possession for the requisite period could reasonably claim that it was for the person who disputed his title to show that he had acquired in bad faith or that the thing had been stolen or taken by force. It is in fact a compromise between the Roman dislike of interference with vested rights and the practical

---

[1] See below, p. 213.

[2] He suggests, by way of illustration, two cases in which he would be able to. I have lent you something and on your death your heir finds it and, assuming it to be yours, sells it. Or a slave woman of whom I have a usufruct has a child. Being ignorant of the law, I suppose the child to belong to me (it really belongs to the *owner* of the slave woman) and I therefore sell it. In each case the buyer can usucapt.

[3] See below, p. 214.

need to give some recognition to established facts. It is a compromise which is achieved by forgoing the absolute certainty in matters of property rights which is the advantage of a strict rule of prescription.[1]

The bonitary owner and the bona fide possessor. The rules of usucapion in effect marked off two classes of possessor as potential owners —the possessor whose title was only formally defective, typified by the recipient of a *res mancipi* by *traditio*, and the possessor whose title was substantially defective because derived from a non-owner. The former is called the 'bonitary owner'[2] and the latter the '*bona fide* possessor'. By the Civil law, however, their rights were no more than potential. Until usucapion was complete they were protected only by the interdicts which were available to any possessor; and these, as we have seen,[3] lay only against the immediate dispossessor. In this state of the law the Praetor intervened, probably in the late Republic. His policy was different in the two cases. The bonitary owner was to be protected against everyone, including the owner; the *bona fide* possessor was to be protected against everyone except the owner. If one considers the possible situations, this policy and the methods adopted to give effect to it explain themselves. There are essentially two situations.

(i) The person on the way to usucapion is still in possession, but the thing is claimed from him. The claim can only be a *vindicatio* and only the owner therefore can hope to succeed. He must obviously be allowed to succeed against the *bona fide* possessor, since otherwise the Praetor would in effect be allowing usucapion without even the short periods of time required by the civil law. On the other hand, to allow him to succeed against the bonitary owner would be to allow him to take advantage of a technicality to upset a conveyance which *ex hypothesi* he himself has voluntarily made; and the consistent policy of the Praetor was to dispense with unnecessary formalities. The defendant is therefore allowed to insert in the *vindicatio* a defence (*exceptio rei venditae et traditae*) requiring the judge to acquit him if the thing was sold and delivered to him by the plaintiff. This defence can

---

[1] See further below, pp. 129 f.
[2] See below, p. 127.
[3] Above, p. 108. But see also the note on that page.

obviously only be made good by a bonitary owner, and the Praetor's object is therefore achieved.

(ii) The person on the way to usucapion loses possession of the thing, but wishes to claim it from the present possessor. For example, P is on the way to usucapion when T takes the thing from him and gives it to D. (If the thing were still in the possession of T, P would be adequately protected by the ordinary law, since he could bring a possessory interdict on the ground simply that T had taken the thing out of his possession.) Here the Praetor's policy must differ according both to whether P is a bonitary owner or a *bona fide* possessor and to whether D is or is not the owner. If D is the owner, then the same considerations apply as in the previous situation: P must succeed if he is a bonitary owner and must fail if he is a *bona fide* possessor. If D is not the owner, P must succeed in either case, since his claim is at least preferable to that of D. This policy cannot, however, be put into effect as simply as it can be stated. For we have been assuming that the Praetor knows what the nature of the plaintiff's title is and whether the defendant is owner or not, and yet it is precisely these issues which the action may have to settle. The action must be so formulated that the right result will follow whichever of the four possible alternatives emerges from the hearing. This action provides a good example of Praetorian methods and therefore merits a more detailed examination.

The action derives its name, *actio Publiciana*, from the otherwise unknown Praetor who first allowed it. It is essentially a *vindicatio* in which the necessary lapse of time is fictitiously presumed. The *formula* begins with an assertion by the plaintiff that if he had continued in possession of the thing for one year, or two, he would have been owner. ('If the plaintiff would be owner of the thing, which was sold and delivered to him, if he had held it for a year [or two years].') Nothing but the lapse of time is presumed. The plaintiff must prove, in so far as they can be proved, the other requisites of *usucapio*. This he will be able to do in either of the situations we are envisaging. There then follows a defence (*exceptio iusti dominii*) asserting that the defendant is the true owner ('then, unless the defendant is owner'). If the defendant can substantiate this assertion, the plaintiff will now fail. This is the desired result if the plaintiff is only a *bona fide* possessor, but not if he is a bonitary owner. The *formula* therefore contains, before the final order to condemn or acquit, a further reply by the plaintiff (*replicatio rei venditae et traditae*) asserting, in the same way as in situation (i) above, that the defendant sold and delivered the thing to him ('and even then if the defendant sold and delivered the thing to the plaintiff, let the judge condemn . . .', &c., as in the ordinary *vindicatio*). This will enable the bonitary owner finally to prevail, but will be of no assistance to the *bona fide* possessor.[1]

The Praetor, though he had in form only added one more action to the list in the Edict, had in substance done much more. He had abolished the need for *mancipatio* and had transformed Roman ownership. Henceforward the recipient of a *res mancipi* by *traditio* was for nearly all practical purposes in the position of an owner.[2] The civil law owner (*dominus ex iure Quiritium*) retained almost nothing but the bare name. This however he did retain. For the Romans could not bring themselves to call the bonitary owner a *dominus*. They preferred a circumlocution: he had the thing among his goods—*in bonis*. It was left to the Byzantine jurists to coin from this the term 'bonitary'. This reluctance to abandon old ways of thinking and speaking was matched by an equal reluctance in the practice of conveyancing to take advantage of the Praetorian reform and abandon the use of *mancipatio*.

The transformation of ownership was, however, wider than this. Ownership in the civil law (*dominium ex iure Quiritium*) was unique and indivisible. A man was either owner or not owner. His title must be good against the whole world or against no one. Hence the bonitary owner or the *bona fide* possessor had, as far as the civil law was concerned, no better title than a mere possessor. But the effect of the *actio Publiciana* was to create two other forms of what could have been called Praetorian ownership. Bonitary ownership differed indeed only technically from *dominium* and could have been reconciled with the uniqueness

---

[1] Like the *formula* of every other action, it is in grammatical structure a succession of conditional clauses governing the order to the judge to condemn or acquit (see above, pp. 24 f.). What are in substance assertions are therefore in form conditional clauses. For the *formula* of the ordinary *vindicatio* see above, p. 101, n. 1.

[2] He remained under some disabilities. See, for example, above, p. 74, n. 1 (manumission) and below, p. 265 (legacy *per vindicationem* before the *Sc. Neronianum*).

of ownership if the Romans had been prepared to give theoretical recognition to the fact that *traditio* of a *res mancipi* passed ownership. Justinian in fact, as we have seen, did so,[1] and bonitary ownership has disappeared from the *Corpus Iuris*. But the essence of *bona fide* possession was its relativity—it was good against everyone except the true owner.[2] The Romans never adjusted their conception of *dominium* to allow for this relative ownership, preferring to turn a blind eye to its existence by simply denying to it the name of ownership.[3]

Longi temporis praescriptio and Justinian's reforms. Usucapion, being a civil mode, applied only to things capable of Roman ownership and therefore not to provincial land,[4] and was only available to Roman citizens. The gap was filled by the institution of *longi temporis praescriptio*, of which we first hear in an imperial constitution of A.D. 199. This was originally not prescription, but merely limitation. By the time of Justinian, however, it had become, like usucapion, a mode of acquisitive prescription, but the time required was much longer: ten years if the parties were in the same district, twenty if they were not.

Theodosius, as has been said above,[5] introduced a general limitation period of thirty years, and Justinian made other changes. When he came to the throne, Italy was in the hands of the barbarians, and usucapion therefore applied in practice only to movables and to such land as enjoyed the privilege of the *ius italicum*.[4] Correspondingly, since the citizenship was universal, *longi temporis praescriptio* applied in practice only to land. He therefore gave the name of *usucapio* to the acquisition of movables, but with the period extended to three years, and gave the name of *longi temporis praescriptio*, with the same periods as before, to land. He also created a new form of acquisitive prescription. Anyone who had acquired a thing in good faith, even if without *iusta causa*, and had held it for thirty years, now became owner. The commentators gave this the name of *longissimi temporis praescriptio*. It applied even if the thing had been at some

---

[1] By abolishing the distinction between *res mancipi* and *nec mancipi* (above, p. 106).

[2] The term '*bona fide* possessor', as used here, is consecrated by usage, but can be misleading. It is a shortened version of the full Latin term, *bonae fidei possessor in via usucapiendi*, but obviously not every *bona fide* possessor is on the way to usucapion.

[3] Gaius does recognize that ownership is divided, but he seems to have been alone in this. The terminology and the conception of *dominium* remained unaffected.

[4] See above, p. 105, n. 4.   [5] p. 122.

time stolen, and so it was now possible after thirty years, as it had never been before, to be certain of one's ownership of movables.

Modern law and the inviolability of ownership. Prescription is an inroad on the inviolability of ownership—the principle that a man should not lose ownership without his consent—and is justified by the public interest, which we have already noticed,[1] that rights *in rem* shall be readily ascertainable. Its importance in any particular system will therefore depend both on the importance which that system attaches to the inviolability of ownership and on the extent to which it makes inroads on it in other ways. Classical law is more extreme in its insistence on the inviolability of ownership than any modern system. It allows no other inroads on it than usucapion and *longi temporis praescriptio*, and the scope of these, as we have seen, was limited. In the law of Justinian *longissimi temporis praescriptio* made a further and more substantial inroad, but the lapse of time required was very long. Other inroads there were none. The Roman law adhered to the rule, which embodies the principle of inviolability, that a man cannot transfer a better title than he has.[2] Modern Civil law is very different. It is far more prepared to sacrifice the inviolability of ownership to the requirement of certainty, but it does so in the main by two methods more drastic than prescription, and in consequence prescription is relatively unimportant. These methods we have already glanced at.[3] As far as land is concerned, registration of title, as in Germany, is conclusive in favour of the *bona fide* possessor. For example, if land which belongs to A is wrongly recorded in the Register as belonging to B, and B sells to C, who is not aware of the error, C acquires title. As far as movables are concerned, most modern systems go very far in the direction of equating *bona fide* possession with ownership. The French Civil Code even declares that 'In regard to movables possession is as good as title', which, if taken at its face value, would deprive ownership altogether of its ordinary meaning. The actual effect of the principle is more restricted, but it means, for example, that if you lend me your book and

---

[1] Above, pp. 103 ff.
[2] 'Nemo plus iuris transferre potest quam ipse habet' or, in the more succinct but less accurate English version, 'Nemo dat quod non habet'.
[3] Above, pp. 104 ff.

I sell and deliver it to X, a *bona fide* purchaser, X will acquire title, and your only remedy will be against me. The justification for such a drastic restriction of ownership is that in a modern commercial society, which depends for its existence on the rapid movement of goods, it is more important that the purchaser should be freed of the necessity to investigate the title to the goods which he buys than that the owner should be protected in the enjoyment of his absolute title. This is once again a case of two innocent parties one of whom must suffer, and modern systems find that the balance of convenience lies in placing the loss on the owner. Roman law thought otherwise. English law, traditionally as jealous of the owner's rights as Roman law, now occupies an intermediate position. It is gradually introducing a system of registration of title to land, and in regard to movables it allows a number of rather arbitrary exceptions to the principle of inviolability without going to the length of modern Civil law.

6. ORIGINAL NATURAL MODES

All the natural modes, with the exception of *traditio*, are original. These original natural modes form a characteristic feature of the Roman law and of all systems derived from it, though the prominence given to them in the *Corpus Iuris* and even in the French Civil Code is hardly proportionate to their practical importance. Moreover, though Justinian expounds them at length in the Institutes, and the jurists in the Digest devote enthusiastic ingenuity to the debating of the problems involved, there is little technical terminology to distinguish and identify the different modes and apparently no systematic classification. The classifications and terminology used by modern writers are therefore for the most part not Roman, and though some are universally accepted others vary from author to author, to the confusion of the student.

Occupatio. This, the archetype of the original modes, is the acquisition of ownership of a thing which has no owner (*res nullius*) by taking possession of it. Its problems are therefore the problems of possession.

A *res nullius* may either never have had an owner or have been abandoned by its owner, but the only *res nullius* which are commonly encountered in everyday life are wild animals, and it is in regard to them that *occupatio* is mainly discussed. They are, moreover, the only things of which ownership and possession are always coextensive. If a new island appears in the sea (which, as every student of the Institutes knows, 'rarely happens') I can acquire ownership of it by taking possession of it, and I shall not lose ownership simply by losing possession. But if I catch a starling and it later escapes, I shall lose ownership of it at that moment. And this will be so no matter how long I have had it and how 'tame' it had become. For there is in law no such thing as a 'tame' starling: wildness is not a matter of the characteristics of the individual animal but of the species to which it belongs. And so, conversely, if my domesticated goose escapes and 'goes wild' I shall still own it, though I shall have lost possession of it. For tame animals are subject to the same rules as any other movable property.

The strict rule that ownership of wild animals was lost when possession was lost was relaxed in the case of animals which 'have the habit of going away and returning', such as homing pigeons. Or rather the strictness of the rule was mitigated by a stretching of the idea of possession. For they were subjected to the same rules as other wild animals, but principle was satisfied by saying, rather quaintly, that the physical control necessary to the owner's possession of them is maintained by their 'intention to return' (*animus revertendi*). Consequently, if a homing pigeon loses the *animus revertendi* it becomes a *res nullius* at that moment. Obviously the *animus revertendi* must in practice be the apparent habit of returning.

English law gives to the occupier of land rights in 'game' on his land, so that if without your consent I shoot a partridge on your land it belongs immediately to you. Roman law, however, has no such rules, and the partridge would belong to me by the ordinary principles of *occupatio* as soon as I had taken possession of it (unless it was in a pen and could therefore be said to be in your possession and consequently in your ownership). I may have committed the delict of *iniuria*[1] in entering on your land, but this will make no difference to my title to the partridge. In other respects, however, the rules of English law as to the ownership of wild animals are the same as and seem to be derived from those of Roman law.

[1] See below, p. 216.

The Roman doctrine of *occupatio* was adopted by the founders of modern international law as the basis of the acquisition of title by states to vacant territory (which was conveniently taken to include territory possessed by 'savage' tribes).

Increment by rivers. A number of problems which arise out of the flow of rivers or changes in their course can be treated together. If some of the problems seem to the English reader rather far-fetched, the explanation, at least in part, is that the rivers of the Mediterranean world are not the placid, orderly streams to which we are accustomed.

(i) *Alluvio.* In the course of time riparian land may be significantly extended by imperceptible increments of soil brought down by the river. Such additions are not *res nullius* but belong to the riparian owner. If the addition is not imperceptible, but a piece of land has been carried bodily down the river (what the commentators call *avulsio*), there is no change in its ownership until it has become permanently attached to the bank (the texts speak of trees on it striking root).

(ii) *Insula nata.* There is much discussion of the ownership of islands which are thrown up by the movement of the river (as opposed both to those which are created when the river divides, thereby enclosing an existing piece of land the ownership of which remains unchanged, and to those which are laid bare by a fall in the level of the water and are treated as part of the bed). The rules are nevertheless not altogether clear. If the island is wholly on one side of the river, it belongs to the riparian owner on that side. If there is more than one riparian owner, the island is divided by drawing vertical lines from the limits of each holding to the island. If the island is not wholly on one side, apparently a line is drawn down the middle of the river and the island divided accordingly. This was the interpretation adopted by modern Roman law, but it leaves unanswered the mathematician's objection that unless the banks are parallel it is impossible to define the middle line.

(iii) *Alveus derelictus.* If a river changes its course, the bed which it abandons becomes the property of the riparian owners in the same way as the *insula nata*, and the new bed becomes public. It logically follows that if the river changes its course again, the second bed will not revert to its previous owner but will be divided in the same way as the first was. Usually this will make no difference since the former owner of the bed will own both banks, but in extreme cases the result can be harsh. For example, if my plot of land is small, it may be entirely taken up by the new bed so that when the river moves again it will belong not to me but to my neighbours on either side. This is pointed out by a text in the Digest, but, adds the hand of Justinian, 'this rule would hardly be applied'.

Merger. Problems may arise when a thing belonging to one person is united to or mixed with that of another, as, for example, if I pour your oil into the same vat as my oil, or if I paint a picture on your canvas with my paints, or weld your silver handle on to my silver cup. If the union or mixture has been made by agreement between us, there is little difficulty: either we will have agreed as to our rights in the resulting whole, or, if we have not, the law will presume that we intended it to be jointly owned in proportion to our contributions. Again, if the union is dissoluble, the aggrieved owner can claim that it be dissolved. For example, if my pearl is set in your ring and you are in possession of the complete ring, I can claim that my pearl be detached; and I can do the same if my wheel is fixed to your cart. But if the union or mixture has not been made by agreement between us (i.e. it has been made by one of us without the consent of the other, or by a third party without the consent of either), and if it is indissoluble, there is more difficulty. The problems are those of ownership and compensation—of rights *in rem* and *in personam*—but the problem of ownership comes first. For it admits of two possible solutions—either the whole belongs exclusively to one of us, or else it belongs to both of us jointly— and it is only if the first of these solutions is adopted that the question of compensation can arise.

The criterion applied is essentially one of identity. If the identity of one thing (the accessory) is merged and lost in the identity of the other (the principal) the owner of the principal is owner of the whole. In the example of the cup and the handle, the owner of the cup is owner of the cup-with-handle. There is said to be *accessio*.[1] If there is no merger of identity, but the

[1] The term is used by some commentators (and, following them, by the French Civil Code) in a much wider sense to include all cases in which there has been an addition to my right, i.e. in which the object of my ownership has increased. The

identity of the whole is the same as the identity of each of the component things, the ownership is joint. This will commonly only occur in the case of liquids or metals (as where my oil and your oil are mixed, or where my gold ingot and your gold ingot are melted together into a larger ingot) and the process is therefore termed by most commentators *confusio* (a pouring or melting together).

Here everything obviously turns on the meaning of 'identity', and this, as philosophers have found, is an elusive concept. In particular, how is the principal thing to be distinguished from the accessory? The distinction will usually in practice be easy enough to draw (as in the case of the cup and the handle), but to formulate a test is difficult. The only simple one the texts offer is that of value, and this is inadequate. For though it is usually the less valuable thing which accedes to the more valuable, it is not always so: if I write on your paper, the letters will accede to the paper, even if they are gold letters. All other tests do no more than to replace 'identity' by some equally elusive term. And, even so, none of them accounts for the answer actually given in the case of my painting on your canvas. For it was eventually held that the canvas acceded to the painting. It is difficult, however, to formulate any principle which will account for this, since the canvas is acceding to something which had no previous existence and could have no existence without the canvas.[1] Gaius says as much, and the reason evidently is the jurists' reluctance to say that a work of art is merely the accessory of a piece of canvas.

owner of an animal therefore acquires ownership of the young of the animal at birth by *accessio,* though in physical terms there has been not an accession but a separation. In this sense *accessio* includes all the original natural modes except *occupatio* and *thesauri inventio.* And there are other, intermediate, meanings. Since *accessio* as an abstract word is not Roman and no clear classification emerges from the texts, no one meaning or classification can be said to be 'right', but those adopted by the French Civil Code are so wide as to be almost meaningless.

It can be argued that some of the cases of 'increment by rivers' fall within even the restricted meaning of *accessio* given above. *Alluvio* and *avulsio* can fairly easily be fitted in (except that there should be *accessio* to the bed rather than to the bank, and the bed is said to be public). But *insula nata* and *alveus derelictus* can only be included by a forced interpretation and it seems simpler to adopt a merely descriptive classification for all these cases.

[1] It is not to the paint that the canvas accedes, but to the painting, as is obvious if one envisages the case of A's painting on B's canvas with C's paint. The problem would have been better dealt with as one of *specificatio* (see below, pp. 136 ff.)—the result would have been the same.

We have so far been considering *accessio* only of movables to movables. There can also, however, be *accessio* of movables to land. If your seed is sown in my land it belongs to me; if your tree is planted in my land it becomes mine when it takes root. The important case, however, is that of building (*inaedificatio*). A builds on A's land with B's materials or A builds on B's land with A's (or with C's) materials. The building accedes to the land. The union is in principle a dissoluble one,[1] but the owner of the materials is debarred from claiming them by a rule of primitive public policy, deriving from the Twelve Tables, that no one should be compelled to pull down a building. He must therefore wait until the house falls down or is voluntarily pulled down, and then he can bring a *vindicatio*. In the case, however, of A's building on his own land with B's materials, B is in the meantime given by the Twelve Tables an action (*actio de tigno iuncto*) against A for a penalty of twice the value of the materials (the same penalty as for theft) for his having wrongfully incorporated B's materials into the land or building.

This brings us to the problem of rights *in personam*. Where the union is indissoluble and the owner of the accessory has therefore lost his ownership, can he claim any compensation? There are two situations in which the law is clear. The first occurs where the union has been made in bad faith by the owner of the principal thing, as when A has fixed B's handle to his own cup, knowing it to be B's handle. In this case A's act constitutes the delict of theft, and B can claim not only compensation, but also a penalty.[2] The second situation occurs when B, the former owner of the handle, is in possession of the whole. In this case, A owns the whole and can therefore bring a *vindicatio* for it, but B is allowed to plead in defence (by *exceptio doli*) that A, even if he acted in good faith, ought to pay compensation for what he has acquired. In other words, if A does not pay compensation he will fail in his *vindicatio*. So far the law is clear, but what if A was in good faith, and B is not in possession? It seems that, in the classical law at any rate, B has no remedy. The only ground on which he might base a claim is that A is unjustifiably enriched at his expense, and, as we shall see,[3] the classical law allowed such claims only in a limited number of cases, of which this was not one. This may seem harsh, and sometimes it would be,

---

[1] See above, p. 133.   [2] See below, pp. 212 ff.   [3] Below, pp. 231 ff.

but by no means always. For how did it come about that A could in good faith fix B's handle to his cup? Most probably he bought it from a third party, in which case, assuming he paid a good price for it, he can hardly be said to be enriched. We are once again faced with the problem of two innocent parties, one of whom must suffer. Moreover, as we have seen,[1] it would rarely happen that a man would lose possession of a movable without his consent unless there had been theft, and therefore A would usually have at least the possibility of an action against the thief. In short, the only clear case of hardship will be the unusual one in which A has come into possession of the handle without paying for it. This case could only be dealt with at the risk of so widening the doctrine of unjustified enrichment that it would become unmanageable. The classical lawyers preferred to allow an occasional hardship than to run this risk. In fact the surprising thing is not that they refused B an action, but that they allowed him to claim compensation by way of defence. For this left the decision as to which of the two should bear the loss to the chance of which was in possession. The explanation is probably that it was possible to allow the *exceptio* to be pleaded to the *vindicatio* without opening the door to wide claims for unjustified enrichment, and the lawyers were therefore more willing to allow it. But the distinction is nevertheless arbitrary.

Specificatio. There remains one other problem involving identity. Two things may be so united that the identity of the resulting thing is different from that of either of the original two. Or a single thing may be so worked upon that its identity is changed. There is, in short, a new thing (*nova species*). For example, A makes his own wine and B's honey into mead, or his own gold and B's silver into electrum; or he makes B's bronze into a statue. As before, if this has been done by agreement there is no difficulty: either the agreement will have decided the question of ownership or, if it has not, the new thing will be owned by A and B jointly. But what if A has acted without B's consent?

In the classical law there was a dispute between the schools. The Sabinians gave the ownership to the owner of the materials, or if, as in the case of the mead, there was more than one owner,

---

[1] Above, p. 124.

to the owners jointly in proportion to their contributions. The Proculians gave the ownership to the maker. He acquired by *specificatio*—by his act of making a *nova species*. There was yet a third doctrine, to which Justinian gave his approval, and which he describes as a compromise (*media sententia*). This gave the *nova species* to the maker only if the materials could not be restored to their former state. The mead would therefore belong to A, but the bronze statue to B, whereas if the statue had been made out of marble it would have belonged to A. The mead would indeed belong to A for another reason. For Justinian introduced a further rule that if the maker had contributed any part of the material, the *nova species* should belong to him— apparently on the ground that he could claim support from both the Proculian and the Sabinian doctrines, since he had not only made the thing but had also contributed at any rate part of the material. If therefore A makes a statue partly out of B's bronze and partly out of his own, the statue will be his. It seems that in all these cases, as in *accessio*, the good or bad faith of the maker is irrelevant to his title.

The problems of compensation are the same in *specificatio* as in *accessio*, and what has been said above applies equally here.

Justinian's *media sententia* has been criticized as taking no account of the relative importance of the materials and of the maker's skill—i.e. of capital and labour—and has been abandoned by most modern systems. The French Civil Code gives the thing to the owner of the materials unless the value of the work far exceeds the value of the materials; the German Civil Code strikes a different balance, giving the thing to the maker unless the value of the work is far below that of the materials.

What is a *nova species*? When is a thing so changed that it becomes a new thing? It is probable that the dispute between the Proculians and the Sabinians reflects a difference of philosophical doctrine, the Proculians following Aristotle in giving the primacy to form or essence and the Sabinians preferring the Stoic view which gave the primacy to matter. Such distinctions are unfashionable now, and 'form' or 'essence' is no easier to define precisely than 'identity'; but there was a practical difficulty also. The plaintiff in a *vindicatio* must identify in words the thing to which he claims title. Is 'marble' a sufficient description of a marble statue, or can the defendant reply that the thing which he possesses is not the thing mentioned in the plaintiff's claim? In short the question 'is there a *nova species*?' can be restated in the form 'would the ordinary man give the thing as it is a name different from that of the thing as it was?'[1] This may be more acceptable to current ways of thinking, but it only shifts on to the ordinary man the burden of deciding when a thing has changed sufficiently to require a different name, and this is no other than the problem of form, essence, or identity.

Acquisition of fruits. The fruits or produce of a thing include both the natural increment of land or tame animals and also rents or similar profits. These are distinguished in modern terminology as natural and civil respectively (*fructus naturales* and *fructus civiles*).

The right to civil fruits is a matter not of the law of property but of the law of contract. If a man hires out land, his right to the rent depends on the validity of the contract, not on his title to the land. Indeed he need have no title: provided he maintains the lessee in enjoyment of the land he is entitled to the rent.

It is with natural fruits that we are here concerned. *Prima facie* they belong to the owner of the parent thing (which we shall assume to be land), but in some circumstances someone else may have a right to them. Obviously a tenant is usually entitled to the fruits, but since his right to the land is only *in personam* so also is his right to the fruits. He has a right that his landlord shall allow him to become owner of the fruits by gathering them (*perceptio*). His gathering them with the consent of the landlord is construed as a *traditio brevi manu*[2] by the latter, the practical consequence being that if he withdraws his consent before the tenant has gathered, the tenant can acquire no title, though he may have an action for breach of the contract of hire.

Equally obviously a usufructuary[3] is by the very nature of his right entitled to the fruits, and he too acquires them by *perceptio*, but since he has a right *in rem* his acquisition cannot depend on the consent of the owner, and there is therefore no idea of *traditio*.

The law is faced with a more difficult problem of policy in

---

[1] The same test can of course be applied to *accessio*: 'Does the thing as it is go by the same name as one only of the things from which it is made?'
[2] See above, p. 119.   [3] See below, p. 144.

the case of the *bona fide* possessor. On the one hand, there is the principle of the inviolability of ownership. (English law applies the principle uncompromisingly and requires the *bona fide* possessor to compensate the owner even for the fruits which he has innocently consumed.) On the other hand, the *bona fide* possessor has reasonable claims to consideration. He may well have spent money and labour on cultivation. This led to the view that he should be entitled to such fruits as need cultivation (*fructus industriales* as opposed to *fructus naturales* in a narrower sense), but the dominant opinion evidently took account of wider arguments—that the *bona fide* possessor will have conducted himself on the assumption that he was owner and that, if he is on the way to usucapion, he has what amounts to a relative ownership—and equated him, so long as he was in good faith, with the owner. He acquired all fruits as soon as they were separated from the parent thing (*separatio*), provided he was still in good faith at that moment. Justinian was much more restrictive and, if the owner asserted his title, required the *bona fide* possessor to hand over or account for all fruits except those which he had in good faith consumed.[1]

The difference between the *bona fide* possessor's acquisition by *separatio* and the usufructuary's or the hirer's acquisition by

---

[1] The innovation was achieved by interpolation and provides a simple example of the compilers' methods. In one text (Dig. 41.1.40) the *b.f.* possessor is said to 'become owner of the consumed fruits'. This is, strictly speaking, nonsense, and even if generously interpreted means that he becomes owner of fruits which he has gathered at the moment when he consumes them; and yet it is at that moment that they cease to be capable of being owned. Obviously the word 'consumed' has been added. By this simple, if clumsy, device a text which originally simply gave ownership to the *b.f.* possessor has been made in effect to deny it and merely to protect him from a claim for compensation—a claim, moreover, from which, at least in the classical law, he needed no protection since it could rest only on unjustified enrichment, and that doctrine did not then extend so far. In another text (Dig. 41.1.48 pr.) the *b.f.* possessor is said to acquire interim ownership. Here the word 'interim' has been put in. To the classical lawyer temporary ownership would have been a contradiction in terms. In the Institutes (II.1.35) the text begins with a statement, taken no doubt from a classical author, that the *b.f.* possessor acquires title; this is then followed by '*and therefore* if later the owner appears and vindicates the land, he cannot claim for the fruits which have been consumed'. But if the *b.f.* possessor has acquired title it should follow that the owner cannot claim even the unconsumed fruits. Other texts are treated similarly.

We are in consequence quite uninformed as to what constituted consumption. Did it include sale, or did the *b.f.* possessor have to account for the price? Probably he did not, since it would then in turn have been necessary to decide whether the price had been consumed, and this would have led to intolerable difficulties.

perceptio becomes of practical importance if the fruit is gathered by someone else. The usufructuary (or hirer) cannot claim them by *vindicatio*, since it was not he who gathered them (they belong to the owner), whereas the *bona fide* possessor can. The explanation of this restriction of the usufructuary's right lies probably in the fact that he has no possession of, or right in, the land itself, but merely a right to use it and to take the fruits. Until therefore he has actually taken them he can have no right in them.

The child of a slave woman was not classed as a fruit, and therefore belonged to the owner. This is presented as a concession to the humanity of the slave, but the more cynical modern view is that the child was too valuable an asset to allow to the usufructuary.

Treasure trove. Treasure (*thesaurus*) consists of valuables which have been hidden so long that their owner can no longer be discovered. Precisely what was included is uncertain. One text speaks of 'money', which is clearly too narrow, and another simply of *mobilia* (movables), but this is clearly too wide and must be a scribe's error for *monilia* (valuables), which occurs in a third text. There is certainly no evidence of the restriction to gold and silver which is found in English law. Hadrian provided that if a man found treasure on his own land he was entitled to it all, and if he found it on another man's land, each was entitled to half, provided the finding was by chance. From a constitution of A.D. 474 we learn that if the finding was not by chance the owner of the land was entitled to the whole.

In feudal Europe treasure trove was reserved to the Crown as the ultimate owner of all land, and this prerogative right still survives in England. On the Continent it has for the most part been superseded by the Roman rules, but without the exception as to deliberate search.

7. SERVITUDES

Introductory—iura in re aliena. We must now turn to rights *in rem* other than ownership. In a simple case the owner himself has all the rights which can be exercised over the thing, but sometimes, and particularly with land, others may have rights over it which, to a greater or less extent, limit his enjoyment of it. If I own a plot of land, *prima facie* I may do with it as I like, subject to the general law, but one of my neighbours may have a right of way over it and another a right to graze cattle on it; my banker may have a mortgage over it which gives him the right in certain circumstances to sell it; or I may have no present enjoyment of it at all, because someone has a usufruct over it. Such rights are commonly described in metaphorical terms as fractions of ownership vested in someone other than the owner, or as encumbrances or burdens on ownership or on the thing owned. The commentators gave them the name of *iura in re aliena*—rights *in rem* over another man's property.[1]

The principal *iura in re aliena* are termed by Justinian 'servitudes', but the two types of right which are included under this head—praedial and personal servitudes—are so different in character and function that they are best considered separately before any attempt is made to explain Justinian's classification.

Praedial servitudes. A man will often be unable to make the most advantageous use of his land or buildings without some rights over those of his neighbours. To take only a few examples, my land may have no water while that of my neighbour has plenty, and I will therefore wish to have the right to use this water and perhaps to pipe it across my neighbour's land; or the most convenient access to the highway from one part of my land may lie over the land of my neighbour; or I may wish to be sure that if I build up to the boundary of my land my neighbour will not subsequently darken my windows by building up to the boundary on his side. I can, of course, achieve my object by making a contract with my neighbour, but this will confer only a right *in personam*, and this will be doubly inadequate. First, if my neighbour sells his land, I shall have no right against the buyer: I shall have to make a new bargain with him, and he will be in a position to dictate the terms. My only protection in this case, as also when a third party interferes with my right, will be by an action against my original neighbour for breach of contract. Secondly, if I sell my land, I shall not be able to pass on my rights to the buyer, and the price I shall get will be correspondingly lower. In other words, it is important not only that

---

[1] The term 'right *in rem*' is English, though derived from the Roman *actio in rem*; the Continental equivalent is *ius in re*, and hence *ius in re aliena*.

the right should be enforceable against any subsequent owner of my neighbour's land, but also that it should be enforceable by any subsequent owner of my land. In the language of English law, not only must the burden 'run with' my neighbour's land, but also the benefit must 'run with' mine. This is the essence of a praedial (or 'real') servitude. It is a right *in rem* over a definite plot of land or a building and annexed to another plot of land or building (i.e. vested in the owner for the time being of the land or building). The land or building over which the right is exercised is said to be 'servient' and that to which it is annexed is said to be 'dominant'. This terminology, like the word 'servitude' itself, expresses the idea of a subjection or burden imposed on ownership.

But there are dangers in the multiplication of such burdens on ownership. There is the danger that the purchaser of the servient land may be unaware of the burdens attached to it (or alternatively that the difficulty of discovering their existence may add greatly to the complexity and expense of transfers of land). This presents merely one aspect of the general problem of ensuring publicity for the creation and transfer of rights *in rem*.[1] Some modern systems meet it by requiring the registration not merely of ownership of land but also of all encumbrances on it. Roman law, of course, had no such system and the problem was hardly met at all. A conveyance was in principle necessary for the creation of servitudes, but, as we have already seen, any effectiveness this may ever have had in ensuring publicity had disappeared long before the classical law.

There is also the danger that such encumbrances, unless they are restricted in number and extent, may so hamper the profitable use of the servient land as gravely to diminish its value; and this will ultimately injure the public interest. Against this danger the Roman law did take effective steps. It is not the Roman habit to formulate, as we have done here, the problems which the law has to meet: the purpose of legal rules is left to emerge from their practical working. But the rules which governed praedial servitudes did have the necessary restrictive effect. The most important of these rules is expressed in the commentators' maxim 'servitus in faciendo consistere nequit'. The owner of the servient land could not be required to do

[1] See above, pp. 103 f.

anything; he could merely be required either to abstain from doing something (e.g. from building so as to darken a window on the dominant land, or from the building or planting trees so as to obstruct the view from the dominant land) or to permit the owner of the dominant land to do something on the servient land (e.g. to walk or drive across it, to take water or sand or chalk from it).[1] This principle prevented the growth of anything akin to the feudal services by which, in France until the Revolution and in other parts of Europe until even later, the servient owner might be required to render certain personal services or to supply certain kinds and quantities of produce from the land.

A further rule required that a servitude should be for the benefit of the dominant land and that it should be used exclusively for that purpose. For example, a servitude of quarrying stone might only be exercised for the needs of buildings on the dominant land: the stone might not be sold or used elsewhere; similarly, a servitude of drawing water extended only to the water needed for the dominant land. This prevented the exploitation of servitudes for industrial purposes. It is sometimes said that the dominant and servient land must also be adjacent, but this seems in truth to be only another aspect of the same rule. If J own land at *x*, it is hardly conceivable that a right of way at *y*, twenty miles distant (say a short cut between two roads), can be of benefit to my land at *x*. It may be of benefit to me because I enjoy walking at *y*, but there is no difference in this respect between me and a man who owns no land at all. My right to walk across the land at *y* can therefore only be obtained by contract.

Praedial servitudes are of two kinds, rustic and urban. Examples of rustic servitudes are rights of way and of water, and of urban servitudes rights of light and of support for buildings. But though the distinction was of some practical importance, most noticeably because rustic servitudes were *res mancipi*, the principle on which it was based is quite uncertain. It is clear at least that the names are misleading, for the distinction is not between town and country (otherwise a right of light would be

---

[1] There was one exception: the servitude *oneris ferendi* gave to the dominant owner the right to have his building supported by (literally to have its burden borne by) a building on the servient land, and the servient owner was bound not only to refrain from pulling his building down but also to take positive steps to keep it in repair.

urban in the town and rustic in the country), but between dominant land without buildings and dominant land with buildings. But a distinction as simple as this would mean that a right of way from one field over another would become urban if a house were built on the dominant field. The principle is perhaps that a servitude is rustic if it serves a predominantly agricultural purpose, urban if it does not.

Personal servitudes. In Justinian's law these were four in number. Usufruct was the right to use and take the fruits and profits of another's property, movable or immovable, without fundamentally altering its character ('ius alienis rebus utendi fruendi salva rerum substantia'). *Usus* was, as its name indicates, a fraction of usufruct, entitling the beneficiary to use, but not to take the fruits of, the property. *Habitatio* and *operae servorum* were merely modifications of *usus*, applicable to houses and the services of slaves respectively. They were probably distinguished from *usus* only by Justinian, the main point of difference being that the beneficiary was entitled to hire out as well as to use the house or the services of the slave. The same principles apply to all four, and since usufruct was the earliest and by far the most important, we shall ignore the other three.

In classical law the term 'servitude' denoted only praedial servitudes. The enlargement of the category to include usufruct and its three derivatives, and the differentiation of the two types of right as personal and praedial, is Byzantine. They are alike in that they are both burdens on ownership which restrict the enjoyment of the owner. They are both fractions of ownership vested in someone other than the owner, rights *in rem* which 'run with' the servient property and can be asserted against the world at large. They are alike also in that they cannot require the servient owner to do anything, and in that they are to a large extent created and terminated in the same ways. But there are marked differences between them. Personal servitudes vest in a person as such, irrespective of his ownership of anything. They are personal to him and inalienable. There is thus a servient thing but no dominant thing. Moreover the servient thing may be either movable or immovable: there may be a usufruct of a slave or a herd of cows as well as of a farm. Again, praedial servitudes, though subject to the restrictive rules which we have discussed, are not limited in number, and are in principle perpetual, whereas there are only four personal servitudes, and they are limited in duration—usually for life, but otherwise for some shorter term. Finally, the function of the two types of servitude is entirely different. Praedial servitudes effect a permanent enhancement of the content of one ownership at the expense of that of another, whereas usufruct effects, after a fashion, a division in time but hardly in content of a single ownership. With *fideicommissum hereditatis*[1] and, in the late law, *emphyteusis*,[2] it constitutes the nearest approach that Roman law ever made to the creation of successive and yet simultaneous ownerships. This aspect of usufruct needs further examination.

By far the commonest purpose of a usufruct was evidently to make a family 'settlement', and accordingly, though it could be created in a number of ways, the continually recurrent example in the Digest is of a usufruct created by legacy. If a testator wished to give property to his wife for life and then to his son, he could do so by leaving it to his son subject to a usufruct in favour of his wife. There was here an approximation to successive ownerships, but a comparison with English law shows that it was a very imperfect approximation. The English land law, with its doctrine that what is owned is not the land but estates in the land, makes fully possible successive and yet simultaneous ownerships. If a man wishes to give Blackacre to his wife for life and then to his son, he can do so by giving his wife a life interest and his son the fee simple (i.e. the ultimate ownership). His wife has the present enjoyment and his son the right to future enjoyment, but both have immediately marketable assets. His wife can alienate her interest, and the person to whom she alienates it will acquire an estate in the land for so long as the wife lives; and the son can likewise alienate his interest. The two interests differ in their present content and in their prospective duration, but both are equally and simultaneously marketable. Moreover, and more commonly, modern English law makes possible the alienation by the wife even of the fee simple, the son's interest (and the wife's also) being transferred to the proceeds of the sale, which are held in trust. It is thus possible to 'tie up' capital without hampering dealings with the specific objects which originally composed the capital. This

---

[1] See below, pp. 268 f.   [2] See below, pp. 148 f.

is obviously important when those objects become inconvenient to manage or depreciate in value. Roman law, which conceives of ownership only of corporeal things, finds such flexibility much more difficult to achieve. The ownership of Blackacre may be divided (as it can also of course in English law) in the sense that X owns half and Y half, or in the sense that X and Y have joint ownership, each having a half share in the ownership of the whole, but ownership cannot be divided in time so as to give X and Y rights *in rem* which are both successive and yet simultaneously marketable. For usufruct achieves only half of this objective. Both the usufructuary and the owner have rights *in rem* which can be asserted against third parties, but only the owner can alienate. His interest only is marketable. The usufructuary can hire out or sell the enjoyment of the usufruct, but this falls short of alienation of the usufruct itself in two ways: it confers on the buyer only a right *in personam*; and the usufructuary is still liable to the owner for any abuse by the buyer of his rights. If the usufructuary could not alienate his interest, still less could he, as we have seen the modern English owner can, alienate the thing itself so as to transfer the owner's rights to the proceeds of the sale. The nearest approach by Roman law to this idea of capital as a fund rather than as specific things was in the institution of quasi-usufruct.[1] This arose to meet the difficulty that since the usufructuary had to return the thing itself to the owner, a usufruct of consumable goods, and in particular of money, was impossible. It was conceded therefore that if a usufruct created by will included such things, the usufructuary became owner of them and was obliged to return only an equivalent in quantity and quality. But the indivisibility and inviolability of ownership stood in the way of any extension of this idea.

The nature of a usufructuary's right to fruits has already been discussed, but the most productive property would very often be slaves, and, quite apart from the exclusion of the offspring of slave women, the profits from their activities did not fall within the category of fruits. The ordinary rule was, as we have seen,[2] that all rights which a slave acquired vested in his master, but the simple application of this rule would have drastically diminished the value of a usufruct in the more skilled type of

---

[1] Cf. F. H. Lawson, *A Common Lawyer Looks at the Civil Law*, p. 109.
[2] Above, p. 71.

slave. It would be of little interest to the usufructuary that the slave was a shrewd man of business if all the profits went to the owner. The rule which was evolved to balance the interests of owner and usufructuary was that any rights acquired in connexion with the property or affairs (*ex re*) of the usufructuary and any remuneration due under a contract made by the slave for the hire of his services (*ex operis*) belonged to the usufructuary, whereas rights acquired in any other circumstances belonged to the owner. Acquisition *ex re* was by far the more important. It would include any transactions made with a *peculium* granted by the usufructuary, any contracts made in connexion with his affairs, in fact any rights acquired when the slave was about the business of the usufructuary. On the other hand, a gift or a legacy to the slave would belong to the owner. Acquisition *ex operis* was much more restricted than the term suggests. It does not cover every acquisition made by the labours of the slave, but only the right to payment for the slave's services where the slave himself has made the contract with the hirer. (The usufructuary would equally be entitled where it was he and not the slave who made the contract, but the right to the payment would in this case not be acquired 'through' the slave any more than the rent of a house is acquired 'through' the house: it is acquired through the contract to which the usufructuary is a party.) If therefore a usufructuary slave has been hired out (or has hired himself out) as an agricultural labourer, and while digging a field belonging to the hirer he finds treasure, the finder's half goes to the slave's owner. The usufructuary has no right, because, though the treasure was acquired through the labours of the slave, it was not acquired *ex operis*, and it was obviously not acquired *ex re*.

A similar conflict of interest might arise between owner and *bona fide* possessor of a slave, and between a free man held in good faith as a slave and his *bona fide* possessor (e.g. A has bought B's slave in good faith from C, or A has bought B, who is, unknown to him, a free man). The conflict was resolved in the same way. A was entitled *ex re* and *ex operis*, B was entitled in all other circumstances.

The Roman law of servitudes and modern law. The influence of the law of praedial servitudes on modern Civil law has been very marked. The modern law is in essentials, and often, particularly in German law and systems derived from it, in details also, manifestly Roman. Even English law here reveals an obvious debt, the law of easements being perhaps the most Roman part of English law. Until the end of the eighteenth century it was very little developed, but what little there was owed much to Bracton's borrowings in the thirteenth century from Roman law; and when the Industrial Revolution called for more elaboration in the law, the courts, and more especially the author of the fundamental book on the subject,[1] turned to Roman law.

Usufruct, with the conception of ownership which it implies, is a fundamental feature of a Civil law system. It could indeed serve as the identifying mark of such a system, just as the doctrine of estates is the mark of a Common law system. It is not, however, always classified as a personal servitude. This is not for any reasons of principle (though these, as we have seen, are not lacking) but because the framers of the French Civil Code shrank from the term as being too likely to recall to the uninstructed the feudal services, abolished by the Revolution, which had involved for the person burdened with them personal servitude in a different sense. The term 'servitude' is therefore, as in classical Roman law but for different reasons, confined to praedial servitudes, but not all even of the codes which derive from the French follow it in this respect.

8. OTHER *IURA IN RE ALIENA*

Emphyteusis and superficies. These two institutions, which are noticeable features of modern Civil law, originated in the public law of the Empire, and were not wholly acclimatized in the private law until Byzantine times. It is perhaps for this reason that they are not classified as servitudes; for they have as good a claim to the name as usufruct has. *Emphyteusis* originates in the practice of granting state or municipal land (*ager vectigalis*) for very long periods, or for ever, in return for the payment of an annual rent. These grants differed from both ordinary leases and usufruct in being inheritable and alienable. And the holder had a 'real' relation to the land in that, unlike an ordinary lessee, he had possession. In the late Empire this holding of *ager vecti-*

---

[1] C. J. Gale, *Law of Easements* (1st edn., 1839).

galis was assimilated to *emphyteusis*, a kindred institution of Greek law, and by the time of Justinian it had been adopted also by private landowners. By this time, too, the holder (*emphyteuta*) had not merely possession, but also, like the owner or the usufructuary, an *actio in rem*, so that, where the *emphyteusis* was perpetual, he was for all practical purposes an owner, except that his holding might be terminated by his dying without successors, or by forfeiture for non-payment of rent or for irremediable damage. In its final form *emphyteusis* is the Roman law's nearest approach to the leasehold estate of English law (which cannot indeed be perpetual, but the ordinary landowner is unlikely to make much difference between 999 years and perpetuity). It survives still in modern Civil law, particularly in systems deriving from the French. But because it drains almost all content from ownership, particularly when it is granted in perpetuity, and therefore conflicts with the Roman and Romanistic conception of the unity of ownership,[1] French law limits its duration to 100 years.

Superficies was a closely similar institution, corresponding to the modern English building lease and serving still in modern civil law a similar purpose. In its eventual form it was a right *in rem* in a building, inheritable and alienable, and lasting either for ever or for a long term. It was a right in the building as opposed to the land on which it was built, and was thus a qualification of the principle that buildings accede to the land.[2] The owner of the land did, it is true, still own the building, just as the grantor of land by *emphyteusis* retained ownership of it, but the right of the *superficiarius*, as of the *emphyteuta*, was so extensive that so long as the *superficies* endured there were in effect two ownerships.

Real security. If one man (the debtor) borrows money from another (the creditor) or incurs towards him some other contractual obligation, the creditor will often wish to have some other way of obtaining satisfaction of the debt than his simple action *in personam* against the debtor. In other words, he wishes to be protected against the possibility that when the debtor is called upon to pay the debt he may either have disappeared or have become insolvent. In legal terms, he wants security for the

[1] See below, p. 157.   [2] See above, p. 135.

debt. This security may be either real or personal. Real security is the granting of either ownership, possession, or a *ius in re aliena* over property of the debtor or of some other person prepared to answer in this way for the debtor. It entitles the creditor at the least to retain or recover the property, and usually also to sell it in satisfaction of the debt. The commonest examples of such real securities in modern England are the mortgage and the 'charge' given (usually to a bank) by the deposit of title-deeds or share certificates. Personal security, on the other hand, is merely the addition of another debtor (the surety), or perhaps several debtors, to the first. The creditor seeks protection in numbers: if the debtor does not pay, he will have recourse against the surety or sureties, and he trusts that not both or all will simultaneously have disappeared or become insolvent. Personal security is therefore pure contract and will be considered in that connexion. Real security is a matter both of contract and of property. It is a matter of contract in so far as the rights of the parties *inter se* are concerned (the duty of the creditor to take care of the thing, to account to the debtor for any surplus resulting from its sale, &c.), and a matter of property in so far as the rights of the creditor *in rem* are concerned. We shall deal here in outline with the latter and, since the two aspects cannot be kept altogether distinct, to some extent also with the former.

The summary description of real security which is given above is, for the modern world, misleading in its emphasis. It suggests that the primary purpose of real security is to ensure the payment of the debt, whereas the modern mortgage is usually an investment. In other words, the mortgagor (the borrower) is concerned to obtain the use of capital for some considerable period and the mortgagee (the lender) is concerned to get an adequate and steady return on his money. Neither, probably, is anxious for an early repayment of the debt, and neither thinks of the mortgagee's realizing his security as anything more than a remote possibility. But for Rome the emphasis is right.[1] The use of real security as an investment seems to have been but little developed; if a man wished to invest in land he seems to have preferred the direct investment provided by an out-and-out purchase to the indirect investment offered by a mortgage.

[1] On what follows see F. Schulz, *Classical Roman Law*, pp. 401–5.

And there is a further marked difference from modern practice. Personal security in modern life is rare; in the Roman world it was very common—much commoner evidently than real security. It was the normal accompaniment of any substantial transaction on credit, as can be seen from the documents which chance has preserved. A sailor in Asia Minor sells a slave child to a warrant-officer, and another sailor goes surety for the price; a soldier on the frontier in what is now Romania buys a slave, and again there is a surety. The explanation of these two marked differences from modern practice is certainly not to be found only in the shortcomings of the law of real security, but these must, as we shall see, have played their part.

The earliest Roman form of real security, like the late medieval English mortgage, was a conveyance subject to a covenant for reconveyance on payment of the debt. The debtor gave ownership to the creditor by *mancipatio* or *in iure cessio* (but not *traditio*), subject to an agreement or trust (*fiducia*) that the creditor would reconvey it if and when the debt was paid. The *fiducia* would also usually contain provisions as to the creditor's right to sell, and the disposal of any surplus arising from such a sale, and so forth. This type of security had little to recommend it to the debtor. The creditor might, it is true, restore to him the possession of the thing to be held at will (*precario*),[1] but there remained two other disadvantages—first, that the debtor took all the risk, in the sense that he retained no right *in rem* and therefore, if the creditor sold in breach of his undertaking, his remedy (the *actio fiduciae*) lay only against the creditor; and secondly, that successive mortgages were impossible. Even if the property was worth far more than the total of the debt it could not be used as security for any other debt. *Fiducia* nevertheless remained in use throughout the classical period, but there grew up side by side with it the informal and more flexible institution of *pignus*.

Pignus involved a transfer not of ownership but only of possession. The debtor therefore was better protected than in *fiducia*, but the creditor, to begin with at least, less well. The remedying of this defect forms part of the development of a variant of *pignus* which gave the creditor neither ownership nor possession but a bare *ius in re aliena*.

---

[1] See above, p. 112, n. 1.

This development apparently began in the practice of a tenant's pledging some property, such as agricultural implements, to his landlord as security for future rent. Such an arrangement would defeat its purpose if the landlord actually took possession of the tenant's property, and the pledge therefore amounted in law to no more than an agreement, not in itself enforceable, that the landlord should be entitled to take possession if the rent were not paid. Such arrangements were given recognition by the Praetor, who gave the landlord an interdict (*interdictum Salvianum*) by which he could claim possession. This was available, however, only against the tenant. The important step, which created in effect a *ius in re aliena* and which ignored the line between contract and conveyance, was the granting, also by the Praetor, of an action *in rem*, the *actio Serviana*, by which the landlord could assert his claim against anyone. This action was later extended to all cases of pledge, whether possession had been given or not. The terminology in the Digest is confused, but according to some texts the term *pignus* is properly applied to that form in which possession is given, and the Greek word *hypotheca* to the simple 'charge' without possession. The terminology is convenient provided the conclusion is not drawn that there were two distinct institutions.

The character of *hypotheca* as a mere 'charge' gave it the advantage also that successive mortgages were now possible, the earlier taking priority over the later.[1] For example, X, who owned land worth £5,000, might give a *hypotheca* on it to A for a debt of £1,000, and subsequently might give other hypothecs for debts of the same amount to B, C, and D, in that order. So long as the value of the land did not fall below £4,000, all the creditors would be adequately secured even though X became insolvent. If the value fell to, say, £3,500, A, B, and C would still be able to realize the full amount owing to them, but D would recover only £500, and so forth. But the character of *hypotheca* as a mere 'charge' revealed also the danger, which besets any right *in rem* and which we have already met more than once,[2] that unless the right is created with sufficient publicity it provides a trap for the unwary. The purchaser of a thing

---

[1] The maxim of English law, 'qui prior est tempore potior est iure', expresses also the Roman principle.

[2] See above, pp. 103 f., 129, 142.

may be unable to discover that it is burdened with a hypothec created by some previous owner; and the creditor who takes a charge on it may not know that it has already been charged for as much as it is worth. Here, as in other similar cases, modern systems require registration. Roman law did not attempt such a system until A.D. 472, and then only in the form of a grant of priority to hypothecs created before a public authority. And even this limited step must have been deprived of much of its value by the proviso that a hypothec created before three witnesses should rank equally with those made publicly. Moreover, no system of registration could have protected the creditor against the increasing number of 'tacit' hypothecs (i.e. hypothecs created not by agreement but by operation of law). For example, the fisc had a tacit hypothec to secure the payment of any debt owing to it, and a *pupillus* likewise had a hypothec over the property of his tutor. No creditor could therefore be secure unless he knew almost every detail of his debtor's life. And even this would not protect him in the later law, when a number of the tacit hypothecs were 'privileged' by the grant of priority even over previously existing express hypothecs. The most important were those of the fisc for taxes and the wife for the return of her dowry.[1] And so, in the example given above, A might appear to be amply secured if the land had been realistically valued at £5,000 and if he had taken the precaution of ascertaining that X was unmarried and had no other debts at the time that the hypothec was created, but his security would become worthless if X subsequently married a woman with a dowry of £5,000 and, having squandered the dowry, died insolvent.

9. OWNERSHIP

We have so far been proceeding in truly Roman fashion and have left undefined our most fundamental concept—ownership. It can indeed be said that ownership is either so simple as to need no explanation or so elusive as to defy definition. At its simplest it is the difference between mine and thine, at its most sophisticated it is the ultimate right, the right behind all other rights. The elusive character of ownership can be appreciated if one attempts to give a precise meaning to the often-repeated

---

[1] See above, p. 89.

statement that Roman ownership is markedly, and to some of its critics excessively, 'absolute'.

The most obvious sense in which ownership may be 'absolute' is that of enjoyment. Though there is no Roman definition of ownership, there is no lack of Romanistic ones, and these are usually in terms of enjoyment. Thus, the commentators adapted the definition of usufruct by adding to the rights of use and enjoyment the right of abuse—*ius utendi fruendi abutendi*. The adaptation is a little forced, since 'abuse' has to include alienation, but it is also, in its emphasis on the plenitude of enjoyment conferred by ownership, misleading. In the first place, no enjoyment can ever be absolute in the sense that it is free from any restrictions whatever. At the very least the use, enjoyment, and abuse of his property by one owner must be reconciled with the equal use, enjoyment, and abuse by all other owners of their property. In a simple sense this is one of the functions of law. Moreover, in all but the crudest system of law there will be other restrictions which, in the general interest, are imposed on the enjoyment of the owner, and the extent of these restrictions will depend very largely on the political and economic ideas of the time. The enjoyment of the modern English owner is far less absolute than that of his Roman predecessor, but this difference in the content of ownership derives from a difference not in the technical legal character of ownership but in the extent to which the public law restricts the rights of the owner in the general interest. For this reason the French Civil Code, though it declares that ownership is 'the right to enjoy and dispose of things in the most absolute way', adds the proviso that such enjoyment must not contravene the general law.

But even when it is thus qualified, a definition in terms simply of enjoyment is misleading. For, as we have already seen, the existence of *iura in re aliena* will sometimes leave the owner with no present rights of enjoyment at all: the owner of a thing which is subject to a usufruct or of land which is subject to a right of *emphyteusis* or *superficies* has no more than an ultimate right to enjoyment. For this reason ownership has been defined as the ultimate residual right in a thing, the right which will remain when all others have expired.

A second sense in which ownership may be said to be absolute is that of title. The owner's right in this sense is not simply relative, not simply better than other competing rights, but the best, or rather the only, right of its kind. This is, superficially at least, true of Roman law. There is nothing intermediate between the right of ownership and the 'fact' of possession. If A has possession, but not ownership, of something which is taken from him by B, he can proceed against B in reliance on his possession; but if the thing is taken from B by C, A has no remedy against C, even though, morally speaking, he has a better right to it than C. For a plaintiff who cannot rely on possession must show ownership. In other words, Roman law has an action asserting ownership and an action asserting possession but no action asserting merely a right to possession. It is otherwise in the English law of movables,[1] which has an action asserting possession and an action asserting a right to possession, but no action asserting ownership as such. The owner only has an action in English law when he also has (as indeed he usually does have) an immediate right to possession. In the example given above, A will have an action against both B and C; but if A has been given possession of the thing by the owner for a term of, say, six months, the owner will have no action at all, because until the six months have elapsed he will have no immediate right to the possession of the thing. For our present purposes, however, the corollary of this is more important—that in Roman law a person asserting title to a thing must show that he is owner, whereas in English law he need only show that he has an immediate right to possession (and also perhaps be prepared to show that his right is better than any other of which his opponent can adduce evidence). Moreover he can show a right to possession merely by showing that he previously had possession and that he lost it without his consent. There is here, superficially at least, a striking contrast. The Roman plaintiff must show an absolute title, the English plaintiff simply a right to possession. But how could the Roman plaintiff prove his absolute title? This is the *probatio diabolica* of the commentators—only the devil would ask for proof of ownership, since what the plaintiff will in the ordinary case have to do is to show that he obtained it lawfully from X, that X obtained it lawfully from Y, and so on until he can trace his title to an original mode of acquisition. A moment's

---

[1] The doctrine of estates (above, p. 145) makes any instructive comparison with the English law of land impossible.

consideration of the things which one 'owns' oneself will show that such an undertaking will very rarely succeed. It is sometimes said that the escape from the plaintiff's dilemma lies in the very short periods of usucapion. But usucapion is no easier to prove than ownership itself. It is true that possession for the requisite period can readily be proved, and that good faith is presumed until the contrary is shown, but there remain the requirement of *iusta causa* and the requirement that the thing should not have been stolen or taken by force. *Iusta causa* will indeed sometimes be provable—particularly where land or a movable of considerable value is concerned—but only a man of unusually careful habits will be able to show how he came by all the things which he claims to own. And even if he can show, for example, that he bought the thing from X many years ago and that he has had possession of it uninterruptedly ever since, he still cannot prove the negative proposition that it has never been stolen or, in the case of land, taken by force.[1] The Romans themselves, with their habitual lack of interest in questions of evidence, never discuss this question, but one is driven to the conclusion that, in spite of the wording of the *vindicatio*, the Roman plaintiff can hardly have been required to do more than his English counterpart, viz. to show a right to possession deriving from possession itself, and to be prepared to show that it was better than any which the defendant could adduce in answer. Both the French and the German Civil Codes in fact formally establish a presumption that the possessor is owner. Indeed it is on reflection obvious that, original modes apart, ownership will only be positively provable if there is in operation either a system of registration of title, or a system of prescription which requires no more than possession and the lapse of time. As we have seen,[2] the former can in practice only apply to land or very special movables, and the latter comes near to equating ownership with possession and therefore makes possible the proof of ownership only by depriving it of its ordinary meaning.

Roman ownership was therefore not absolute in the sense that the plaintiff in a *vindicatio* was required to prove that he had the

---

[1] In the law of Justinian he will indeed be able to say after thirty years' possession that *longissimi temporis praescriptio* has purged any 'vice' of theft that may have existed. See above, p. 128.   [2] Above, p. 104.

best and the only right. The significance of the Roman idea of absolute title lay rather in the absence of any remedy to protect the *tertium quid* between ownership and possession—the right to possession which can make no claim to be ownership. A man is either owner or he is not owner. But even this characteristic of ownership, which we have referred to as its uniqueness or indivisibility, is, as we have seen, only verbally true. The Romans certainly adhered to the dogma of the uniqueness and indivisibility of *dominium*, but they were able to do so only by turning a blind eye to the claims of bonitary ownership and *bona fide* possession to be classed as forms of ownership. Both are clear exceptions to the principle of indivisibility. Each is a *tertium quid* between ownership and possession, the bonitary owner being owner in all but a few technical details, and the *bona fide* possessor being in effect a relative owner—an owner as regards everyone except the *dominus*. The Roman lawyers here never came to terms with their own creations.

We have seen also that usufruct might have constituted a threat to the indivisibility of ownership, but was prevented from doing so by the lawyers' insistence on its inalienability and also by their failure to grasp the advantages held out by the idea of quasi-usufruct. *Emphyteusis* and *superficies*, on the other hand, being freely alienable, did make a serious inroad on the indivisibility of ownership, but they were admitted to the private law too late for any theoretical account to be taken of this inroad. The lawyers of the late Empire were content to leave them simply as institutions *sui generis*.

The absoluteness of Roman ownership can, perhaps, be better seen in what we have called its inviolability—in the principle that a man cannot lose ownership without his consent, with its corollary that a man cannot pass a better title than he has. We have seen that the only exception to this principle of inviolability was prescription, and that even that was a very limited exception when contrasted with the practice of the modern civil law. In this feature the individualism of Roman law is most marked, but since it is a feature which to a considerable extent English law still shares, it is perhaps less noticed by the English student than by his colleague in the countries of the Civil law.

IV

LAW OF OBLIGATIONS

INTRODUCTION

We come now to the second division of the law of things, that which is concerned with obligations. 'Things', we have seen, are a man's economic assets, and, in the language of rights, these assets are either what he owns or what he is owed; they are either rights *in rem* or rights *in personam*. Rights *in rem* are the province of the law of property, rights *in personam* of the law of obligations.

As a thing, therefore, an obligation is a right, but the term 'right' denotes only one side of the relationship which is embraced by the Latin term *obligatio*. To every right *in personam* there must obviously be a correlative duty: if A has a right that B shall give him a book, B must be under a duty to give A the book. The term *obligatio* denotes sometimes the right, sometimes (like the English 'obligation') the duty, but more properly it denotes the whole relationship. Thus, etymologically it signifies a tying together—the bond which unites creditor and debtor. It is a bond by which one party is bound, and the other entitled, to some act or forbearance, third parties being, in principle at least, unaffected.

Gaius classifies obligations under two headings. They arise either from contract (*ex contractu*) or from delict (*ex delicto*). We may provisionally define a contract as an enforceable agreement, and a delict as a wrongful act which is not, or not exclusively, a breach of contract. Thus, if A agrees with B to buy B's book, an obligation arises *ex contractu*: B is under a duty to give A the book, and A is under a duty to pay B the agreed price, each duty having, as we have seen, its correlative right. And if C steals D's book, an obligation arises *ex delicto*: C is under a duty to pay D a penalty and D has a right to the payment of the penalty. Most obligations fell clearly into one or other of Gaius' two categories, but there remained a certain number which did not. To accommodate these Justinian's

Institutes added two further categories: they were said to arise either *quasi ex contractu* or *quasi ex delicto*, according as they had more affinity with one or other of the main categories. The justification for these categories will be considered later.

I. CONTRACTS

1. HISTORICAL DEVELOPMENT

The idea of debt. We have provisionally defined a contract as an enforceable agreement, and the later classical lawyers would probably not have demurred to this definition. But we shall misread the history of Roman law if we imagine that the idea of contract as an agreement was always present. It is an idea which emerged slowly, as it did also in English law. The early law probably had no more than an undifferentiated idea of debt—that one man owed another man a certain thing or sum. The debt might be owed because the one man had injured the other or had damaged or stolen his property, or because a formal act had been performed which created the debt, or, finally, because the one man had conveyed to the other a sum of money or a thing which the other was not entitled, or no longer entitled, to retain (e.g. a loan of money). The three debts were eventually differentiated—the first as arising *ex delicto*, the other two as arising *ex contractu* or *quasi ex contractu*—but for the primitive law in all three cases alike there was merely a debt. The presence or absence of agreement was not a significant factor.

Roman law was indeed precocious in that, as early as the Twelve Tables, it had a formal act which embodied the bare external essentials of agreement. This was the *stipulatio*, an exchange of a question and answer in formal words. In its earliest form the prospective creditor said 'Do you solemnly promise [to pay me 500, or, to convey to me your horse]?' and the prospective debtor replied 'I solemnly promise.' ('*Spondesne . . .? spondeo.*') But the validity of a *stipulatio*, like that of any formal act, came from its form and not from the agreement which the form no doubt embodied. For agreement was neither necessary nor sufficient. It was not necessary, and therefore the debtor could not plead that he was mistaken, that his mind did not go with the act; it was not sufficient, and therefore if the form had been defective (e.g. because the debtor said '*promitto*' instead of '*spondeo*'),[1] the creditor could not plead that there had nevertheless been an agreement in substance.

Similarly, if we take as an example of the third type of debt a loan of money which has not been repaid, the later classical lawyers saw here an agreement. The borrower had agreed to repay the money, and it was the breach of this agreement which was the basis of the lender's claim. But for the early law there was simply a debt: the basis of the lender's claim was that he had paid to the borrower a sum of money which he, the lender, now ought to have. The difference between the two approaches can be seen if one takes another example. If X pays a sum of money to Y in the mistaken belief that he owes it, he may reclaim the money from Y. For the later classical lawyer, as for the modern lawyer, this is not a contract, since there has been no agreement; the obligation arises, in Justinian's classification, *quasi ex contractu*. But in the eye of the early law there is no significant difference between this and a loan—in each case a debt arises from the payment of a sum of money which the recipient is not entitled to retain.

Promissory and 'real' debt. The origins of contract lie probably in these two types of debt, the one deriving from a formal act, the other from an informal payment or transfer. But their scope was limited. The latter was clearly confined to debts of a specific thing or sum, and it is likely that the *stipulatio* was similarly restricted to promises to convey specific things or money.[2] Nevertheless there is a vital difference between them. The debt by *stipulatio* is a promissory debt, whereas the other is a 'real' debt, i.e. it is limited to the return of something already received from the creditor. The satisfaction of a promissory debt changes the *status quo*, whereas the satisfaction of a 'real' debt serves only to restore it.

For the development of commerce the concept of the promissory debt is essential. That this is so can be seen from a glance

---

[1] Cf. below, p. 193.

[2] The other important formal acts were *nexum*, an act *per aes et libram* of which the details are obscure and which was early obsolete, and the literal contract (see below, p. 196). Both were confined to money debts.

at the fundamental commercial contract of sale. A merely cash sale, i.e. one in which the thing sold and the price are exchanged simultaneously, and in which, therefore, there is no promissory element, raises few problems in the early law. Until the exchange is made there is nothing for the law to recognize; after the exchange is made there is little or nothing for the law to enforce.[1] But for anything more than the most rudimentary commerce a cash sale is not enough; what is needed is a promissory or credit sale, i.e. one in which either the payment of the price or the transfer of the thing or both are to take place at a later date. The seller or the buyer or both must be able to bind the other to the performance of a promise.

For the essential promises of buyer and seller (to convey the thing and to pay the price) the *stipulatio*, even with its restricted scope, was sufficient, but other commercial transactions require more than promises to convey a thing or pay a sum of money. Such are the many transactions involving the performance of services as, for example, the building of a house or the carriage of goods. For these, as for undertakings incidental to a sale (e.g. that the thing sold is free from defects), something more flexible is necessary. The first step was apparently to adapt the content of the *stipulatio* without formally extending its scope: the promisor promised to pay a penalty if he failed to perform the service in question. What was in substance a promise of a service was formulated as a promise of a sum of money. This formulation remained in use long after the scope of the *stipulatio* had been extended to include promises of any kind, a development which had occurred by the first century B.C.[2]

The consensual contracts. Meanwhile, however, there had been a development of a different kind—the emergence of the principle

---

[1] The thing sold may be defective, but the buyer should have seen to that before he bought—*caveat emptor*. It may turn out that the seller did not own the thing, with the result that the true owner reclaims it from the buyer; here, in the case of *res mancipi*, the early law did give a remedy (*actio auctoritatis*) to the evicted buyer, but the claim was for a penalty of twofold the price, and the underlying idea is hardly one of contract or promise.

[2] The formulation had advantages. In an action on such a *stipulatio* the promisee was relieved of the possibly difficult task of showing what damage he had suffered, and by a procedural device (*sponsio et restipulatio tertiae partis*) he could obtain not merely the sum promised but a penalty of one-third in addition. Cf. below, p. 192, n. 2.

that in certain typical transactions (which we call the consensual contracts, e.g. sale and hire) the parties could be bound by a mere formless agreement. The acceptance of this principle was one of the most important factors in the adaptation of the law to the commercial needs of a vast empire. And here, as in the earlier development of the *stipulatio*, Roman law was precocious. English law did not finally recognize a purely executory agreement (i.e. one in which neither party has yet performed his side of the bargain) until the seventeenth century, and Greek law never did so. At how early a date the principle was accepted in Roman law it is impossible to say. The consensual contracts were certainly established in the first century B.C., but our knowledge of the course of legal history in the second century, which in this and in many other respects must have been the great formative period, is far too exiguous to permit of anything but conjecture.[1]

Unilateral and bilateral contracts. There was a further difference between the *stipulatio* and the 'real' debt on the one hand and the consensual contracts on the other. To use modern terms, the former were unilateral, the latter bilateral. A unilateral contract is one which creates only rights in one party and only duties in the other; a bilateral contract is one which gives rise to reciprocal obligations, each party having both rights and duties.[2] In a loan of money, for example, the lender has a right to the repayment of the loan, and the borrower a duty to repay it, but the borrower has no rights and the lender no duties. Similarly, in a *stipulatio* one party is promisor and the other promisee. Of course, the substance of a bilateral contract could be expressed in two stipulations, in one of which, for example, the buyer promised to pay the price, while in the other the seller promised to deliver the thing; but there would still in law be two unilateral contracts, with the result that the buyer, for example, could claim the thing even though he had not paid the price. The seller would have to claim the price in a separate action, with the risk that the buyer would prove to be insolvent.[3]

[1] See below, p. 165, n. 5.
[2] The English lawyer sometimes uses these terms in a different sense, a bilateral contract being one which is purely executory and a unilateral contract one which has been performed on one side but not on the other.
[3] Once the *exceptio doli* was admitted (see below, p. 164), the seller would in such

It was only in a bilateral contract that the duties of the parties were fully reciprocal.

Stricti iuris and bonae fidei actions. It is not only for the principle of the purely executory contract that the consensual contracts are important, but also for the concept of good faith (*bona fides*) upon which they rest. *Bona fides* colours every aspect of these contracts, but it is in form and in origin a matter of the formulation of the actions by which they were enforced.

Unilateral contracts were enforced by *stricti iuris* actions and bilateral by *bonae fidei* actions.[1] The distinction is one of both pleading and substance, but it derives simply from three additional words in the *formula* of a *bonae fidei* action.

We have seen that in the classical system of procedure pleading was strict:[2] no issue could be argued before the *iudex* unless it either appeared in the regular *formula* of the action or had been added to it by way of *exceptio, replicatio,* &c. This was equally true of both types of action, but whereas in a *stricti iuris* action the issue was simply whether the defendant was in law liable or not,[3] in the *formula* of a *bonae fidei* action three words were added; the *iudex* was directed to determine this question in the light of the requirements of good faith (*ex fide bona*).[4] This meant that in a *bonae fidei* action any plea involving good faith could be raised before the *iudex* without the need for an *exceptio,* &c. In the classical law this was simply a matter of pleading— of the moment at which each party's case must be defined— though obviously there must often have been a tactical advantage in the delay which the *bonae fidei* action allowed. But in the early years of the *bonae fidei* actions[5] it had been a fundamental

circumstances be able to bar the buyer's claim. But by this time the consensual contract was in existence.

[1] Some quasi-contractual actions (e.g. on *negotiorum gestio* and *tutela*) were also *bonae fidei.* The term *stricti iuris* is not classical.

[2] For what follows, see generally above, pp. 23 ff.

[3] See the *formula* of the *condictio,* p. 24 above.

[4] The *formula* given in the note on p. 24 above is that of a *bonae fidei* action (the *actio venditi*).

[5] They originated perhaps in the second century B.C. and perhaps in the Edict of the Peregrine Praetor. In the classical law they, and therefore the contracts which they enforced, were considered to belong to civil law and not to Praetorian law, but it is probable that in origin they were Praetorian creations, the contrast being between *stricti iuris* actions which enforced duties deriving from the law (i.e. the traditional civil law) and *bonae fidei* actions which enforced duties deriving not

matter of substance. For it was not until the middle of the first century B.C. that bad faith was allowed to be relevant in a *stricti iuris* action: it was only then that the defence of fraud or bad faith (*exceptio doli*)[1] was admitted to the Edict. Until then the defendant in an action on a stipulation, for example, could not plead that his promise had been induced by the plaintiff's fraud; he was strictly bound.

Once the *exceptio doli* was admitted, the difference of substance became less fundamental, but it remained important. In matters of interpretation, and in other ways, the idea of good faith entered far more fully into the *bonae fidei* contracts than into those which were *stricti iuris*. For example, it was possible, as we have seen, to make a contract of sale either by a consensual contract (*emptio venditio*) or by two separate stipulations. But the incidents of the contracts would be very different. If, for example, the seller knew, and the buyer did not, that the thing was defective, or if the seller knew that the thing was significantly different from what the buyer thought it to be, this was sufficient to give the buyer in a contract of *emptio venditio* a cause of action, even though the seller had done nothing to induce the buyer's mistake. But if the contract had taken the form of two stipulations, the buyer had no remedy. He had stipulated for that particular thing and the seller had delivered it; the seller had fulfilled the letter of his promise and the buyer had therefore no ground for complaint.

The idea of good faith does inevitably fit more easily with bilateral contracts than with unilateral. For in a bilateral contract the duties of one party are the counterpart of the duties of the other. In arriving at his decision the judge must strike a balance, and in doing so he can readily take account of matters of good faith. In a unilateral contract, on the other hand, the duty of the defendant has no counterpart in a duty of the plaintiff. The judge has no balance to strike.

The classification of Gaius and Justinian. In the Institutes of Gaius the outcome of the historical development which we have been considering is expressed in a fourfold classification of obligations

---

from the law at all but from the moral concept of good faith. Thereafter this concept acquired, with use, sharper outlines and came to be accepted as a part of the ordinary law.   [1] See above, p. 22, n.1.

ex contractu. They arise, he says, either *re* (by the transfer of a thing—the primitive 'real' obligation in a contractual framework), *verbis* (by the uttering of formal words, as in the *stipulatio*), *literis* (by the use of a documentary form), or *consensu* (the consensual contracts of which we have already spoken). Save for an enlargement of the category of obligations arising *re*,[1] Justinian in his Institutes follows Gaius, and it is accordingly customary to speak of real, verbal, literal, and consensual contracts. And it is in this order that Gaius and Justinian treat of them. The order has little, however, to recommend it,[2] and since the verbal and the literal are formal contracts and the real and consensual are informal, it is more convenient to rearrange them accordingly. But first we must consider the principal characteristic of the Roman system—that it is a law of contracts and not a unitary law of contract.

Law of contracts, not law of contract. The definition of a contract as an enforceable agreement is misleading, not only for the period of development but also, in a different way, for the mature law. It suggests a greater unity than in fact there was. Modern systems have a single concept of contract; Roman law had a list of contracts. In modern law it can, very loosely, be said that any seriously intended agreement is a contract, no matter what its content. In Roman law an informal agreement was not a contract unless it satisfied the requirements of one or other of the listed contracts. For example, the consensual contract of sale (*emptio venditio*) required that the parties be agreed on a specific thing to be bought and sold and on a fixed price. An agreement which did not satisfy one or both of these requirements (e.g. an agreement to 'sell' for a reasonable price) was not a contract of sale.

The practical consequences of this lack of generalization were three. In the first place, the lawyers were able to work out in detail the 'incidents' of each type of contract. The parties to a contract will rarely have the foresight to lay down in advance what their rights and duties shall be in all possible eventualities, and the law must supply what they have left unsaid. The Roman system, by isolating under a small number of headings

[1] See below, pp. 167 ff.
[2] It probably derives from the not very rational order of the Edict.

the characteristic transactions of life, was able to assign to each of them those legal consequences which seemed, commercially and otherwise, most appropriate. Once it had been determined that a given transaction fell under a particular heading, the established rules of that type of contract could be applied. And equally, the parties, in entering into the agreement, could know what consequences would follow where they were silent. Even modern law, in spite of its generalization in theory, resorts in practice to the regulation of typical contracts.

The second consequence is a technical one of the law of actions, but for that reason it was one which mattered much to the classical lawyer. We have seen that the classical law was a law of actions—that the question a lawyer asked was not whether a man had a right but whether he had a remedy. And we have also seen that for each cause of action there was in principle a form of action. Each type of contract, therefore, had the appropriate form or forms of action, and the choice of the wrong form would lose a man his case. It was not sufficient for a plaintiff to prove to the *iudex* that he had entered into a contract. He must prove that he had entered into the type of contract specified in the *formula* of his action. It would avail him nothing, for example, to show a contract of hire if his action were one of sale, even though, on the point in issue, the incidents of the two contracts might be the same.

The third consequence is the most obvious—the possibility of gaps in the law. An agreement, though seriously intended, might fall within none of the recognized headings and therefore have no legal effect. An example of this is the one already given of an agreement to sell for a reasonable price. This shortcoming was, however, mitigated by the existence among the recognized headings of the *stipulatio*, which embodies a different principle.

Methods of contracting and types of contract. The *stipulatio* was, as we have seen, a formal contract. It was not this, however, that gave it its importance (the other formal contracts are of little consequence), but the fact that it was a method of contracting rather than a type of contract. Any agreement could be made legally effective by being cast in the form of a stipulation. The agreement to sell for a reasonable price, for example, would become a contract if this simple step were taken. Equally, as we have seen, an agreement which did satisfy the requirements of one of the informal contracts, such as an agreement to sell for a fixed price, could be cast in the stipulatory form. The stipulation, in short, supplied the element of generality which otherwise was lacking in the Roman system of specific contracts.[1] It could thus claim, as we shall see, the central position in that system.

2. THE INFORMAL CONTRACTS

(a) The Real Contracts

The individual contracts. In Justinian's classification there are four real contracts: *mutuum, commodatum, depositum, pignus.* Their common characteristic is merely that an obligation arises not from an agreement alone, though agreement is essential, but from the delivery of a *res corporalis.*[2]

Mutuum, the pattern of the primitive 'real' debt,[3] was a loan for consumption, not simply for use, i.e. a loan of things, such as money, food, and drink, which can ordinarily be used only by being consumed.[4] It accordingly involved a transfer of ownership, and obliged the borrower to return not the thing itself but its equivalent in quantity and quality. It was, as we have seen, a unilateral contract, and was actionable by the *condictio,* a *stricti iuris* action. The obligation being simply to return, no claim for interest could arise from the *mutuum* itself.

---

[1] The innominate contracts eventually supplied an element of generality in a different way. See below, pp. 189 ff.

[2] We have seen, however (above, pp. 118 ff.), that the distinction between delivery and mere agreement is not easy to maintain.

[3] See above, pp. 159 f.

[4] It is often described as a loan of fungibles, i.e. of things belonging to a class all the members of which are identical, or sufficiently similar to be freely interchangeable, but this can be misleading. Obviously every *mutuum* must be a loan of a fungible, since the nature of the borrower's obligation presupposes the existence of an equivalent in quality, but not every loan of a fungible is a *mutuum.* For many fungibles (e.g. a piece of crockery which is made in large numbers) are ordinarily used without being consumed. Modern mass-production has greatly enlarged this category of fungible, but it existed also in the ancient world. The test can only be whether the parties intended that the borrower should return the thing itself or only its equivalent; if the latter, the contract is *mutuum,* if the former, *commodatum.* Again, 'consumption' must be understood in a wide sense. A brick or a nail can ordinarily only be used in such a way that although it is not literally consumed, it cannot be returned.

Any agreement for interest had to be clothed as a separate *stipulatio*.

Commodatum was a loan for use only. *Depositum* was the handing over of a thing for safe-keeping and not for use. The two contracts were otherwise closely similar. The borrower or depositee received neither ownership nor possession but simply detention.[1] And both contracts were gratuitous. If the borrower was to pay for the loan or the depositor for the deposit, the transaction was either hire or what was eventually called an innominate contract.

Pignus was, as we have seen,[2] the giving of real security by the transfer of possession.

Obligations re in Gaius. For Gaius the category of obligations contracted *re* is much narrower. It includes, in fact, only *mutuum*. *Commodatum, depositum,* and *pignus* are not mentioned, though they certainly existed at the time. The reason for this narrow classification is probably to be found in Gaius' further statement that there is also an obligation arising *re* where something has been paid over in the mistaken belief that it is owing; though, he adds, the obligation does not arise *ex contractu*, since the person making the payment intended rather to terminate than to create a legal relationship. Here we have two typical instances of the early 'real' debt, but differentiated now in terms of the intention of the parties or, as we should put it, in terms of the presence or absence of agreement. Gaius does not, in the Institutes, complete the process of differentiation, since he has no category to accommodate the non-contractual obligation *re* (of which the payment of what is not owing is only the typical example), but Justinian makes good the omission by classifying them as quasi-contractual.

The classification which we find in Gaius is therefore a transitional one. The emergence of agreement as the common factor of contractual obligations causes him to distinguish the contractual from the non-contractual obligation *re*, but he still sees the foundation of both in the old idea of the 'real' debt; and the old unity is for him still preserved in the single action which sanctions such debts, the *condictio*.[3] *Commodatum, depositum,* and

---

[1] See above, p. 112.   [2] Above, pp. 151 f.
[3] See further below, pp. 229 ff.

pignus, on the other hand, have no connexion with the old idea. They involve no transfer of ownership; they are bilateral[1] and *bonae fidei*; and they are in origin Praetorian. It is easy therefore to see why they were excluded from the category of obligations *re* as Gaius understood it. It is less easy to justify his failure to mention them at all in his treatment of contracts.

Relative unimportance of the real contracts. These contracts are less important than their prominence in the Institutional classification suggests. *Commodatum* and *depositum*, being gratuitous, could be of no commercial significance, and a loan or deposit between friends will only rarely give rise to litigation. The existence or not of such a contract would, however, be indirectly relevant if a third person took possession of the thing. For it would determine which party could sue and for what.[2] *Pignus*, on the other hand, is obviously a business transaction, but its importance lay less in its contractual aspect than in its effect on third parties.[3] Again, a loan of any substantial sum of money will usually be a business transaction, but, if it is, the lender will expect to receive interest; and since for the exaction of interest on a *mutuum* a *stipulatio* was necessary, it would obviously be convenient to embody both the undertaking to repay the capital and the undertaking to repay the interest in the same *stipulatio*, and thereby to enable both to be claimed in the same action.

Standards of care. In *mutuum* the borrower was bound to return the equivalent of what he received, no matter what became of the thing itself. He was the owner, and the risk of loss or damage was on him. In the other three contracts, however, it was necessary to determine what amount of care the recipient must show in looking after the things or, in other words, what degree of

---

[1] More precisely, they are imperfectly bilateral (or semi-bilateral), i.e. the duties of one party are only contingent. For example, in a contract of *depositum* the depositee's duties are to take care of the thing and to return it on demand; the depositor's duties are to make good to the depositee such expenses as he may incur in keeping the thing and to compensate him for any harm which the thing may cause and which the depositor could by taking care have prevented. The depositee's duties exist in any such contract, whereas the existence of the depositor's is contingent on the depositee's incurring expenses or suffering harm.

[2] See above, pp. 110 ff., and below, pp. 214 ff.

[3] It is for this reason that it, and the closely related *fiducia* and *hypotheca*, have been treated in the law of property (above, pp. 149 ff.).

fault would make him liable for its loss or damage. Similar questions will of course arise in nearly every contract, and the scheme of degrees and standards of care which eventually emerged was not confined to the real contracts, but it is convenient to consider it here.

It is probable that the classical lawyers distinguished three degrees of liability: for *dolus* (fraud or bad faith), for *culpa* (fault or negligence), and for failure to exercise *custodia*. *Dolus* and *culpa* are abstract and generalized. They represent a failure to conform to the objective (though not of course precisely definable) standards of, respectively, good faith and the care shown by the reasonable man (*bonus paterfamilias*). *Custodia*, on the other hand, which was probably the oldest of the three, is defined in a much more concrete and casuistic way. A man was liable for loss caused in certain typical ways (e.g. ordinary theft) whether or not he had taken reasonable care to prevent it, but he was not liable for loss caused in certain other typical ways (e.g. theft with violence). It can, however, be approximately defined as a strict liability (i.e. liability irrespective of fault) for all loss not caused by *vis maior* (which included both superior force and what we call acts of God).

It is not certain to which contracts the requirement of *custodia* originally applied, since in the law of Justinian it had been confined to a few special cases and replaced by liability for *culpa*. At the same time, within the concept of *culpa*, a distinction had been made between *culpa levis* and *culpa lata*, and, within *culpa levis*, a further distinction between what modern commentators have called *culpa levis in abstracto* and *culpa levis in concreto*.

Culpa lata (gross fault or negligence) is hardly to be distinguished from *dolus*. It is, says a text, 'not to understand what everyone understands'; it is carelessness so gross as to suggest bad faith.

Culpa levis in abstracto (judged by an abstract or objective standard) is the original, undifferentiated *culpa*—a failure to show the *diligentia* of a *bonus paterfamilias*. *Culpa levis in concreto* (judged by a concrete or subjective standard) is a failure to show *diligentia quam suis rebus* (sc. *adhibere solet*)—the care which the particular individual habitually shows in his own affairs. The difference is therefore not, as is the difference between *culpa levis* and *culpa lata*, one of degree: the individual may be habitually either more or less careful than the *bonus paterfamilias*. But such is the wisdom after the event which is attributed to the 'reasonable man', that *diligentia quam suis rebus* is in fact sometimes treated as applying a lower, rather than simply a different, standard than that of the *bonus paterfamilias*.

Whatever the standard applied, *mora* (delay) would displace it. If a party through his own fault failed to fulfil his duty at the proper time, he was strictly liable for any loss or damage which occurred thereafter, even if occasioned by *vis maior*.

The texts are often in conflict as to the standard required in particular types of contract, and it is difficult to detect any consistent principle. There are suggestions that the incidence of *culpa levis* or *culpa lata* depended on whether the party in question took a benefit under the contract or not. Thus most texts make the depositee liable only for *culpa lata*, whereas the borrower in *commodatum* and the pledgee in *pignus* were liable for *culpa levis* (*in abstracto*), and perhaps originally for *custodia*. There are exceptions, but the principle is useful as a rough guide. Again, we are told that the reason why the contract of *societas* (partnership) required *diligentia quam suis rebus* was that a man has only himself to blame if he chooses a careless partner (the argument being presumably that *societas* is a peculiarly personal relationship). But this is an elusive principle: it could apply equally to *commodatum*.

(b) *The Consensual Contracts*

The consensual contracts were four: *emptio venditio* (sale), *locatio conductio* (hire), *societas* (partnership), *mandatum* (mandate). Their common characteristic was that they arose by mere agreement (*nudo consensu*), i.e. without the need for any form or for any physical act, such as the delivery which was necessary for the real contracts. It was in the consensual contracts that the idea of *bona fides* had its most fruitful application, and in them, and more particularly in sale and hire, that most of the important transactions of commercial life could be expressed.

(1) *Sale* (*emptio venditio*)

Sale claims a more detailed treatment than the other contracts, not only because it is the fundamental commercial contract, but also because the Roman law of sale has had great influence on modern Civil law, and even on the Common law.

Formation of the contract. As we have seen, the essential elements of the contract were that the parties should be agreed on a thing and a price.

(i) *The thing.* The typical object of a sale was a *res corporalis*, movable or immovable, but it might also be an incorporeal thing, such as a praedial servitude, or even a right of action against a third party. In short, there could be a sale of any right which the seller was capable of transferring to the buyer. But if what was being transferred was not a right but simply the benefit of the 'seller's' services or of the use of a thing, the contract was not sale but hire (*locatio conductio*). For while the incidents appropriate to a sale of a corporeal thing could be extended without much difficulty or incongruity to incorporeal things, the same could not be said of bargains for services or for the use of a thing. But the drawing of a line between the two types of transaction did inevitably involve some fine distinctions. If I engage a goldsmith to make me a ring, is this a sale of the ring or a hire of his services? Opinions differed, but the answer was eventually held to depend on which of us supplied the material—if it were I, then the contract was hire, if the goldsmith, then it was sale. The underlying principle is that the typical sale is an agreement to transfer the ownership of a thing, and it is only when the maker supplies the material that there can be such a transfer. It must be for a similar reason that it was further held that if I agree with a builder that he will build a house on my land, the contract is hire even though the builder supplies the materials. In such a case there is indeed a transfer of ownership, but it occurs, quite independently of any agreement, by the operation of the principle of *accessio*.

The thing must exist at the time of the agreement. If it did not, either because it had never existed or because it had by then been destroyed, there was no sale. This was an application of the much wider principle, expressed in the maxim *impossibilium nulla obligatio*, that there could be no contract to do the impossible.

The most restrictive requirement was that the thing must be identified, in the sense that it must be either specific ('my

slave, Stichus', 'that cask of wine'), or what is nowadays sometimes called semi-specific, i.e. part of a specified mass ('ten
gallons of the wine in that cask') or one of a number of specific
things ('one of my slaves'). There could be no sale of 'generic
goods', i.e. of things defined only by reference to their *genus*
('a cask of wine', or 'a slave'). Such a transaction could, of
course, be made effective by means of two stipulations, but it
could not, it seems, constitute *emptio venditio*. This rule looks like
a survival from the primitive cash sale, but it is surprising that
so thriving a commercial society as imperial Rome should have
retained it. The explanation lies perhaps in the ease with which
a stipulation could be made.

Even within these limits, however, a sale of some 'future
things' was possible, e.g. next year's crop from a specified field.
But such a transaction presents a problem. If the crop fails, the
principle that there can be no sale of a non-existent thing should
make the contract void, and the seller should not be able to
claim the price. This will be a proper result if the contract was
intended to be conditional on the crop's coming into existence,
i.e. if the parties intended that the seller should take the risk of
there being no crop. But they may well have intended that it
should be the buyer who took this risk, the price being fixed
accordingly. For the interests of the merchant, who buys, and
the farmer (particularly the peasant farmer), who sells, are
different. The farmer seeks protection from the vagaries of the
weather and the market, whereas the merchant makes his
fortune by risking his capital. The farmer may be willing to
accept a low price in return for a secure income, and the merchant may be willing to risk a big loss in return for the chance
of a big profit. The difficulty was met by making a distinction
between *emptio rei speratae* (the sale of an expected thing) and
emptio spei (the sale of an expectation). If the parties must have intended that the seller should take the risk of total loss, there was
an *emptio rei speratae*, and the ordinary principle applied: if there
was no thing there was no contract. But if the intention must
have been that the buyer should take the risk, there was an
emptio spei. The transaction was construed as the sale not of a
res but of a *spes*—not of a physical thing but of an expectation.
The difference between the two will commonly be reflected in
the way the price is formulated. In an *emptio rei speratae* the

price will be proportionate to the actual yield (e.g. so much a bushel), whereas in an *emptio spei* the price will be fixed at so much per acre or so much for the whole crop, the same price being payable whatever the yield.

(ii) *The price.* There must be a money price. This requirement meant that *permutatio* (exchange or barter) was not sale. The Sabinians had held otherwise, but the Proculians prevailed. Their argument was that if the price were not in money it would be impossible to distinguish buyer from seller, the implication being that since their duties, and the actions by which they were enforced, were different, the law would then be unworkable. It seems at first sight surprising that so old a transaction as barter should have been excluded from the Roman list of typical contracts, but it must be remembered that if part of the price were in money the Proculian objection would be met and the contract would be one of sale. And an exchange in which there is no balance payable in money is not likely to be either common or commercially important.[1]

The price must be fixed (*certum*). There could be no sale for what English law calls a 'reasonable price', i.e. a price to be fixed by the parties in their subsequent dealings or, in default of this, by the court. Moreover, the price was sufficiently fixed only if it were either known or immediately ascertainable at the time of the agreement (e.g. 'today's market price'). To this rule there was one exception, disputed in the classical law but admitted by Justinian, that the price was sufficiently *certum* if it were left to be fixed by a named third party. But if, in the event, the third party did not fix it, the contract was void.

The requirement that the price be fixed is more easily defended than the requirement that the thing be specifically identified. Many of the incidents of a contract must, as we have seen, be supplied by the law, but in its essentials it should be the work of the parties. The law should not make their bargain for them. And one of the essentials of a sale is clearly the price.

For the same reason, the parties were free to fix their own price, subject only to the rule that it must be seriously intended and must not merely mask a gift. Inadequacy of price was

---

[1] *Permutatio* fell under the eventual heading of innominate contracts. See below, pp. 189 ff.

therefore ordinarily irrelevant, but might invalidate the transaction if the parties were husband and wife.[1]

In the late law, however, there appeared the doctrine of what is called *laesio enormis* (literally 'abnormal injury'), the intended scope of which is uncertain, since it appears only in two constitutions concerned with individual cases. Both are sales of land and in both the seller is allowed to rescind the sale on the ground that the price agreed was less than half the real value of the land. Later civilians have usually confined the doctrine within these limits, refusing to extend it to sales of movables or to cases in which it is the buyer who complains that he has paid too much. In this form, though with modifications in detail, it survives in some modern Civil law systems, especially those derived from the French. Even so, its application presents considerable difficulties, and we may think that the classical law (like the Common law) chose the better course in refusing to consider the adequacy of the price unless bad faith or incapacity was shown. In the sphere of contracts, more than in other parts of the law, it is less important that the law should in every case be just than that it should be certain. The law of contract provides the framework for commercial life, and in commercial life the taking of risks is inevitable. It is probably better that some sellers should be saddled with unfair, though not fraudulent, contracts than that a man who has taken a risk and lost should be able to escape from his bargain.

(iii) *Consent*. This element was found. in the eventual analysis, in all contracts, but the Roman law, unlike the modern Civil law, did not isolate and generalize such concepts. It preferred to deal with them casuistically in connexion with individual contracts. It is thus that some problems of defective consent are discussed particularly in connexion with sale.

Consent involves the meeting of two minds, the concurrence of two intents. The first need is therefore to determine what these intents are. In doing this one meets the possibility of a divergence between a man's real intent and the manifestation of that intent—between what modern lawyers sometimes call subjective and objective intent. For example, there may be an apparent agreement to buy and sell a horse but the buyer may have had in mind horse A and the seller horse B, neither party

[1] Since gifts between husband and wife were void. See above, p. 90.

being aware of the disagreement. There is here, subjectively, no consent. But it may be that the natural interpretation of what passed between the parties, the interpretation of the reasonable bystander, is that they were agreed on horse A. Objectively there is consent. Modern systems differ. The older view, resting on the philosophical doctrine of the autonomy of the will (i.e. that the binding force of a contract derives from the human will, which is its own law) requires subjective consent. The more recent view asserts that the validity of a contract comes not from the individual will but from the law, and that the law is concerned with a balancing of interests. It emphasizes the difficulties of proof and the importance of stability and certainty in commercial transactions: each party should be able to assume that the other will be held to the objective interpretation of the transaction.

The Roman lawyers, with their habitual disregard of questions of evidence, give little attention to matters such as this, but seem tacitly to assume a subjective interpretation, qualified only by such principles as that a man may not profit from an ignorance which comes from his own gross carelessness.

Granted that the intents of the parties are known, the second need is to determine to what extent those intents must concur, or, in other words, what defects of consent will vitiate a contract. Such defects are of two kinds. Either there is no consent, as to the whole or some part of the transaction, or even though there is consent, it has been obtained in such a way that the law will not enforce it. Defects of the first kind arise from *error* (mistake), those of the second from *dolus* (fraud or bad faith) or *metus* (duress).

In a *bonae fidei* contract such as sale, both *dolus* and *metus* came within the wide heading of bad faith so as to enable the *iudex* to hold that *ex fide bona* the innocent party should not be held to his contract. And it was bad faith not only if one party actively deceived the other on some material point, but even if he did no more than passively to acquiesce in the other's self-deception.

Error gives rise to greater difficulties. It may be classified either with reference to the states of mind of the parties or with reference to the content of their mistake.[1] The states of

---

[1] Such classifications, although the materials for them, and to some extent the

mind of the parties may be defective in two principal ways. Either both parties make the same mistake (e.g. both believe that the cup they are dealing with is gold when in fact it is brass) or, more commonly, one party has one intent and the other another (e.g. the case of the horses, above). Within this latter category there is indeed a further distinction: either the mistake of one party is known to the other, or else neither is aware of the divergence of intent. But to acquiesce in another's mistake is, as has just been said, bad faith, and can be more simply and readily dealt with as such.

Obviously not every mistake can be allowed to prevent the formation of a contract. To use the modern term, not every mistake can be allowed to be 'operative'. To produce this drastic result the mistake must be as to some fundamental matter. But what meaning are we to give to 'fundamental'? This is the problem of the content of mistake. The traditional Civil law treatment, which has had a considerable influence on the Common law also, simply classifies the types of operative mistake which are to be found in the Roman texts.

Error in negotio occurs when one party thinks he is entering into one type of transaction and the other thinks he is entering into another (e.g. sale as opposed to hire). There can then be no contract. *Error in pretio* (where the parties intend different prices) and *error in quantitate* (where they intend different quantities) are, however, only partially operative. Neither party can enforce the contract at his own figure, but each can, if he wishes, enforce it at the other's. Thus, if the seller intended a price of 10 and the buyer a price of 5, the seller can enforce the contract if he is prepared to accept 5, and the buyer if he is prepared to pay 10. *Error in persona* occurs where one party is mistaken as to the identity of the other. Surprisingly, however, it is hardly mentioned in the texts. *Error in corpore* is mistake as to the identity of the thing sold, hired, &c. (e.g. the case of the horses, above). It must be distinguished from *error in nomine* where the parties are in fact agreed on the particular object, but give it different names or descriptions.

In all these cases the mistake must obviously be of the second category mentioned above: it must result from divergent intent.

terminology, can be found in the Roman sources, inevitably distort the casuistic approach of the Roman jurist.

In *error in substantia*, however, it may fall into either category. This, the most controversial and elusive type of mistake, occurs when the parties are agreed as to the physical identity of the thing sold (i.e. there is no *error in corpore*) but are mistaken as to some essential characteristic. The jurists seem sometimes to be thinking in terms of the philosophical distinction between substance and accident, but the illustrations offered of operative mistake (where bronze is mistaken for gold, but not where gold-alloy is mistaken for gold; vinegar for wine, but not sour wine for good wine; a silver-plated table for a solid one, but not—according to another text—a gilt dish for a gold one) make it difficult to spell out a coherent principle in terms of the philosophical doctrine. Again, the term *substantia* is sometimes replaced by *materia*, but a simply material test cannot account for the opinion that the purchase of a female slave in mistake for a male is void. The texts seem to have been altered, and the original doctrine or doctrines are probably irrecoverable. Its modern descendant, however, is of considerable importance, especially in French law. 'Substance' has there thrown off any material connotation and is that essential quality of the thing which determined the buyer to buy. The purchase of an imitation for a genuine Rembrandt, of a modern reproduction for an antique table, or of an old horse for a young one, will therefore all be void. Since the mistake may be, and usually will be, that of the buyer alone, there is an obvious danger that the doctrine may be used, as it were as an after-thought, in an attempt simply to escape from a bad bargain. It must therefore be shown that the seller knew at the time of the contract that the quality in question was in the buyer's eyes essential. English law is even more restrictive. If it admits the doctrine at all—and this is very doubtful—it requires that the mistake be the mistake of both parties.[1]

Effects of the contract. (i) *The passing of title.* This was, strictly, an effect not of the contract but of the consequent conveyance. For we have seen[2] that Roman law insisted on the distinction

---

[1] French law, unlike Roman law, does not treat passive acquiescence in the buyer's self-deception as fraud. But, provided the requirement of 'substance' is met, such passive acquiescence is sufficient to constitute an operative mistake. In English law, however, the seller must, it seems, not simply acquiesce in the buyer's mistake; he must share it.   [2] Above, pp. 103 ff.

between contract and conveyance, with the result that owner-ship did not pass to the buyer when the contract was made, but only when the thing was actually conveyed. Moreover, at least in the law of Justinian, it was necessary not only that the thing be delivered, but also that the price be paid or security given for its payment. The effect of this rule should have been to protect the seller against the buyer's insolvency, since until the price was paid he could assert title to the thing, no matter into whose hands it had come, but we are also told that even the giving of credit was sufficient, and this seems to deprive the rule of all effect. For it is only when the seller has given credit (i.e. has delivered the thing without requiring payment of the price) that he needs the protection provided by the rule.

(ii) *The passing of risk.* Outside the contract of sale the rule is that the owner takes the risk of accidental loss or damage (*res perit domino*). For example, we have seen that the borrower in a contract of *commodatum* was, at least in the law of Justinian, liable for loss or damage only if it were caused by his negli-gence. Otherwise the risk was on the lender. In sale, however, the rule was different. The risk (*periculum*) passed to the buyer as soon as the contract was complete even though he did not be-come owner until the thing was conveyed. In other words, pro-vided the seller looked after the thing with due care in the period between contract and conveyance, he could claim the price from the buyer no matter what happened to the thing. And conversely the buyer had no claim against the seller if, without his fault, the thing was destroyed or damaged before convey-ance.

The need to define the moment at which the contract was complete so as to pass the risk gave rise to a number of detailed rules, but the broad principle was that nothing should remain to be done except the delivery of the thing and the payment of the price. For example, a sale of twenty bottles from a larger stock was not complete until the particular twenty were identi-fied; and a sale of 'all my wine' at so much a bottle was not complete until the bottles had been counted and the price thereby determined.

The separation of title and risk is often cited as an illogicality and a defect in the Roman law, and most modern systems have in consequence rejected it. But the Roman rule corresponds to the underlying economic facts. Until the contract is complete the seller retains an economic interest: in the example given above of a sale of twenty bottles from a larger stock, until the particular twenty are identified the seller has a power of choice which may be economically valuable. And similarly, once the contract has been completed, the seller, though he still has a legal interest in the thing, has no further economic interest in it. If there is a rise in the market price it is the buyer and not the seller who is entitled to take advantage of it by selling the thing.[1] And conversely, of course, the buyer takes the risk of a fall in the market price. It is for the same reason that he takes the risk of loss or deterioration.[2]

With the risk, on the same principle, go any accruing fruits or other benefits (*commodum*). For example, if between the sale and conveyance of a mare she foals, the buyer has a right to the foal. This right is, of course, *in personam*: the seller still owns the mare and therefore owns the foal, but he is under a duty to convey both to the buyer.

Duties of the seller. (i) *Care and delivery.* The seller, we have seen, was bound to deliver the thing and until delivery to take care of it. He may originally have been liable for *custodia*, but at least in Justinian's law he was required to show only the care of a *bonus paterfamilias*.

(ii) *Warranty against eviction.* The typical sale is an agreement for the transfer of the ownership of a thing, but the fact that the seller is not owner does not in itself vitiate the sale. He is required only to abstain (in this as in all aspects of sale) from bad faith, and to maintain the buyer in undisturbed possession until, if ever, he becomes owner by *usucapio*. If therefore the

---

[1] He can sell it even though he is not the owner. See immediately below. It is important here to keep questions of rights *in personam* arising from the contract distinct from questions of rights *in rem* arising from the conveyance. The seller is not entitled to resell, in the sense that if he does so he commits a breach of his contract with the first buyer and is liable in damages to him; but if nevertheless he does sell and deliver the thing, he will pass title to the second buyer. To adopt the terminology of current legal theory, he has no right to sell, but he has a power by selling to pass title. Conversely, the first buyer has a right to sell, but no power to pass title. Having, as yet, no title, he can pass none.

[2] It might therefore seem simpler to allow the title to pass with the risk on the completion of the contract, but, whatever the intrinsic merits of the separation of contract and conveyance, this creates other difficulties. See above, pp. 102 ff.

seller knows that he is not owner and the buyer does not, the buyer has a remedy, but on the ground of the seller's bad faith, not of his lack of title. Whereas if the seller is in good faith the buyer has no remedy unless and until he is evicted by the owner. In most cases, of course, this will be a distinction without a difference, since the buyer will usually become aware of the seller's lack of title only when the owner asserts his title, but exceptionally the rule can cause hardship. For example, if it is certain that the seller was not the owner but uncertain who is, or if the owner cannot be found, the buyer can neither claim against the seller nor, since he is aware of his lack of title, resell. The origin of the rule is much debated, but its survival into the classical law is surprising. It has disappeared from modern Civil law.

(iii) *Warranty against latent defects.* The original principle of the civil law was *caveat emptor.*[1] The seller was not liable for any defects in the thing unless he had by *stipulatio* expressly undertaken such liability. The development of the idea of good faith imposed a considerable qualification on the rule by making him liable for any defects of which he knew but which he had not revealed. Moreover, since the requirement of good faith was inherent in the contract itself, the seller could not contract out of this liability. Such a high standard of honest dealing is not imposed on the English seller.

The further development of the seller's liability came from the Aedilician Edict. In exercise of their jurisdiction over the market the Aediles issued edicts regulating market sales of slaves and beasts of burden. Sellers were required to display on a board a statement of any physical defects and, in the case of a slave, certain other defects also (if he was a vagabond or a runaway or burdened with noxal liability[2]). If a defect appeared which had not been so declared the buyer, if he sued within six months, could claim rescission of the sale by the *actio redhibitoria*, and, if within twelve months, could claim the difference between the price paid and the actual value of the defective slave or animal by the *actio quanti minoris*. In both actions the knowledge or ignorance of the seller was irrelevant: liability was strict. The seller could, however, exclude all such liability

[1] The maxim is not, however, Roman.
[2] See below, p. 223.

if he made clear his intention to do so, though he would still be liable for bad faith.

By a process which remains obscure, this Aedilician liability was extended to sales outside the market, and eventually, but only by Justinian, to sales of every kind of thing, including land. This all-embracing strict liability, with its two actions, survives in the *Corpus Iuris* alongside the older liability under the civil law for what had been expressly warranted and for bad faith. The forms of action were no longer significant, but it was presumably intended that where more than one remedy was available, the buyer should choose whichever was most advantageous to him.

Duties of the buyer. The buyer's principal duties were to pay the price (a duty which was concurrent with the seller's duty to deliver, in the sense that if one party sought to enforce the other's duty he must either have performed or be ready to perform his own), and to compensate the seller for any expenses he incurred in looking after the thing between contract and delivery.

(2) *Hire (locatio conductio)*

Scope and character. Into the framework of this single contract the Roman law fitted a wide range of transactions. There may at first sight seem to be little in common between a lease of land and a contract of employment, but in the Roman analysis both were *locatio conductio*. Within the single Roman category later civilians distinguished three types: *l.c. rei, l.c. operarum, l.c. operis.* In *l.c. rei* one party (*locator*) places a thing, whether movable or immovable, at the disposal of another (*conductor*) for his use or enjoyment; in *l.c. operarum* the *locator* places his services (*operae*) at the disposal of the *conductor*; and in *l.c. operis* the *locator* places out a piece of work (*opus*) to be done by the *conductor*, the work having always, it seems, a physical object—a slave to be taught, a house to be repaired, and so forth—so that the texts speak of the thing being placed out to be worked upon.

The key to an otherwise confusing terminology lies in the idea of *locatio* as a placing out. It is for this reason that, although both *l.c. operarum* and *l.c. operis* are contracts for the performance of work, in the former the work is done by the *locator* and in the latter by the *conductor*. In the former the *locator* places out his services, in the latter he places out the job to be done.[1] In a somewhat similar way we sometimes speak in English of placing or letting out the contract for, for example, the construction of a building. The difference of substance between the two contracts can be defined as a difference of control and responsibility. Whether a contract for the repair of a house is *l.c. operarum* or *l.c. operis* will depend on the degree of control which the house-owner is to exercise over the carrying out of the work. If he merely specifies the character and quality of the work to be done and leaves its detailed execution to the other party, the contract will be *l.c. operis*, but if he is to have supervision of the work from moment to moment it will be *l.c. operarum*. In a different context English law makes a distinction on these lines between an independent contractor and a servant.

Such is the civilian classification, but neither in terminology nor in substance are its distinctions clearly made in the Roman texts. This is not to say that the jurists were unaware of the differences between hiring a thing and hiring a man's services, or between hiring a man's services and commissioning the performance of a piece of work, but rather that they never arrived at a systematic analysis of them. This may seem surprising. The virtue, we have said, of the Roman system of specific contracts was that it made possible the elaboration of a scheme of incidents appropriate to each type of transaction, and the three types of *locatio conductio*, although broadly similar, were sufficiently different to call for differing incidents. This is obvious where the contrast is between the lease of land and the hire of services, but it is also true where the contrast is between *l.c. operarum* and *l.c. operis*. If, for example, a house under construction is accidentally burned down and work has to begin again, or if the work is held up by bad weather, the incidence of the risk of these misfortunes must depend on the character of the contract between the parties. The jurists, of course, knew this, but they did not, as they did elsewhere, arrive at a set of clear-cut distinctions.[2] Moreover, the threefold classification

---

[1] This has a consequence in terms of actions. In the former the person doing the work will have the *actio locati* and in the latter the *actio conducti*.

[2] For this reason the outcome of the texts on such matters as risk and the duties of the parties cannot be simply stated. These matters are therefore omitted in the discussion of the effects of the contract, below.

towards which they were working does not represent the limit of useful analysis. Within the category of *l.c. rei* the incidents appropriate to the hire of, for example, furniture will differ from those appropriate to a lease of agricultural land. For this reason modern Civil law systems commonly distinguish either between contracts in which the lessee is entitled to the use of the thing and those in which he is entitled both to its use and to the enjoyment of its fruits, or, more simply, between those relating to agricultural land and those relating to other things.

These shortcomings are only an aspect of what seems to us a wider lack of thoroughness in the Roman treatment of *locatio conductio*. Buyer and seller are commonly economic equals, but landlord and tenant or employer and employee may well not be. In our eyes, therefore, there is a greater need to regulate their relationship in order to prevent the economically more powerful party from abusing his position. In the ancient world this inequality was more marked: the agricultural tenant was commonly a small-holder who eventually, in the later Empire, degenerated into a serf (*colonus glebae adscriptus*), and the disparity of bargaining power between employer and employee was accentuated by the much greater extremes of wealth and poverty, and by the institution of slavery. But the jurists were not social reformers. They were conservative members of the wealthy class, and saw no need to make things other than they were. To blame them for this is to blame them for having lived when they did, but the consequence was that they devoted less interest to *locatio conductio* than its social and economic importance seems to us to deserve. Their treatment of it is much less thorough than their treatment of, for example, legacies.[1]

Formation of the contract. The rules as to the thing, the price, and consent were much the same as those of sale, in so far as they could be applied. The insistence on a money price did, however, yield sufficiently to admit the share-cropping tenancy (*colonia partiaria*). And the scope of the contract for services was limited by the exclusion of what we should call the professions and the liberal arts. For it offended Roman ideas of propriety that persons of good social standing should be paid a reward. The

---

[1] It is true that much of the modern English law on the subject derives not from 'lawyers' law' but from statute; but imperial legislation is almost silent.

contract for their services was, if anything, mandate. The social distinction between professions and trades and between arts and crafts was, however, differently drawn in the ancient world. Painting and medicine, for example, were commonly the occupations of slaves.

Effects of the contract.[1] In *l.c. rei* the *conductor* had only detention of the thing. He acquired, in other words, nothing but his right *in personam* against the *locator*,[2] on whom he was therefore entirely dependent. He had no remedy directly against a third party who interfered with his occupation, but could only sue the *locator* for breach of his duty to accord him undisturbed enjoyment. This was so even if the third party were a purchaser from the *locator*. The *conductor* had no protection against the purchaser, who could enter as of right, leaving the *conductor* to his remedy against the *locator*. The *locator* would usually insert a term in the contract of sale requiring the purchaser to respect the tenancy of the *conductor*, but the purchaser's breach of this term would give a remedy only to the *locator*. This was expressed succinctly, though inaccurately,[3] in the medieval maxim 'sale breaks hire'.

(3) Partnership (societas)

Formation of the contract. Societas was an agreement between two or more persons to co-operate for a common purpose. Its earliest form involved a merger of all the assets of the parties (*societas omnium bonorum*)[4] but it came to include any agreement for joint activity, great or small, brief or prolonged. Since Roman law had no concept of a corporation, every joint commercial venture necessarily took the form of a *societas*, but the making of a profit was not an essential part of the common purpose. In this respect *societas* was wider than English partnership. It would include, for example, an agreement to share the expenses of a journey or to buy land to preserve it as an open space. In this last case, and in many others, the partners would be joint owners,

---

[1] See above, p. 183, n. 1.
[2] See above, p. 110.
[3] The sale did not terminate the hire: it enabled the purchaser to exclude the *conductor* from the enjoyment to which, as against the seller, the hire entitled him.
[4] For *consortium* as a probable forerunner of this, see Jolowicz, *Historical Introduction to Roman Law*, 2nd edn., pp. 309 ff.

but joint owners are not necessarily partners: they may well, as in the case of joint heirs, have no common purpose.

Each party must make some contribution, either of capital, skill, or labour. Otherwise the transaction will be one not of partnership but of gift. For the same reason the *societas leonina* (so-called from the fable of the lion and the ass), in which one party was excluded from sharing in the profits, was, after some dispute, held to be void. It was otherwise, however, with a *societas* in which one party was excluded from bearing any loss: such a transaction was not a gift, since his participation might be worth securing at that price and it was not for the law to assess the value or adequacy of the parties' contributions. It was in accord with this principle that, unless it was otherwise agreed, the parties shared equally in both profit and loss, whatever their contributions.

The purpose must, as in all contracts, be lawful. One of a band of robbers could not, we are told, assert a partnership in order to obtain his share of the proceeds.

Incidents of the contract. The relationship between partners was treated as an especially personal one, the relationship between brothers being invoked as an analogy. The law therefore left the incidents of the contract to a considerable extent to be regulated by the broad principle of good faith. Like sale and hire it was perfectly bilateral, but whereas in sale and hire, as the doubling of their names in Latin indicates, the interests of the parties were different, it was of the essence of *societas* that their interests should be the same. In both sale and hire, therefore, there were two different sets of duties and two different actions, but in *societas* the duties of all partners were in principle the same and there was accordingly only a single action, the *actio pro socio*. Moreover litigation between partners was held to be incompatible with the 'brotherly' character of the contract, and therefore the bringing of the action by any partner terminated the contract. The action was in consequence a general winding-up action rather than a remedy for the breach of a particular duty. A partnership could never be brought to court until it had been terminated.

The personal character of the contract appeared also in the other ways in which it could be terminated. Any partner could at any time bring the partnership to an end by a unilateral renunciation. He could, it is true, be called to account in the *actio pro socio* if his purpose was to avoid bringing into the partnership some expected gain, or to avoid sharing in some expected loss, but the renunciation was nevertheless effective. The contract was likewise terminated by the death, *capitis deminutio*, or bankruptcy of any partner.

To the English lawyer the most surprising feature of *societas* is that it created relationships only between the partners themselves. It gave a third party who contracted with one partner no rights against the others, even though they might have expressly authorized the contract. They were bound to make good to the contracting partner their share in any loss he might suffer, but he alone was liable to the creditor. The English creditor, by contrast, can claim the whole debt from any or all of the partners. But the Roman rule was only one aspect of the general principle, discussed below,[1] that obligations were strictly personal.

(4) Mandate (*mandatum*)

Mandatum existed when one person (*mandatarius*) agreed to perform a service gratuitously for another (*mandator*) at his request. The service might be of any kind but consisted commonly in entering into a contract or some other legal transaction with a third party. Mandate was imperfectly bilateral,[2] the *mandatarius* being bound to perform the service, and the *mandator* being contingently bound to indemnify him for his expenses. The *mandatarius* was also bound to account to the *mandator* for any incidental benefits he derived from the performance of the service. If the service was the making of a contract, he satisfied this duty by assigning[3] to the *mandator* his action on the contract.

To the English lawyer, accustomed to the idea of contract as necessarily a bargain, the surprising feature of mandate is its gratuitous character. The *mandatarius* could indeed with impunity withdraw from the contract before he had begun to carry it out, but thereafter he was bound, even though he had no interest. The origins of the contract are hidden, but they lie

---

[1] pp. 199, 201 ff.   [2] See above, p. 169, n. 1.
[3] Also by mandate. See below, p. 203.

perhaps in the extra-legal relationship between friends, which could make far greater demands in Rome than it does in the modern world. It is still surprising that such social obligations should have acquired legal force, but the transformation was no doubt made easier by the importance of the transaction which the agreement might embrace, and also by the existence of the intermediate concept, part social or moral and part legal, of good faith. Moreover in the later classical law the gratuitous character of the contract had come to be a matter of form rather than of substance. For it was possible to agree for the payment of an *honorarium*, and this *honorarium* could be claimed by *cognitio extraordinaria*.[1] The mandate itself was still, however, gratuitous in the sense that the claim to an *honorarium* could not be used as a set-off or a defence to an *actio mandati* brought by the *mandator*. The *mandatarius* must submit to judgment in the *actio mandati* and claim his *honorarium* separately in a different court. In the time of Justinian, when the distinction between the two methods of proceeding had long since disappeared, one would expect mandate to have ceased to be gratuitous even in this sense, but the classical statement of the law is preserved and we do not know what happened in practice.

Although the *mandatarius* could claim no reward under the contract he might nevertheless have an interest in its execution. If, for example, he were asked to lend money at interest to a third party, he would derive an advantage to the extent of the interest on the loan. It was in cases such as this that there arose a further problem: how was mandate to be distinguished from mere advice? The answer was that a mandate in the interest of the *mandatarius* alone was not binding. If, therefore, A told B that he should employ his money by lending it at interest, or by investing it in some other way, and B incurred a loss, A was not liable. But what if A told B to lend his money to a particular person (C)? If A himself had an interest (e.g. because C intended to use the money on some project in which A was concerned) there was no difficulty: the mandate was not in the interest of the *mandatarius* alone. There was greater hesitation where A had no such interest, but it was eventually held to be sufficient that C had an interest. This made possible a useful means of suretyship. For if A gave a mandate to B to lend to C,

[1] See above, p. 27.

and C failed to repay the loan, B could claim to have his loss made good by A. A was in effect acting as surety for C.[1]

Mandate, like *societas*, was ended by the death of either party, but the rule was stretched to allow the *mandatarius* to claim compensation for expenses incurred up to the moment when he learned of the death of the *mandator*. The consequences would otherwise be harsh, as English law, which makes no such concession, shows.

'*Mandator*' and '*mandatarius*' may be loosely rendered 'principal' and 'agent', but there is this fundamental difference that the English agent when he contracts on behalf of his principal creates a relationship directly between the principal and the third party—a relationship to which he is ordinarily not even in law a party. The strictly personal character of the Roman obligation, however, made agency in this sense impossible, and the *mandatarius* alone was both liable and entitled on any contract which he made. The extent to which this principle was circumvented is discussed below.[2]

(c) *Innominate Contracts*

The four real and four consensual contracts, together with the contracts *verbis* and *literis*,[3] exhaust the Institutional list of contracts, but the list leaves gaps and uncertainties. It leaves gaps because it excludes several common types of agreement, such as exchange or any agreement which calls for the payment of a reasonable price (e.g. an agreement for the making of repairs the extent of which cannot be exactly foreseen). It leaves uncertainties because, while it may be clear that a given agreement is a contract, there may be a doubt as to the particular heading under which it should be placed. We have encountered examples of this on the borderline between sale and hire, and there were others. Of these the transaction called *aestimatum* is an example. We should call it an agreement for sale or return: one party provides the other with a thing on the terms that if the other sells it he will pay an agreed sum, and that if he does

---

[1] The modern name of this type of suretyship is *mandatum qualificatum*. Another reason given for its validity is that B would not have lent to C if it had not been for A's mandate, but this could equally well apply to the case where A simply told B that he should employ his money by lending it at interest (to no one in particular). It leaves the distinction between mandate and advice to the elusive test of the intention of the parties.   [2] pp. 201 ff.   [3] See below, pp. 193 ff.

not he will return it. This has affinities, if not with mandate and *societas*, at least with sale and with hire (both of a thing and of services), but does not clearly fall within the limits of any.

The stipulation provided, as we have seen, a way of escape from these difficulties, but if this way were not followed the *ius civile* offered only limited assistance. Where one side of a bargain consisted in the conveyance of a *res*, and that side had been performed but the other had not, a *condictio* could be brought for the return of the *res* on the ground that it had been given for a purpose (the securing of the performance of the other side of the bargain), which purpose had not been achieved, and that therefore the recipient was not justified in retaining it. This is, in Justinian's classification, a claim *quasi ex contractu*.[1] It is a claim for restitution and not, as is a contractual action, for damages for non-performance. For example, if the transaction is an exchange of a horse for a cow, the horse having been conveyed but the cow not, the owner of the horse will secure by the *condictio* the restitution of the value of the horse, whereas a contractual remedy would have given him what he had lost by not receiving the cow. This will normally, of course, be the value of the cow, but if he has suffered any consequential loss it will include that also. The practical difference between the two types of remedy will therefore depend on the market value of horses and cows at the time when the action is brought, and on whether the plaintiff has suffered any consequential loss.

The *condictio* thus provided only a partial remedy. It was confined to agreements which had been performed on one side and in which the performance consisted in a conveyance, and it was directed to restitution and not to performance. Where there had been no performance, or the performance consisted in an act rather than a conveyance, the aggrieved party could bring a Praetorian *actio de dolo*,[2] but he would then have to show that the breach was due to the defendant's bad faith.

Such was probably the law at the end of the Republic. By the time of Justinian, however, there had grown up a general action which went by various names but which is most often

---

[1] See below, pp. 227 ff. It is the *condictio ob causam datorum* (sc. *causa non secuta*), which is given in the later law (and by modern Civilians) the untranslatable name of *condictio causa data causa non secuta*. Another name is *condictio ob rem dati*.

[2] See below, p. 223.

called *actio praescriptis verbis*. This action lay whenever one party
to an agreement had performed his side of the bargain but the
other had failed to perform his (provided, of course, that the
agreement did not fall within any of the recognized types of
contract). A general principle had thus evolved that an agreement which is executed on one side is a contract. The principle
emerges clearly from texts in the Digest and is important as con-
stituting a break from the system of typical contracts, but since
Justinian's compilers did not revise the traditional classification,
it remained without express recognition, and the contracts without a name. The term 'innominate (i.e. nameless) contracts' by
which they are now known occurs first in Theophilus.[1]

The more important types in fact have names, such as *permutatio* (exchange) and *aestimatum*, but this must not be allowed to
obscure the significance of the innominate contracts, which lies
precisely in the generality of the principle which they represent.
For this principle goes a long way towards filling the gaps and resolving the uncertainties left by the system of typical contracts.

The steps by which this general principle was developed are
obscure, but the ultimate generalization is the work of Justinian's compilers. It is for this reason that in the *Corpus Iuris*
both the *condictio* and the *actio praescriptis verbis* exist side by
side as remedies for the same situation. Nowhere else is there
this concurrence of quasi-contractual and contractual remedies.
In a contract of sale, for example, the unpaid seller cannot elect
to bring a *condictio* for the return of the thing (a course which
would be advantageous if the value of the thing increased since
the sale); he is confined to his action on the contract. The same
rule should logically have applied to innominate contracts, but
the work of expunging the *condictio* from the texts was beyond
the capacity of the compilers,[2] and they simply added the *actio
praescriptis verbis*.

(d) Pacts

Bare pacts. The original meaning of *pactum* and related words is
that of a compromise—an agreement not to sue. It was a rule

---

[1] See above, p. 45.
[2] It would have been extremely difficult in any case, since the *condictio ob causam datorum* was only one application of the *condictio*, and the scope even of the *condictio ob causam datorum* was wider than that of the innominate contracts. See
below, p. 230.

of the Civil law that such a *pactum* completely extinguished any obligation arising *ex delicto*, and the Praetor extended the principle by allowing an *exceptio pacti* to be pleaded in bar of any action. Meanwhile the meaning of *pactum* had widened to include any agreement, and there was coined the maxim, which is fundamental to the Roman system of contracts, that a bare pact (i.e. an agreement which does not fall within the limits of any recognized contract) begets a defence but no action.[1] In the informal contracts this principle was relaxed so far as to allow agreements made at the time of the contract (*pacta continua* or *in continenti facta*) to be treated as part of the contract. But all agreements made subsequently (*pacta ex intervallo*), and in stipulations *pacta continua* as well, were effective only by way of defence.

Clothed pacts. In a few cases, however, the Praetor, and later the Emperors, gave actions on agreements which did not fall within the list of contracts. In modern terminology these are called *pacta vestita* (clothed pacts) and are distinguished as *pacta praetoria* and *pacta legitima* respectively. Only one need be mentioned here.

Constitutum debiti was an agreement to pay an existing debt at a fixed time. If, for example, a debt owing under a *mutuum* were due on 1 January, but at the debtor's request the creditor allowed six months' grace, this agreement would be a *constitutum*. By suing on the *constitutum* the creditor could obtain payment of the debt and of a penalty of one-half in addition, whereas in the *condictio* which lay to enforce the original *mutuum* the penalty was only of one-third.[2] The difference in effect compensated the plaintiff for his inability to claim interest. The agreement could also, however, relate to a debt owed by a third party to the promisee (*constitutum debiti alieni*), the promisor becoming in this way a surety for the debt of the third party.[3]

---

[1] 'Nuda pactio obligationem non parit sed parit exceptionem.'

[2] These penalties, obtained by procedural wagers on the outcome of the action, are a peculiar feature of Roman law, but were confined to a few actions. The wagers took the form of stipulations. Cf. above, p. 161, n. 2.

[3] Cf. below, p. 205.

3 THE FORMAL CONTRACTS

(a) *The Contract* verbis—*the* stipulatio[1]

The traditional *ius civile* was characterized by formalism, and in its choice of forms it resorted habitually to the use of spoken words. It is not surprising therefore that the central contract was formal and that its form was oral. What is more surprising is the extreme simplicity of the form and its precocious development. For we know that it existed already in the time of the Twelve Tables.

Classical form. The earliest form was apparently the *sponsio*, i.e. a question and answer using the solemn verb *spondere* (*spondesne?* —*spondeo*),[2] and this form, perhaps because of religious associations, was always confined to citizens. In the classical law, however, the question and answer could be expressed in other words, perhaps in any words, provided a few requirements were satisfied. The question and answer must be spoken; the answer must follow immediately on the question; both parties must be present throughout; and the question must exactly correspond with the answer, both as to the promissory word used (if the promisor, for example, answered *promitto* to the promisee's question *spondesne?* there was no contract) and as to content (e.g. if the promisee asked for 50 and the promisor promised 100, there was again no contract). No witnesses were necessary,[3] though obviously the wise promisee would see that he had some evidence of the transaction, in the shape either of witnesses or of a document.

The form was thus minimal, but it served its purpose. The formal question ensured that the promisor knew when the decisive moment had come; the requirements that the whole take place at the same time and with both parties present, and that question and answer exactly correspond, ensured as far as possible that the parties were agreed on the same thing at the same time.

Function. The importance of the stipulation lay in the fact that it was a method of contracting rather than a contract. Any

---

[1] Other verbal contracts (*dotis dictio, iusiurandum liberti*) are of such limited importance that they can be ignored here.   [2] Cf. above, p. 159.

[3] For the reason for the contrast, in this respect, with *mancipatio*, see above, p. 104 and below, p. 256.

agreement (provided it was not illegal, immoral, or impossible) could be made enforceable by being cast in this form. It was not necessary, of course, that the whole agreement be framed in a single interrogatory sentence. A simple agreement, e.g. to pay a sum of money (*centum dari spondes?*), ordinarily would be so framed, but commercial agreements are rarely simple. All that was necessary was a recital of the terms of the agreement, which would then be taken up in a single promise (e.g. 'do you promise that all these things will be done?').

A stipulation might thus be used either because the agreement entered into did not fall within one of the recognized types of contract, or because the parties preferred the stricter incidents of the stipulation, or, finally, because they wished to make express the subsidiary terms of a contract.

Degeneration. The Roman law of specific contracts was founded on the distinction between an agreement and a contract. But since any agreement would become a contract if cast in the form of a stipulation, the crucial distinction was that between an agreement and a stipulation. If that distinction were whittled away the foundation of the law of specific contracts would be lost: any agreement would be a contract. That this came eventually, in centuries after Justinian, to be the law—or at least that any agreement in writing was a contract—is certain. What is less clear is how far this process of degeneration had gone in Justinian's own time and before.

The main agent in the process of degeneration was the use of writing. Here, as in the case of *mancipatio*,[1] what originates simply as evidence of an oral act comes eventually to take the place of that act. Roman forms, as we have seen, were predominantly oral, but convenience, and the example of Greek law in which the use of writing was common, led to the use of documentary evidence. As early as the first century B.C. the use of such evidence had become so common that Cicero could speak loosely of the stipulation as a written act. We have no means of knowing how far the parties to such written acts continued to observe the prescribed oral form, but, as in the case of *mancipatio*, it would be surprising if they did not sometimes let the record do duty for the act. There thus opens up the

[1] See above, p. 117.

possibility of a divergence between principle and practice—between what is in principle oral but in practice written. The possibility becomes a certainty after the *constitutio Antoniniana* of *c.* A.D. 212, when vast numbers of new citizens who previously had followed the Greek practice of written acts found it necessary to accommodate themselves to Roman forms. Finding that, to all appearances, the Roman law was satisfied by a written contract to which was appended, in words which were common form, an allegation of the exchange of a stipulatory question and answer, they simply added to their documents this common form phrase. Here begins the vulgar law.[1] In the pure Roman law, whatever the actual extent of the divergence between principle and practice, the principle still entailed at least the negative practical consequence that proof that no words had been spoken would destroy the value of the document. But in the provinces even this consequence was either never understood or soon forgotten. Practice alone prevailed and therefore gave birth to a new principle, the principle of the vulgar law that a written document, or at least a written document incorporating the stipulatory phrase, was a contract.

It remains uncertain how far the imperial law followed the same path. We may guess, however, that, even in classical times, although in principle the *iudex* was free to accept or reject any evidence he chose, he would in practice require something more than the defendant's simple allegation before he was satisfied that no words had been spoken. To prove this negative the defendant would have to prove an inconsistent positive, and (leaving out of account the unlikely possibility of one or both parties' being either dumb or stone deaf) the only possible inconsistent positive was that the parties were in different places when the contract was made. It seems likely that by the time of Justinian practice here too had become principle, and that a document alleging a stipulation could be overthrown only by proving that the parties had not met.[2] To attempt even this was characterized by Justinian as dishonest, and he therefore made the requirements of proof more rigorous: the defendant must adduce unimpeachable evidence not merely that one or

---

[1] Cf. above, p. 36.
[2] There is a further problem: was a clear distinction possible between a document alleging a stipulation and one alleging simply an agreement?

other party had been elsewhere but that he had been in a different township for the whole of the day in question. The oral principle thus survived, but in so attenuated a form as to be scarcely recognizable.

In view of this progressive assimilation of the stipulation to the document which recorded it, the degeneration of the oral form itself is less important. Controversy centres on an obscurely worded rescript issued by the Emperor Leo in A.D. 472 which apparently removed the need for any 'formality of words'. This might refer simply to the use of special words, leaving unaffected the need for a question and a corresponding answer. But it is commonly accepted that this was already the classical law. If that is so, we can only conclude that after A.D. 472 not even a question and answer were needed—that any agreement was a stipulation. In preserving the classical system of specific contracts Justinian was therefore guilty of an anachronism. The scale and theoretical importance of such an anachronism would indeed be immense, but it must be admitted that to recast the entire law of contracts would have been an undertaking beyond the capacity of the compilers in the time at their disposal.

(b) The Contract literis

The classical contract. Our knowledge of this contract is derived from a very brief account in the Institutes of Gaius and a few references elsewhere. Many questions are therefore left unanswered. Its function was limited to the renewing or transforming of an existing obligation in one of two ways. Either it converted one or more existing obligations, *bonae fidei* or not, into a single *stricti iuris* money debt, or it transferred a debt from one debtor to another. That it was a formal contract—i.e. that its validity depended on the existence of a certain form of writing rather than on the existence of the facts which that writing recorded—is clear, but we do not know precisely what the form was. Gaius speaks of 'transcriptive entries', and it is possible that the contract consisted of fictitious entries by the creditor in the traditional Roman account book.

The brevity of Gaius' treatment suggests that the contract was obsolescent in his day, perhaps because the old account book itself was obsolescent, and in Justinian's time it had evidently been long forgotten.

The contract of Justinian's Institutes. Faced with the disappearance of the old literal contract, the compilers of the Digest simply expunged all reference to it, and reduced the types of contracts in the traditional classification to three (*re, verbis, consensu*). The compilers of the Institutes, however, perhaps out of enthusiasm for a fourfold pattern (four types of contract, four delicts, four real contracts, four consensual contracts) found what they claimed was a new literal contract. The claim seems, however, on examination to be unjustified.

Imperial legislation had attempted to deal with the problem of the written acknowledgement of the wholly or partly non-existent debt. The facts might arise either from the creditor's bad faith in extracting the document in advance and then failing to make the loan which it recorded, or, more probably, from an attempt to evade legal restrictions on the rate of interest by recording a capital sum larger than the one actually lent. The document might record a debt owing by stipulation or by *mutuum*, but it is with the latter only that the Institutes are concerned. The problem with which the legislation attempted to deal was akin to that of the document alleging a stipulation which had never been orally made. If the 'creditor' brought an action, the 'debtor' would be put to the almost impossible task of proving a negative—of showing that the money had never been paid. He was therefore allowed to plead a special defence (*exceptio non numeratae pecuniae*) which reversed the ordinary burden of proof and required the plaintiff to prove the debt independently of the document. This was a powerful weapon, which could work injustice on an innocent creditor who, relying on a truthful document, had allowed the debt to remain un-enforced for a considerable time, only to find in the end, when proof by other means was almost impossible, that the debtor could in effect tear up the document by pleading the *exceptio non numeratae pecuniae*. The *exceptio* was therefore subjected to a limitation period, which in Justinian's time was two years.[1] Thereafter the defendant can no longer plead the *exceptio* and, so runs Justinian's argument, he will therefore be obliged to pay. And his obligation, since it cannot arise from a *mutuum*,

---

[1] This in turn led to other devices to prevent further injustice. The moral of the complicated story of these devices seems to be that it is unwise to tamper with the 'natural' burden of proof.

which *ex hypothesi* has never existed, must arise from the document. If it were true that the defendant would be in law bound to pay, this argument would raise an often-debated question of legal classification: whether a conclusive presumption (i.e. one which it is not permissible to rebut) is better expressed as a rule of evidence or a rule of substantive law; or, in other words, whether we should look to the facts which actually happened or to those which the law presumes to have happened. If after two years the law raises from the mere existence of the document a conclusive presumption that its contents are true, it is indeed more realistic to say that the defendant is bound by the document. On the other hand, systems of law not infrequently resort to such conclusive presumptions or fictions in order to simplify classification by bringing exceptional situations under established headings. Justinian's example is a case in point. The facts are exceptional and unimportant. To erect them into an independent class of contract unnecessarily complicates and distorts the law.

There is, however, a prior objection to Justinian's arguments: the presumption does not seem to have been conclusive. There is nothing to show that after the expiry of the two years the defendant was debarred from contesting the existence of the loan alleged in the document. The burden of proof would, it is true, be on him, and he would in the ordinary case find it impossible to discharge, but there is a crucial difference between a presumption which the defendant cannot in fact rebut and one which he may not in law rebut.

4. DISCHARGE OF OBLIGATIONS

An obligation might be discharged without the consent of the parties in a number of ways, such as by supervening impossibility (e.g. destruction of the thing owed) or in a few cases (e.g. *societas*, *mandatum*) by death, but discharge would ordinarily be by a voluntary act of the parties.

To us it seems evident that performance must discharge an obligation, but the formalism of early law seems to have required that a bond which has been formally created should be formally dissolved. Hence we find formal acknowledgements of performance, both *verbis* (*acceptilatio*) and *literis* (*accepti relatio*), corresponding to the stipulation and the literal contract. Thus in *acceptilatio* the debtor asks the creditor whether he has received satisfaction and the creditor replies that he has. In the classical law, however, performance by itself had become sufficient, and *acceptilatio* was simply a method of release without satisfaction, the acknowledgement being fictitious. But for such a release the formal act was necessary: a simple agreement was effective only by way of *exceptio pacti*.[1] On the other hand, an obligation *ex consensu*, since it was created by agreement, could be released simply by a contrary agreement.

Discharge by novation is considered below.

5. PRIVITY OF CONTRACT

The principle. What English law calls the principle of privity of contract requires that a contract should affect only the parties to it, and that third parties should therefore acquire neither rights nor duties under it. In Roman law, save that all acquisitions made by a slave or *filiusfamilias* vested automatically in the head of the family (and in Roman eyes this was no exception), the principle was rigidly applied. If X promised Y that he would pay T, T could not claim, because he was not a party to a contract. If P authorized A to contract with T, P was neither entitled against nor liable to T. If C owed A, A could not without C's co-operation transfer his right against C to B.

That a third party could acquire no rights under a contract was an aspect of a wider principle which excluded all acquisitions through an *extranea persona* (i.e. a person outside the family). Within the law of property this principle yielded ground, but it remained unmodified in the law of obligations. That a third party could acquire no duties under a contract derived perhaps from the strictly personal and indeed physical character of an obligation in early law, when execution was against the person of the defaulting debtor, and the debt, it seems, died with the debtor.

Novation and delegation. It is no exception to this principle that the rights or duties created by a contract could be transferred to a third party by a fresh contract between the third party and

[1] See above, p. 24 f. Apart from the need expressly to plead the *exceptio*, however, the practical differences between the civil law extinction of the debt and the Praetorian barring of the action were largely whittled away. If, for example, the debtor paid in ignorance of the availability of the *exceptio*, he paid what was in law owing, but nevertheless he was able to claim it back.

one of the original parties. There was then said to be a novation,[1] the old contract being extinguished and replaced by the
new. The new contract conferred no rights or duties on anyone
who was not a party to it, but it did extinguish the rights or
duties of the original contract. If therefore the novation effected
a change of creditors, the consent of the original creditor was
necessary, since he was being deprived of a right. On the other
hand, if it effected a change of debtors, the original debtor could
not be prejudiced by the extinction of his debt, and his consent
was therefore not neccessary.

The most important application of this type of novation was
in what is called *delegatio*. For example, if D owes C and C owes
X, C can direct D to promise to pay X. D's promise to pay X
will novate and therefore extinguish C's debt to X. In this way
C can satisfy his debt to X by substituting D for himself, but
such a substitution requires the consent of all three parties.

Assignment. In modern English law such a substitution can be
effected without the consent of the debtor (D) by what is called
assignment. C simply assigns, or transfers, his right against D
to X and, subject to certain provisos, D is then bound to pay X.
Such an assignment of rights would in Roman law have involved
too great an inroad on the personal character of obligation, but
what was in substance the same result was achieved by a variant
of procedural representation. A litigant who was unable or
unwilling to conduct his own case could appoint by mandate
a representative to do so. The Praetor gave effect to this without doing violence to the civil law by a simple change of name
within the formula: the action was brought (or defended) in
the name of the principal, but the *iudex* was directed to give
judgment for or against the representative.[2] To convert this

---

[1] For there to be a novation the new contract must effect some change in the old.
The change might be either, as here, in the parties, or in the form (e.g. one or more
informal contracts might be novated by a single stipulation, which would be more
easily either sued upon or released), or in the content, or in more than one of these.
The novation must be by stipulation. The classical literal contract performed a
similar but not, it seems, identical function, since the new obligation was apparently
not dependent, as it was in novation, on the validity of the old.

[2] If, for example, A alleges that B owes him money, but has appointed C to act
for him, the skeleton of the *formula* will be: 'If B owes A, condemn B to pay C.'
This *formula Rutiliana* (named after an otherwise unknown Praetor Rutilius) was
used in other cases in which it was desired to transfer a burden or a benefit. See,
for example, below, p. 203.

representation into an assignment of the action (*cessio actionis*), all that was necessary was for the principal to waive the representative's duty to account to him for the proceeds of the mandate. There was then said to be a *mandatum* or *procuratio 'in rem suam'* (for his own benefit). This simple device suffered however from two defects. On the one hand, the authority to sue, like any other mandate, was revocable, and the assignor could therefore go back on the assignment at any time up to *litis contestatio* (joinder of issue) between the assignee and the debtor. And the assignment would be similarly destroyed by the death of either party. On the other hand, in the eyes of the law the debt was still owed to the principal (i.e. the assignor) who could therefore at any time before *litis contestatio* release it or accept satisfaction of it. Both defects were eventually remedied, though perhaps not completely until Justinian's time. The first was met by allowing the assignee an *actio utilis* in his own name. This action was unaffected by the assignor's revocation or his death, and in the event of the assignee's death it passed to his heirs, but it was still subject to the second defect. This was met by the device of notice. If the assignee gave notice of the assignment to the debtor, the latter could no longer obtain a discharge of his debt by dealing with the assignor. In this circuitous way Roman law seems eventually to have arrived at an effective system of assignment.

Agency. In modern law, if an agent enters into a contract on behalf of his principal with a third party, he creates rights and duties directly between principal and third party, and himself incurs neither. Roman law had no concept of agency in this sense, though eventually it evolved a system which yielded some of the same results. The slowness of the evolution and the inadequacy of the outcome may have been due in part to the facts that business agents were often slaves and that within the family the law yielded fairly satisfactory results at quite an early stage of its history.

(i) *Within the family.* The law was in essentials the same for sons and daughters *in potestate* as it was for slaves, and we shall therefore for the sake of simplicity speak only of slaves. We have seen that by the civil law the rights but not the duties under a slave's contracts vested in the master. If the contract were bilateral the master could not of course enforce his rights unless he were prepared to perform the duties, but this still left in his hands the decision whether the contract should be effective or not, and in such circumstances few would be prepared to enter into contracts with slaves. From as early as the second century B.C., however, the Praetor began to grant remedies against the master on his slave's contract. The device employed to prevent an open breach with the civil law was, as in assignment, the change of names within the *formula*. The claim alleged the appropriate debt or contract between the slave and the third party (the plaintiff), but directed the *iudex* to condemn or acquit the master.[1] There were eventually three of these Praetorian remedies. One made the master liable in full when it was with the master's authority that the third party had contracted with the slave. The other two applied where there had been no such communication between the master and the third party, but were confined to cases in which the slave had a *peculium*, and limited the master's liability to, at the most, the value of the *peculium*. They made possible in effect what we know as limited liability trading. But in neither was the underlying idea that of agency. In one the master must have known that the slave was trading with part or the whole of his *peculium*, but in neither was it necessary that the master should have authorized the contract: he might indeed have forbidden it. Moreover there was no question of transferring the slave's liability to the master. The primary liability remained, as the *formulae* of the actions show, in the contracting party.[2] The actions created only an additional liability. (They have therefore borne since medieval times the name of *actiones adjecticiae qualitatis*.) The underlying idea is not therefore one of agency but rather one of apportioning risks according to benefits: the master takes the

---

[1] Cf. above, p. 200, n. 2. Since a slave could not in any event incur civil rights and duties a fiction of freedom was also necessary and the skeleton of the *formula* (of a *condictio*) would be 'If B, who is the slave of C, were a free man, then if he would owe A, condemn C to pay A.' If the action were on a sale, hire, &c., the *formula* would vary accordingly, and its further details would depend on which of the Praetor's remedies the plaintiff had invoked. If the contract had been made not by a slave but by a *filiusfamilias*, no fiction would be necessary.

[2] Though in the case of a slave it is only a 'natural' liability (i.e. one which will bar recovery if he pays the debt after becoming free), and in the case of a son is one which, in the absence of *peculium castrense*, cannot be effectively enforced until he becomes *sui iuris*.

benefits to be derived from his slave's activities, and he should therefore take the burdens.

(ii) *Outside the family.* Two other *actiones adjecticiae qualitatis* extended the same principle outside the family. If one man appointed another, whether a slave or son of his or not, as manager of a business undertaking (*institor*), he was liable in full by the *actio institoria* on contracts made in connexion with the business; and the owner or charterer of a ship was similarly liable, by the *actio exercitoria*, on the contracts of his captain. If, however, the relationship between principal and agent were more limited in scope, the third party had no remedy against the principal until late in the classical law, when the *actio institoria* was extended by analogy (*actio ad exemplum institoriae*) even, it seems, to cases in which the relationship existed only for a single transaction.

In this way the liability of the principal was eventually established, but his entitlement was not. There was no corresponding action which the principal could bring against the third party. His remedy had to be found in assignment. We have seen that the agent was bound to account for the proceeds of his agency, and that this duty to account imported a duty to assign any action he had against the third party. The principal then sued as the agent of his own agent. In the ordinary case therefore both principal and third party would have an effective remedy against the other, the third party by the *actio institoria* or *ad exemplum institoriae*, and the principal by assignment of the agent's action. The remedy by assignment, however, had its defects: the agent might revoke the assignment or die before the principal had brought the action to *litis contestatio*, or he might simply refuse to make the assignment. We have seen that the effect of revocation or death was in the end nullified by giving the assignee (i.e. the principal in this case) a remedy in his own name. If the same course had been followed in the case of refusal to assign, the whole process of assignment would have become superfluous. Wherever there was a relationship of principal and agent the principal would have been able to sue on the agent's contract in his own name. And since the third party was correspondingly able to sue by the *actio institoria*, &c., the substance of agency would have been achieved, except that the agent would have remained both liable and entitled.

But even Justinian seems not to have been prepared to take this last step.[1] For him the principle of privity of contract was apparently still too strong: the principal's remedy must still be primarily against the agent for failure to assign, and only if this remedy was in the particular case valueless (i.e. if the agent were insolvent, or had disappeared, or had died without heirs) could he sue the third party directly. This was purposeless pedantry—to waive circuity where it would injure the principal, but to insist on it where it would not.

6. SURETYSHIP

A feature of Roman law which is at first sight surprising is the prominence of personal security or suretyship, and the variety of forms it could take. Its prominence has already been discussed.[2] The explanation of it is partly, as we saw, legal—the defects of the law of real security—and partly social—the same sense of the duties of friendship that accounts for the institution of mandate. The variety of types of suretyship, in a system otherwise characterized by economy in such matters, is explained by the special features of each.

The two earliest forms of suretyship (called *sponsio* and *fidepromissio* from the formal words used) were by stipulation, and were in most respects subject to the same rules, *sponsio* being however confined, as it was when used to create a principal debt, to Roman citizens. But they were both subject to several limitations and defects. They could only be used when the principal debt itself was created by stipulation; the obligation died, as did probably all primitive obligations, with the person who undertook it; it was extinguished in any case two years after it was created; and if there were several sureties for the same debt, each was liable only for his proportionate share of the principal debt, even if one or more of his co-sureties were insolvent. These last two restrictions, and some others, were the result of legislation which was evidently intended to relieve the lot of sureties. But it defeated its own purpose by making these two forms too unattractive to creditors. In the late Republic therefore there emerged a third form, *fideiussio*, which was also a stipulation, but was subject to none of the defects and limita-

---

[1] He made no express pronouncement, and the texts are confused.
[2] Above, p. 151.

tions mentioned above: it could guarantee any debt, however created; it bound the heirs of the surety and was subject to no limitation period; and if there were several sureties the creditor could claim the full debt from any of them. This last feature was indeed modified by Hadrian to the extent that a surety could, if he wished, claim the privilege (*beneficium divisionis*) of paying only his proportionate share of the debt; but in the calculation of the share those sureties who were insolvent at the time the action was brought were ignored. In other words, the risk of a surety's insolvency was on the other sureties, whereas in *sponsio* and *fidepromissio* it fell always on the creditor.

Fideiussio was thus far more favourable to the creditor than the other two, and it alone of the three survived in the law of Justinian. We have already encountered two other, informal, methods of effecting suretyship—by mandate and by *constitutum*. Since both came into existence simply by agreement, and laymen habitually do not express their agreement in legal terms, the substantial difference between the two was that in mandate the agreement must precede the creation of the principal debt and in *constitutum* it must follow it.

These contracts of suretyship created, of course, relationships only between creditor and surety. If there were to be any claim by the surety who paid the debt against either the debtor or his co-sureties, it must rest on some other ground. As between surety and debtor, if the surety had incurred his obligation to the creditor at the debtor's request the ground would be mandate, and if he had done so of his own accord it might be *negotiorum gestio*.[1] It is significant of the early origin of *sponsio* that the remedy of the *sponsor* against the principal debtor was provided by statute. As between co-sureties the relationship would be one of *societas* if they had acted in concert, but if they had not the law provided no remedy. After Hadrian's introduction of the *beneficium divisionis*, however, this cannot have been a matter of much importance.

7. MODERN CIVIL LAW

We have seen that the foundation of the Roman system of specific contracts had by the time of Justinian been undermined

[1] See below, pp. 227 ff.

by the principle, implicit in the degenerate *stipulatio*, that any agreement, or at least any agreement in writing, was a contract. Justinian's compilers either did not recognize what had happened or were unwilling to undertake the work of reconstruction, and they therefore left the conflict of principle unresolved. To the medieval and later Civil lawyers this course was not open. The form of the *stipulatio*, along with the other Roman forms, was dead. The Canon law insisted on the moral principle that agreements should be carried out. The system of specific contracts could not survive. So it is that modern Civil law systems proceed from the premiss that, in effect, any seriously intended agreement is a contract.[1] Other fundamental principles have likewise been abandoned. The tangle of technicalities in which the Roman law of agency was caught could not survive the disappearance of the Roman world, and modern Civil law accepts without question the principle of representation. The principle that a third party cannot sue on a contract, even when made expressly in his favour, was longer-lived, but in the last century the needs of modern business, and in particular of insurance, have made great inroads even on this principle.

And yet the law of contract remains one of the most markedly Roman branches of the Civil law. In evolving the principles of their unitary system of contract the Civilians drew heavily on Roman sources and in particular on the very fully worked out law governing the *stipulatio*. For, once freed of its form, the *stipulatio* could be seen as simply the model contract. Moreover the Civil law contrives to enjoy both the advantages of a unitary system of contract and those of a system of typical contracts. For within the framework of the unitary system it still retains, with some modifications, the typical contracts of the Roman law. The existence of these typical contracts no longer of course entails the consequence that an agreement not falling within them is no contract, but it does retain the great advantage of providing for the most usual transactions of life a ready-made set of 'incidents'.

Nor is it only in the Civil law that the influence of the Roman law of contracts has been felt. Even the Common law has here and there made borrowings—in the law governing mistake, for

---

[1] For the doctrine of *cause*, see Buckland and McNair, *Roman Law and Common Law*, 2nd edn., pp. 223 ff., 228 ff.

example, or in the law of sale—though these borrowings have more often been at second hand from the Civilian commentators than directly from the Roman sources.

II. DELICT AND QUASI-DELICT

I. INTRODUCTION

While the Roman law of contracts can be transposed without much difficulty into modern terms, there is in the law of delicts a great deal which is quite foreign to our ways of thought, and even to those of a Roman of the time of Gaius or Justinian. In any system of law which has not undergone a radical revision or codification there will be fossils—features which reveal and preserve ideas deriving from a way of life which has otherwise disappeared. English law, for example, at the beginning of the nineteenth century contained a great number of such fossils, and, though many have since then been removed by the hand of the legislator, some still survive. In Rome the legislator had, until Justinian's reign, little interest in such revision of the law, and Justinian himself left much undone.

The most obvious fossils are to be found in the formal acts, such as *mancipatio*, with its weighing out of uncoined bronze, and the act before the *comitia curiata*. These are at worst inconvenient and at best picturesque. The fossils to be found in the law of delicts, however, are of a different kind, and affect the character and substance of the law. But here again the most obvious, such as the survival, even in the law of Justinian, of noxal liability or the distinction between manifest and non-manifest theft, are less important than the survival of the principle which underlies them all, the principle of vengeance. The history of this part of the law can be seen as a movement, never completed in Roman times, from the principle of vengeance for an injury to that of compensation for damage done.

Crime and delict. Modern law makes a distinction between, in English terms, a crime and a tort, or more accurately, since the same act (e.g. theft) may be both a crime and a tort, between the criminal and tortious aspects of an act. Broadly defined, the distinction is between an act which endangers the order or security of the state, and one which is an infringement of an individual's rights (but is not exclusively a breach of contract). And to the difference in the character of the act there corresponds a difference in the sanction. In a criminal proceeding the primary purpose of the sanction is to punish the wrongdoer, and if there is an incidental benefit to be derived from the punishment, as in the case of a fine, it goes to the state and not to the person, if any, who has suffered from the act; but in a proceeding in tort the purpose of the sanction is normally to compensate the injured party and not to punish the wrongdoer. It is for this reason that a criminal conviction does not normally bar a remedy in tort.

The corresponding distinction in Roman law is between crime, which falls within the province of the public law, and delict, which is a matter of private law. But there is this important difference between delict and tort that the delictal sanction, which originated as a substitute for private vengeance, retained to the very end, though in varying degrees, a punitive character. It is for this reason that, for example, even in the law of Justinian three distinct proceedings could be brought against a thief: a criminal prosecution, a delictal claim for a money penalty to be paid to the victim, and either a claim *in rem* for the return of the thing or a claim *in personam* for its value. It is the last two remedies, and not the claim in delict, which correspond to the action in tort. Elsewhere—in the case of wrongful damage to property, for example—there was no separate compensatory remedy and the delictal action served both purposes, but it still retained, as we shall see, some penal characteristics.

It is a common generalization that in primitive law the criminal sanction develops later than the delictal (in the sense of the exercise of private vengeance or its substitute). Whether this was wholly true of Roman law we cannot tell, for already in the Twelve Tables some very serious offences, such as murder, treason and arson, entailed what we should call a criminal sanction, since the penalty (death) was imposed by direct intervention of the public authority without any hint of its being a substitute for private vengeance. But the number of such offences was small, and until the last century of the Republic the law of delict did very largely discharge what we should

consider to be the functions of the criminal law. In the disturbed conditions of the late Republic, however, the private
sanction was no longer adequate and there was a rapid expansion of the criminal law. There came thus to be two punitive
sanctions for the same act (though of course not every crime
was also a delict, nor every delict a crime). This in turn led to
a shift of emphasis in the law of delict. In theft, for example, the
delictal sanction was probably little used, and in other delicts
the law thought increasingly, but never exclusively, in terms
of compensation.

Penal character of delictal actions. The Twelve Tables preserve all
the different stages in the development of the private penal
action which are commonly found in primitive systems, with
the exception of group liability—the law of the vendetta—of
which there is no trace. Self-help still survives, subject to differing degrees of control. In its crudest form this control amounted
to no more than a definition of the circumstances in which a
killing should be guiltless. Thus, if a thief came by night or if,
even by day, he defended himself with a weapon, the victim of
the theft might kill him, provided only that he called out,
presumably so that the neighbours might verify the lawfulness
of the killing. In the case of the manifest thief—the thief caught
with the goods in his hand—the control was slightly more
positive. There was still no trial, since the guilt was plain,[1] but
the victim might not wreak his vengeance on the thief until
he had brought him—no doubt with the goods still on him—
before a magistrate, who had him scourged (here the element
of 'criminal' sanction intrudes) and then formally assigned him
to the victim. In the case of severe bodily harm (*membrum
ruptum*) on the other hand, there apparently was a trial, and
the victim was entitled not to the entire physical subjection of
the wrongdoer but only to retaliation in kind—the *lex talionis.*
He could indeed accept a money composition, as could the
victim of manifest theft, but he could not be compelled to do so.
In other delicts, however, this stage of merely voluntary composition had been passed, and the victim was bound to accept
a sum of money. This was either an arbitrary amount (300

---

[1] There is a close parallel here with the 'hand-having' thief of Anglo-Saxon
law; cf. Pollock and Maitland, *History of English Law,* vol. ii, p. 579.

asses for the breaking of a bone—*os fractum*—25 *asses* for lesser assaults) or a multiple of the loss suffered (twofold the value of the thing for non-manifest theft), or else was assessed by the *iudex* at the trial. It was only in default of payment that the victim could take execution on the person of the wrongdoer (a proceeding which was indeed open to all creditors at this time).

Delictal actions were classified as penal (*ad poenam persequendam*) by contrast with all other actions, whether *in rem* or *in personam*, which were *ad rem persequendam* (sometimes rendered in English as 'reipersecutory'). A reipersecutory action commonly results in the payment of compensation, and a penal action in the payment of more than compensation, but the essential distinction is to be found in the punitive or vindictive character of the penal action. This had four main practical consequences. If a delict was committed by two or more persons jointly, each was separately liable for the full amount. The purpose of the action being punitive, it was irrelevant that in this way the victim would be paid several times over. Similarly, as we have already seen in the case of the theft, the bringing of a penal action did not bar a reipersecutory action. Again, if the wrongdoer died before the action was brought, it would not lie against his heir: the victim could claim to revenge himself only on the wrongdoer. (In the language of the civilians, the action was 'passively intransmissible'.) On the other hand, if it was the victim who died, the action normally did lie (it was 'actively transmissible'), but an exception was made in the case of the action for *iniuria*,[1] because of its peculiarly vengeful character. Finally, if the wrongdoer was a slave or a son *in potestate* the action was noxal.[2] These characteristics were common to all penal actions. In addition, most praetorian penal actions were subject to a limitation period of one year, perhaps on the ground that resentment should in that time have run cold.[3]

The classification of the Institutes. Justinian follows Gaius in listing only four types of delict: *furtum* (theft), *rapina* (robbery), *damnum iniuria datum* (loss wrongfully caused), and *iniuria* (insult). The classification is unsatisfactory, both in what it includes and, more particularly, in what it leaves out. On the one hand

---

[1] See below, pp. 215 ff.   [2] See below, p. 223.
[3] The civil law had, in principle, no limitation period. See above, p. 122.

rapina is hardly more than a variety of *furtum*, and does not deserve a separate mention in so short a list, and on the other hand, while it was reasonable to leave out the many minor penal actions, civil and Praetorian, the omission of the two major Praetorian actions—for *dolus* (fraud) and *metus* (duress)—left the student with a quite inadequate picture of the resources of the law.[1]

2. *FURTUM* AND *RAPINA*

The law of theft is one of the least commendable parts of the mature Roman law, both because many archaic features were allowed to survive and because the delict was at times given so wide a scope as to defy definition. The archaic survivals are of great interest to the student of anthropology and primitive law but are strangely out of place in a system as sophisticated as the classical Roman law; and it is obviously unsatisfactory that the law should penalize an act which it cannot define. The reason for both defects may be, in part at least, the same: that the law of theft was of little practical importance. A thief in any society will not usually be solvent, or at least not provably solvent, and the multiple penalties of the Roman law must therefore usually have been illusory; and even if the Roman of imperial times had retained a taste for revenge, the old power of personal execution had long since been restricted to a form of private imprisonment of the debtor by the creditor. It would, in short, be much more satisfactory to leave punishment to the criminal law. It is true that if the thief were a slave the victim could be sure of some satisfaction, since he could require his master either to pay the penalty or to make noxal surrender of the slave, but a thievish slave would not be an asset of much value. It may well be, therefore, as one text indeed suggests, that civil actions were rarely brought. The law of theft would then have been of practical importance only indirectly, in determining whether a thing had been stolen and was therefore incapable of being usucapted. However this may be, it is at least difficult to believe that the more archaic remedies were often employed. These we may now briefly consider.

---

[1] Justinian was simply following Gaius. It is more difficult to know what reasons Gaius had. See de Zulueta, *Institutes of Gaius*, Part II, pp. 196 f., and Schulz, *Classical Roman Law*, s. 789.

Archaic features. The most obvious of these is the distinction between *furtum manifestum* and *furtum nec manifestum.*[1] The old savage penalty for manifest theft had gone, as had the summary proceeding without trial, but the distinction was still preserved, the penalty being now a fourfold money payment. Indeed, now that both forms of theft were the subject of an ordinary trial, the old difference in the mode of proof was forgotten and a dispute developed as to how soon after the act the thief must be caught in order to be liable to the fourfold penalty. Even Justinian did no more than settle this dispute. But the fact that it survived all through the classical period suggests that the *actio furti manifesti* was not often brought.

And there were other actions. The victim could demand to make a search with witnesses of any premises on which he thought the goods were hidden. If the search was refused, he could exact a fourfold penalty from the occupier (by the *actio furti prohibiti*). If the search was allowed and the goods were found, the occupier of the premises was liable (by the *actio furti concepti*) to a threefold penalty even if he knew nothing of the matter.[2] He could in turn obtain a threefold penalty (by the *actio furti oblati*) from the man who had left the goods on the premises, but only if he had done so to escape detection. Thus a householder could apparently be penalized without any such recourse if, for example, a guest of his had innocently bought stolen goods and had then left them behind in his house. It is unlikely that so crude a rule was ever put into practice in classical times. The whole apparatus of actions was obsolete before Justinian's time, and was not revived by him. Search was now a public matter, and no special provision was needed for the knowing receipt of stolen goods, since in the wide Roman conception of theft the receiver was simply a thief.

What constitutes furtum. A clear definition is impossible, but the constituent elements can be isolated.

---

[1] See above, pp. 209 f.

[2] By the law of the Twelve Tables, if the victim found the goods after making a search clad in nothing but a loin cloth and carrying a platter, the occupier was treated as a manifest thief. This curious ritual (which was clearly obsolete in the time of Gaius), and in particular its relationship to the search which resulted in the *actio furti concepti*, is the subject of much conjecture. See de Zulueta, *Institutes of Gaius*, Part II, pp. 201 ff.

(i) *The act.* In spite of its obvious derivation from the verb *ferre*, meaning 'to carry', *furtum* did not in the classical law require, as does the English crime of larceny, a taking away of the thing. The jurists use the term *contrectatio*, which strictly denotes a handling, but which seems to have included any meddling or dealing with the thing. Hence, as has just been said, the receiver was a thief, as also was the borrower who used the thing in an unauthorized way or to an unauthorized extent. (This is the so-called *furtum usus*, or theft of the use of a thing.) Likewise, embezzlement (the fraudulent appropriation of what is entrusted to one) or even, according to some jurists, the knowing acceptance of a mistaken payment of what was not owing, was theft. Since such a payment transferred not merely possession but also ownership, and since no one, and least of all the thief, could acquire ownership of stolen property, it was really a contradiction in terms to treat this last case as theft. The appropriate heading was *dolus*.[1] But it is nevertheless impossible to find a clear distinction in the opinions actually given in the Digest.

(ii) *The intent.* The texts sometimes speak of an *animus furandi* or intention to steal, an expression borrowed also on occasion by English law, but since it offers a definition in terms of what is to be defined, it is of no assistance except as an indication that the defendant must be in some sense in a wrongful state of mind. In the ordinary case this will be sufficiently defined as the lack of an honest belief that the owner would consent if he knew. Thus, in the case of *furtum usus*, mentioned above, the borrower will be liable unless he honestly believed that the owner would have no objection. But what if the defendant had no such belief, but the owner in fact had no objection? Gaius puts the case of the man who urges a slave to steal goods from his master and hand them over. The slave tells his master, who, in order to trap the dishonest man, bids the slave collaborate with him. Gaius held that there was neither theft, since the master had consented, nor the delict of corruption of a slave, since the slave was not in fact corrupted. Justinian, with the impatience of the legislator, reversed this particular decision but without resolving the more general problem of which it was simply an illustration.

[1] See below, p. 223. In a similar context English law distinguishes between larceny, in which the wrongdoer obtains possession, and false pretences, in which he obtains ownership.

From the requirement that the act be done against the wishes of the owner it should follow that an owner could not steal his own property. This was however not so. If he took it from a person to whom he had, for example, pledged it, or from a *bona fide* possessor, he committed theft (the so-called *furtum possessionis*).

An intention of a different kind is sometimes required—an intention to make a gain. This would obviously commonly be present, and would serve to distinguish theft from wanton destruction—a necessary distinction since the latter was a case of *damnum iniuria datum*.[1] It also served to exclude the compassionate release of a chained slave, which the jurists were reluctant to stigmatize as theft. The requirement was not, however, consistently carried through, and in an interpolated text it is given so wide an interpretation as to make it virtually meaningless: a man who lends a thing which he himself has borrowed is held to gain because the man to whom he lends it will feel bound to do him a good turn.

(iii) *The thing.* Any movable thing which had an owner could be the object of theft. Even children *in potestate* or a wife *in manu* were included—no doubt a survival from the primitive law in which a distinction had not yet been made between *potestas*, or *manus*, and *dominium*. Since the classical law rejected any requirement of a carrying away, the exclusion of immovables is surprising. No justification for it is offered, and some jurists thought otherwise, but their opinion did not prevail.

The plaintiff. As *furtum possessionis* shows, it is not only the owner who may bring an *actio furti*. Gaius says that anyone who has an interest in the safety of the thing may sue. This is broadly speaking true, but not every interest will suffice. An unsecured creditor, for example, cannot sue, although he has, in a sense, an interest in the safety of his debtor's property. For if the debtor is deprived of it he may be unable to pay the debt. Modern writers distinguish between a positive and a negative interest. The owner has a positive interest—his right of use, enjoyment, &c.—and so do beneficiaries of *iura in re aliena*. Any such person may sue, and the measure of the penalty will be the value of his interest. On the other hand, those persons have a negative

[1] See below, pp. 218 ff.

interest who hold the thing under a contract with the owner
(e.g. *commodatum*) which makes them liable to him if it is stolen.[1]
There are many difficulties, but it is probable that anyone who
had a negative interest could sue, provided he was not insolvent
(when his liability would be merely illusory) and provided his
liability did not arise from his *dolus*. For, ran the maxim, no one
may acquire an action by his own *dolus*. Since liability was the
criterion, and since if he were liable at all it would be for the
full value, the plaintiff with a negative interest had the action
to the exclusion of the owner.

Reipersecutory actions. If he could trace the thing, the owner had,
of course, a *vindicatio* against the present possessor, but, whether
or not he could trace it, he had an action *in personam* (*condictio
furtiva*) against the thief or his heirs. As in any *condictio*,[2] the
formula alleged that the defendant was under a duty to convey
the thing to the plaintiff, a conveyance which, since the plaintiff was still owner, was, strictly speaking, impossible, but the
illogicality was admitted, says Gaius, 'out of hatred of thieves'.
Both actions being reipersecutory, the bringing of one would bar
the other, but neither would bar, or be barred by, the bringing
of the penal *actio furti*.

Rapina. In the disturbed years of the late Republic (*c.* 77 B.C.)
a Praetor introduced an action for a fourfold penalty for violent
damage to property by armed bands. The wrong envisaged
was thus an aggravated form of *damnum iniuria datum*. It came,
however, to include also theft with violence, even if committed
by a single person, and in the settled conditions of the Empire
this was treated as the characteristic case, the action being
termed *actio vi bonorum raptorum*. It was thus simply theft with the
added element of violence, and with a penalty of fourfold. In the
law of Justinian, however, the action was treated as 'mixed',
i.e. as both penal and reipersecutory, and therefore a reipersecutory action could not be brought in addition.

3. *INIURIA*

Classical scope of the delict. In its widest sense the word *iniuria*
denotes simply unlawfulness or the absence of a right. As the

[1] See above, p. 170.   [2] See below, p. 229.

name of a particular delict, however, it bears in the classical law a more specific, but still compendious, meaning. If it is to be translated by a single English word, 'insult' or 'outrage' may serve, but neither suggests the full width of the Roman idea, which embraced any contumelious disregard of another's rights or personality. It thus included not merely physical assaults and oral or written insults and abuse, but any affront to another's dignity or reputation and any disregard of another's public or private rights, provided always that the act was done wilfully and with contumelious intent. It was *iniuria*, for example, to prevent another, without lawful justification, from moving freely in a public place, or from fishing in the sea or other public water. It was likewise *iniuria* to interfere with his use of his property or to enter unauthorized into his house or on to his land. Again, it was *iniuria* to affront a woman's modesty. Indeed such an affront might lay the wrongdoer open to more than one *actio iniuriarum*: if the woman were married, but still in *patria potestas*, not only she, but her husband and her father as well, could sue, since the affront was considered to affect them all. And *iniuria* might take more devious forms: we are told that maliciously to claim payment from my surety when I am solvent, or falsely to advertise a pledge for sale as being mine, is actionable, since my credit is impugned. Even an insult to a corpse or the defamation of the dead was actionable as an affront to the heir, though, as we have seen, an *iniuria* committed in the lifetime of the dead man gave no right of action to the heir.

Earlier development. The width and flexibility of the classical delict was the result, however, of a remarkable process of Praetorian and juristic development. The Twelve Tables provided only for physical assaults, retaliation being, as we have seen, the penalty for grave wounding, and fixed money payments for lesser injuries. In the later Republic retaliation had long been obsolete, and the fall in the value of money had deprived the fixed penalties of their efficacy. This is aptly illustrated by the story of the Roman who devised a novel amusement for himself. Followed by a slave with a purse, he went about slapping the faces of respectable persons and bidding the slave tender to each the statutory penalty of 25 *asses*. This, we are told, drove the Praetors to intervene. They did so by providing an action not for a fixed penalty but for damages. There was here no extension of the delict, but simply the provision of an alternative remedy, which caused the penalties of the Twelve Tables to fall into disuse. Subsequently, however, other remedies were introduced into the Edict for specific acts, such as public insults, affronts to the modesty of a woman, and more generally, and therefore more fruitfully, any attack on the reputation of another which might cause him to suffer *infamia*.[1] The structure of the Edict necessarily left these, and the original remedy in damages for *iniuria*, as specific and unrelated provisions, but before the end of the Republic the jurists had undertaken their characteristic work of interpretation and generalization. They held that the various acts dealt with by the Edict were simply particular applications of a general principle, implicit in *iniuria* and therefore in the original action for damages, that any affront to the dignity of the individual was actionable. It was this fertile generalization which gave birth to the classical law of *iniuria*.

Penal character. Although the Praetorian remedy was for what we should call damages, the essence of the delict was not loss but insult, and therefore the money payment must usually have represented not compensation in the ordinary sense, but rather solace for injured feelings or affronted dignity. The action had also, of course, all the other characteristics of a penal action, with the additions already noticed[2] of active intransmissibility and one year's limitation. Moreover if the Praetor considered the *iniuria* to be aggravated (*atrox*), either by the nature of the affront or by the place in which it was offered (e.g. an insult in the theatre) or by the disparity of social standing of the parties (e.g. assault on a senator by a man of low degree, or on a patron by his freedman), he would intervene to fix the damages at an enhanced figure. It would thus, in principle at least, be *atrox iniuria* to shout abuse at the Consul in the forum, whereas in English law, in which damage to the reputation and not insult is the essence of defamation, it would be no tort to offer a similar affront to the Prime Minister.[3]

---

[1] This was a penalty, entailing certain civil disabilities, which was attached to a variety of forms of disgraceful conduct.   [2] Above, p. 210.
[3] This is not to say that such conduct might not entail a criminal sanction.

4. *DAMNUM INIURIA DATUM*

While the essence of the delict of *iniuria* was insult, the essence of *damnum iniuria datum* was loss (*damnum*), and while *iniuria*, like other delicts, required a wrongful intent, it was sufficient for *damnum iniuria datum* that the loss should have been caused by culpable conduct (*iniuria datum*) whether intentional or merely negligent. For this was the wide meaning which the word '*iniuria*' came to have in this context. But not every loss was actionable, and the scope of the delict can best be understood by a study of its historical development.

Lex Aquilia. The foundation and framework of the delict were provided by two provisions, or 'chapters', of the *lex Aquilia*, passed probably in the third century B.C. The first chapter of the *lex* dealt with the killing of slaves and cattle, and imposed a penalty of the highest value that the slave or animal had had in the year preceding the killing. The purpose of this mode of calculation was probably to protect the plaintiff from fluctuations in market values, but it also had the result, for example, that if a man killed a slave who was blind when killed, but who had lost his sight only within the previous year, he would be liable for a great deal more than the loss he had actually caused.

The third[1] chapter was more general and therefore eventually more important. It provided that, in cases not covered by the first chapter, if a man caused loss to another by 'burning, breaking, or destroying' his property, he should be liable for the loss he had caused, the assessment being in this instance made at the highest point in the last[2] thirty days.

Essential elements of the delict. From these provisions the essential elements of the delict emerge. The act must be a direct application of force. (This is plainly implicit in the words 'burn, break, or destroy' and, perhaps less obviously, in 'kill'.) It must be done *iniuria*. It must result in *damnum* to the plaintiff. And the

---

[1] The second dealt with a different matter.

[2] Or the next? The provision would then have been intended to allow for the possibility that the full extent of the injury to a slave or animal might not be apparent at once. On this and other difficulties see de Zulueta, *Institutes of Gaius*, Part II, pp. 211 ff., and F. H. Lawson, *Negligence in the Civil Law*, pp. 8 ff., with references.

thing damaged must be the property of the plaintiff. All these elements were, in varying degrees, the subject of juristic or Praetorian extension in the centuries which followed the passing of the *lex*.

(i) *The act.* The earliest extensions were the work of the jurists, but these amounted to little more than an admission that the word 'destroy' (*rumpere*) must be allowed to include other forms of direct physical damage (*corrumpere*). The jurists were soon relieved of the need to force the words of the *lex* any further by the intervention of the Praetor, who granted an action on the analogy of the *lex* (*actio utilis*, also referred to as *actio in factum*) where the damage had been caused only indirectly. The jurists were thus faced with the need to distinguish between direct damage which would found an action on the *lex* (*actio directa*) and indirect damage for which the *actio utilis* was the appropriate remedy.[1] The Digest preserves many of the examples which they debated. If a midwife gave a slave-woman a drug from which she died, this was admitted (by *interpretatio*) to be 'killing' if the midwife administered the drug with her own hands, but if she gave it to the woman for her to take it herself it was only the 'providing of a cause of death' and therefore actionable by the *actio utilis*. To overdrive a mule so that it was injured, to lock up a slave so that he starved to death, to persuade him to climb a tree with the result that he fell, to cut the painter of a boat so that it was wrecked, to push one man so that he damaged the property of another—all these were held to be instances of indirect damage.

It is obvious, particularly in the last example, that the substantial issue is one of causation, and that there is a third possibility, that the damage may be so indirectly related to the act as to found no liability at all, even under the *actio utilis*. The jurists' approach is, however, characteristically casuistic, and no attempt at a systematic analysis of the problem is made. All that we have is a large number of not always easily reconciled (because unreasoned) decisions of individual cases. Moreover the question whether the act was the cause of the damage can also be expressed as one of whether the actor was at fault or not. For example, the case is put of the man who, while playing a

---

[1] Older English law made the same distinction between trespass and case, and was faced with similar problems.

game, hits the ball so hard that it hits the hand of a barber who is shaving a slave, and the slave's throat is cut. The discussion is of which party was at fault.

A related question is that of the distinction between an act and an omission. Clearly an omission could not found liability under the *lex*, but was it sufficient for the *actio utilis*? Here again the Roman contribution consists rather in the posing of the question than in the formulation of the answer. Nor is the answer easy, as modern systems have found. To penalize omissions is to impose a duty to act—a positive duty—and it is arguable that, in the absence of a contract, the policy of the law should be to impose only negative duties. To impose on me a duty to act whenever, in the infinitely variable circumstances of life, my failure to do so is likely to result in loss or injury to another, is to impose—so the argument runs—an unwarranted restriction on my freedom. Not every system is prepared to adopt so extremely individualistic an attitude, but from the scanty evidence it seems that Roman law did so—as certainly does modern English law. Even so there remains the difficulty of defining an omission, of distinguishing between a positive and a negative duty. The distinction is to some extent of course a matter of formulation. We may say, for example, that the driver of a vehicle is under a duty to drive carefully, but this is more exactly expressed as a duty not to drive carelessly. The law does not require him to drive at all, and if damage results it is caused not by an omission but by an act—the act of driving carelessly. At the other extreme, if, coming by chance upon a stranger lying bleeding in the road, I pass by on the other side, and he bleeds to death, the question whether I am responsible for his death can hardly be formulated except in terms either of the existence of a positive duty or of the imposition of liability for an omission. English law thinks in terms of the former; Roman law, since it did not employ the concept of a duty, thought probably in terms of the latter. The distinction is most difficult to make where a man voluntarily undertakes to perform an act and then does nothing (e.g. if, after one surgeon has performed an operation, another undertakes to see to the after-treatment but in fact does nothing). English law declares the second surgeon liable because he voluntarily assumed a positive duty. Roman law also made him liable, probably on the ground that by undertaking to see to the treatment he led the first surgeon to leave the case and was thus the cause of the damage.

Such questions apart, there remained outside both the action on the *lex* (for direct physical damage) and the *actio utilis* (for indirect physical damage) a third category of loss, namely that which is caused without there being any physical damage to property of the plaintiff. The troublesome case of the compassionate release of the slave[1] recurs here: the owner has suffered loss by the slave's escape, but there is no damage to the slave. It is probable that the classical law excluded such loss from the scope of the *lex Aquilia*, even as extended by the Praetor, but that in particular cases, such as that of the release of the slave, a special action on the facts was given. In the Institutes, however, Justinian sweepingly includes this third category also, and appropriates to it a remedy which he labels *actio in factum*. In effect, any loss caused by the wilful or careless act of another is declared to be actionable. But it is unlikely that he realized quite how sweeping this innovation was capable of being. No modern system has yet adopted so wide a rule, and for good reason. The law would in substance be undertaking to insure the individual against any loss which is not either purely fortuitous or the result of his own act. The example of commercial competition shows that such a rule would be unworkable. The trader who enters an existing market intends to take trade away from his competitors, or at least can foresee that this is a probable result of his act, but it would obviously be against the public interest to make him liable for the loss he causes. And is a man to be liable for all the economic consequences of a misstatement which he carelessly makes? This is not to say that it is impossible to devise a more restricted, and therefore workable, principle governing such purely pecuniary loss, but English law, at least, has not yet done so, and it is doubtful if Justinian was even aware of the problem. The classical lawyers had been content to remain in general on the firm ground of the requirement of some physical damage, allowing only occasional special actions where there was indeed no physical damage but loss had resulted from an interference with a physical thing (as in the case of the released slave). Justinian probably intended to do no more than to make express this very limited principle.

[1] See above, p. 214.

(ii) *Iniuria.* The act must be done *iniuria.* This originally meant simply *non iure*—without justification. The actor was liable unless he could show some justification, such as self-defence, necessity, or lawful authority. But it was apparently early admitted that it was sufficient to show that the damage was unavoidable; and from 'I could not help it' it is a short step to 'It was not my fault'. At any rate, in classical law *iniuria* was treated as equivalent to *dolus* or *culpa* (fault), and it was for the plaintiff to show one or the other. Questions of *culpa* are, as we have seen, not always easily distinguishable from questions of causation, and the treatment is again casuistic. *Culpa* is in one text defined as a failure to foresee what a careful man could have foreseen, but the jurists otherwise prefer to delimit its meaning by the decision of typical cases. If a man digs a bear-trap into which another's slave falls and is injured, he is liable if he dug it where people commonly go, but not if he dug it in a place where such traps are commonly placed—and so forth.

(iii) *Damnum.* The plaintiff must have suffered loss. We saw that at least in the late law an action lay for loss without damage, but at no time did an action lie for damage without loss. Normally of course damage results in loss, but exceptional cases are possible. To give a slave a black eye is to damage him but his master will not necessarily suffer any loss.

(iv) *The plaintiff's title.* The thing damaged must be the property of the plaintiff. A usufructuary, therefore, or a pledgee had no action on the *lex*, although he had suffered loss. But in these and similar cases the Praetor allowed an *actio utilis.* A much more important consequence of the strict rule was that there was no action for negligent injury to a free man not *in potestate.* 'For no one can be said to be owner of his own limbs.' (A wilful injury would constitute the delict of *iniuria.*) The free man who was negligently run down and injured in the streets of Rome had therefore no remedy. Even in this case, however, an *actio utilis* was eventually given, but probably not until the time of Justinian.

5. PRAETORIAN DELICTS

There were, as has been said, other minor delicts deriving from the civil law, and in addition the Praetor created a number of penal actions. The acts thus penalized are commonly called

Praetorian delicts.[1] We need consider only the two most important of them.

Dolus embraced any fraud or deceit practised to the detriment of another. The action was for restitution or damages in default. Because of its wide and fluid character, *dolus* might have subverted the careful structure of the other delicts, and of the law of contract as well, and it was presumably for this reason that the action could be brought only if no other of any kind were available. In the language of the civilians, it was a 'subsidiary' action.[2]

Metus was duress. If a man was induced by threats to act in some way to his own detriment, an action lay for fourfold his loss. This action had two features which, in view of this large penalty, are curious. The defendant could, as in the *actio doli*, escape liability by making restitution; and the action seems to have lain against a third party who, even innocently, acquired property which had been extorted from the plaintiff.

6. NOXAL LIABILITY

Noxal surrender. If a slave or a son *in potestate* committed a delict the master or father was liable for the penalty, but could avoid it by making 'noxal surrender' of the wrongdoer to the injured person. This, at least, was the way the classical lawyers expressed the law, but it in fact reverses the original order of ideas. The liability was that of the wrongdoer, and the injured person could take vengeance on him. But this produced a clash between the right of vengeance of the injured person and the *potestas* of the master or father, which was resolved by allowing the latter as it were to 'buy off' the injured person by paying the penalty. The true character of this noxal liability is plain from the rule that it followed the wrongdoer (*noxa caput sequitur*). This meant that if the slave was, for example, manumitted before the action was brought, he himself was liable to an ordinary action; or if he were sold, the noxal action lay against his new owner. It was even sufficient for the master to surrender the slave's dead body, and one macabre text debates whether merely his hair and

---

[1] The term is not Roman.

[2] Much the same principle was invoked in English law until the seventeenth century to justify restricting the scope of 'case'. But 'case' eventually broke through and took over the field of other actions, whereas the *actio doli* remained 'subsidiary'.

nails would suffice (probably for their magical significance as symbols of life and growth).

Damage by animals. It is at first sight paradoxical to speak of the 'liability' of a slave since he was in law a thing, but the noxal liability of slaves and sons is only one aspect of what may be called 'thing-liability', which is commonly found in primitive law. The thing that did the act—the weapon, for example—is tainted and must be surrendered.[1] Roman law, indeed, did not apply the principle to inanimate things, but it did recognize noxal surrender of animals. If an animal did damage, its owner could be required, by the *actio de pauperie* deriving from the Twelve Tables, either to compensate the injured person or noxally to surrender the animal. The efficacy of this remedy in the case of wild animals was marred by the principle that once they had escaped they had no owner, and the Aediles accordingly, in exercise of their jurisdiction over public ways, forbade the keeping of wild animals near such ways, and gave actions for any damage which resulted from disregard of this prohibition. In the late law there intrudes into the law of *pauperies* the curious principle that there is liability only if the animal acted in a way which was contrary to the nature of its species. It can be said therefore that just as a man must act as a reasonable man or be liable for any physical damage he causes, so also a horse must act, if the expression be permitted, as a reasonable horse. Wild animals are now altogether excluded, since it is in their nature to do damage.

7. QUASI-DELICT

The Institutes add the category (which in the Digest is attributed to a work of Gaius) of obligations which arise *quasi ex delicto*.[2] Four of these are listed. The judge who misconducts a case or gives a wrong decision (*qui litem suam fecerit*, meaning literally 'who makes a suit his own') is liable to the party who is

---

[1] In English law the surrender was to the Crown (originally for pious uses, as the name 'deodand' shows) and was not abolished until 1846, when the possibility of the surrender of a guilty railway engine drove Parliament to action.

[2] The noun 'quasi-delict' and its counterpart, 'quasi-contract', were given currency in the Middle Ages, but both are found in the Paraphrase of the Institutes by Theophilus.

thereby prejudiced. The occupier of a building is liable for double the damage caused by anything thrown or poured out of the building, no matter by whom, on to a public place. He is similarly liable to a penalty, at the suit of anyone who cares to claim, if he keeps any object suspended from the building which would do damage if it fell. Finally, a ship-owner or the keeper of an inn or stable is liable for any theft or damage caused by slaves or employees, or, in the case of the innkeeper, of permanent residents.

Why were these four cases, and these four alone, placed in this category? This question has been debated down the centuries, but no wholly satisfactory answer has been found. The most influential, in that it has found its way into French law and some of the systems derived from it, and into Scots law, is that a delict is an intentional wrong, and a quasi-delict a merely careless one. The obvious objection to this answer is the fact that *damnum iniuria datum* did not require a wrongful intent.[1] Another answer is that the essence of quasi-delict is vicarious liability: the occupier of a building, the innkeeper, &c., are liable for acts committed by others. But, on the one hand, noxal liability should then also have been included, and, on the other, the liability of the judge can be treated as vicarious only by a rather forced interpretation—that by 'making one party's suit his own' he assumed that party's liability. A third answer is that the essence is strict liability, i.e. liability without fault, but to this the case of the judge is again an obstacle. For the texts attribute to him at least imprudence or lack of skill, and, as we have seen, lack of skill was treated as *culpa*. In the classical law, however, it seems that his liability was indeed strict, and if the Digest's attribution of the category to Gaius is correct this may have been its original basis, but in the time of Justinian it must have been forgotten. For the text as it is presented in the Digest and in the Institutes offers both the first and the second of the answers given above, but without explaining how they are to be reconciled. The first is used to explain the cases of the judge and of the ship-owner, innkeeper, and stable-keeper (the latter should have chosen their employees and permanent residents with more care), and the second to explain the others.

[1] The devices adopted to escape this difficulty cannot be discussed here. On this and other points, see an article by P. Stein in *International and Comparative Law Quarterly*, 4 (1955), pp. 356 ff.

8. MODERN LAW

Civil law. We have seen that the Roman law of delicts, like the law of contracts, had no general principle. It was a law of specific wrongs. Two stand out, however, for their generality: *iniuria* and *damnum iniuria datum.* On the basis of these the Civil law has built a general theory of civil wrongs. The extreme example of this generality is provided by the French Civil Code, which devotes only five of its 2,281 articles to 'Delict and Quasi-delict'. This brevity has, however, cast upon the courts a burden which, by the standards of a codified system, is excessive. Other codes are more explicit but still adhere to the principle of generality. Needless to say, the penal character of the Roman law has quite disappeared.

Common law. English law has a system of specific torts and is therefore at first sight more akin to the Roman law than is the modern civil law. There is, however, an important difference (apart from that between penalty and compensation) which must be understood before any comparison is attempted between the law of delicts and the law of torts. The English common law has no actions *in rem* in the Roman sense and no purely possessory remedies. The remedies for the law of property are provided by the law of torts. Thus, if a possessor wishes to assert his possession against a person who disputes it, he must claim that the latter has committed the tort of trespass; if it is title (to goods) that is in issue, he must allege the tort of conversion or detinue; or if it is his right to an easement, he must allege nuisance, and so forth. And since it must be possible to assert such property rights against even a defendant who acts in good faith or who is unaware that he is interfering with them, these torts are of strict liability[1]—they are independent of fault. So it is that the tort of conversion, for example, which bears some resemblance to *furtum,* can be committed by one who believes in good faith that the goods are his. Moreover, since interference with property rights may occur without the plaintiff's suffering any loss, damage is not of the essence of these torts. On the other hand,

---

[1] Or used to be: the growth of the tort of negligence is having its influence on these torts also.

the remedies are not exclusively proprietary in function. The plaintiff may be concerned not to assert his title (which the defendant may not dispute) but to secure compensation for damage done. They are two-faced remedies, serving sometimes to assert title, sometimes to obtain compensation for a wrong. The Roman law, on the other hand, keeps clearly distinct the two functions. For although in an action on the *lex Aquilia*, for example, the plaintiff's title may be in issue, since he must be prepared to show that he is owner, the essence of the action is the wrong and the damage, and conversely, while in a *vindicatio* the plaintiff may obtain compensation for the deterioration of the thing, the central issue is one of title. It is only with those torts therefore, such as defamation and negligence, in which compensation is the exclusive purpose of the remedy (or, to put it in another way, in which the plaintiff need show no title, but simply damage) that any strict comparison is possible.

III. QUASI-CONTRACT

The basis of this category, though unsatisfactory, is at least clear. There remained a certain number of obligations which could not be said to arise *ex contractu*, since there had been no agreement, and could even less well be said to arise *ex delicto*, since the person obliged had done no wrongful act (and was amenable not to a penal but to a reipersecutory action). These obligations were therefore said, rather lamely, to arise *quasi ex contractu*. The basis is purely negative, though the use of the noun 'quasi-contract'[1] has sometimes encouraged an explanation in terms of an implied or fictitious contract.

Some of these obligations are merely incidental to the law of persons, things, or succession, and therefore need not be further discussed here. They are the obligations between *tutor* and *pupillus*, between joint-owners or joint-heirs, and between heir and legatee. The others, however, are of considerable importance, and are among the most characteristic of the Roman contributions to modern Civil law.

Negotiorum gestio. The history and classical form of this institution are in many respects obscure, and it is therefore possible here

---

[1] See above, p. 224, n. 2.

only to give an outline of it as it appears in the *Corpus Iuris*. It is the voluntary and unauthorized 'management of the affairs' of another, and it creates an imperfectly bilateral relationship[1] akin to that resulting from mandate. The primary duty is that of the 'manager' (*gestor*) to carry through what he has undertaken, and in doing so to show the care of a *bonus paterfamilias*, and to account for any proceeds. But for the history of legal ideas it is the contingent duty of the person whose affairs have been managed (whom we shall call 'the principal') which is the more important. He must reimburse the *gestor* for such reasonable expenses, if any, as he incurs.

The term 'management of affairs' can be misleading. Even an isolated act will constitute a *gestio*. The *gestor* may, for example, have shored up a building which was in danger of collapse, or have treated a sick slave; he may have collected a debt owing to the principal, or made himself surety for a debt which the principal owed; or he may in any other way have cared for the principal's property or protected his rights.

But more is needed than simply a voluntary and unauthorized *gestio*. The law does not require the principal to pay the cost of every unauthorized service he receives. The *gestio* must have been 'useful', in the sense of being something which the principal himself would have done, and the principal must have been absent, or at least incapable of expressing his wishes. (If he was both present and capable, and made no objection, this will amount to a tacit mandate.) But if the *gestio* was 'useful' when first undertaken, the principal could not object that he had nevertheless derived no benefit from it (e.g. because the slave who was treated nevertheless died, or because the building which was shored up caught fire and was destroyed). For the underlying purpose of the law was to encourage the protection of absentees' interests by indemnifying those who undertook neighbourly acts.

The state of mind of the *gestor* is relevant in two ways. In the first place, he must have been aware that the 'affair' was that of another. The man who, for example, has made repairs to a building in the erroneous belief that it is his own, cannot claim

---

[1] See above, p. 169, n.1. The primary duty is sanctioned by the *actio negotiorum gestorum directa* and the contingent by the *actio negotiorum gestorum contraria*. Both actions are *bonae fidei*.

to have 'managed an affair' of the owner.[1] On the other hand, it will be no obstacle that he thought the building belonged to A, whereas in fact it belonged to B. For in this case he knew the 'affair' was that of another and was mistaken only as to the identity of that other. In the second place, the *gestor* must have expected to be indemnified, or, to put it in a more realistic way, he must not have acted exclusively from motives either of liberality or personal advantage.

The kinship with mandate is close, so that if the principal, when he becomes aware of the *gestio*, accepts it, this will constitute a ratification so as to make him liable to an *actio mandati* and, what is more important, to debar him from subsequently questioning the 'usefulness' of the *gestio*.

Negotiorum gestio, with some alterations and extensions, has passed into all Civil law systems, and constitutes one of the most marked divergences, though a minor one, between the Civil law and the Common law. The latter insists on the individualistic principle that a man should not be required to pay for a service for which he has not asked, and holds that to encourage the rendering of such services would be to encourage the 'officious intermeddler'. The requirements of *negotiorum gestio*, however, and in particular that of 'usefulness' coupled with the restriction of the action to the recovery of expenses, offer in fact little scope for such officiousness.

The condictio. We have already encountered this remedy more than once. It was a *stricti iuris* action claiming a certain sum of money or a certain thing, and it was unique in that its *formula* stated no cause or ground; it simply alleged that the defendant was under a duty to convey to the plaintiff a certain sum or a certain thing.[2] Its scope was therefore wider than that of other actions. Its applications, as far as we know, were three. It lay to enforce the obligation arising from a stipulation (provided, of course, that it was for a certain sum or thing) or from a literal contract, and any obligation created *re*, in the older and more restricted sense of the term. It is with this last aspect that we are here concerned.

---

[1] If he is still in possession of the building he will be adequately protected (see above, p. 135). See also below, pp. 231 f.

[2] See above, pp. 24 f.

We have seen that, in the classification which Gaius eventually rejected, the obligations arising both from *mutuum* and from the receipt of what was not owing were classed together, as being sanctioned by the *condictio* and as arising from a transfer of ownership by the plaintiff to the defendant. In both cases the defendant owned what the plaintiff ought to own, and therefore he was bound to make restitution. This is the basis of the *condictio* in this context. *Mutuum* was, as we have seen, eventually isolated as contract, leaving the receipt of what was not owing to fall into the category of quasi-contract. This was, however, only one example of the quasi-contractual applications of the *condictio*. There were others also. Since the *formula* of the *condictio* was the same in all cases the classical law had no clear-cut classification, but the treatment in the *Corpus Iuris* adopted certain headings which passed into the language of the Civil law and are still often used, particularly in German law.

The *condictio indebiti* lay in the case of a payment or conveyance of what was not owing. The *condictio ob causam datorum* or *causa data causa non secuta* applied principally to the situation eventually classified as an innominate contract, and it has been considered in that context,[1] but it applied also where there was no contractual element. This was the case of *donatio sub modo*, i.e. a gift to be applied in a certain way. If A gives B property to be held as *dos* on his expected marriage to C, and the marriage does not take place, A can claim restitution. The *condictio ob turpem vel iniustam causam* lay where the payment or conveyance had been made for an immoral or illegal purpose (e.g. to induce the recipient not to commit a crime, or to return what he had borrowed and was wrongfully refusing to return). But the plaintiff must not be equally tainted by the 'turpitude', as he would be, for example, if the payment had been made to induce the recipient to commit a crime.

In all these cases the basis of the claim was that there was no justification (*causa*) for the defendant's retaining what he had received. Justinian, however, added the further heading of *condictio sine causa*. This, if taken literally, would embrace all the preceding cases, but it seems to have been intended merely as a residual category, to accommodate cases which might not fall precisely under any of the other headings, and, in particular,

[1] Above, pp. 189 ff.

the case where there had initially been a *causa* for the defendant's retaining what he had received, but that *causa* had subsequently ceased to exist (e.g. where he retained the plaintiff's written acknowledgement of a debt after the debt had been paid).[1]

Thus far the *condictio* enforces restitution only where the defendant unjustifiably retains a certain sum or thing which has been conveyed to him by the plaintiff. This duty of restitution is, however, declared to be founded on a much wider principle of 'natural justice', that no one should be enriched at the expense of another. This principle of 'unjust enrichment' is one of the entirely original Roman contributions to legal thought. It has become a part of all Civil law systems, but has hitherto been rejected by English law.[2] It deserves therefore further examination.

Unjust enrichment. The hostility which the principle arouses and the difficulties which it encounters derive from the fact that it claims to correct the law by an appeal to justice. Thus, where A has conveyed a thing to B in the mistaken belief that it is owing, the conveyance is valid, but the injustice is rectified by allowing A a *condictio*. The law could simply have declared the conveyance to be void, but this would have had the inconvenient result that, for example, C, a subsequent purchaser from B, would have found himself without title. The law, therefore, prefers to give one answer in terms of rights *in rem*, and another in terms of rights *in personam*. In this instance this is obviously reasonable, and English law does likewise, but more difficult cases may arise. If, in the example given above, C paid less than the value of the thing or received it as a gift (and B, we may suppose, is insolvent), can it be said that C is unjustly enriched at the expense of A? Or if A lends money to B, who lends it to C, who spends it, can A claim from C if B is insolvent? To do so would be to allow him to circumvent the rule of privity of contract, at least to the extent that C is enriched. Again, if A, unasked, renders B a service which is not sufficiently 'useful' to constitute *negotiorum gestio* but nonetheless enriches B, can A claim from B? Or what if A makes improvements to B's house in the belief that it is his own, but is no longer in possession?

[1] Civilians call the remedy in this type of case *condictio ob causam finitam*.
[2] Its fortune has been different in the United States.

The law has accorded B the right *in rem*, but cannot A assert a right *in personam* to the extent of B's enrichment?[1] And, if so, could it not be said that where B has acquired A's property by prescription the law likewise intends only to determine the question of the right *in rem*, leaving open that of the right *in personam*?

In cases such as these—and the list could be almost endless—the simple principle that a man should not be unjustly enriched at the expense of another is an uncertain guide, and unless settled rules of law are to be freely subverted, the principle requires restriction and definition. The classical law met this need by allowing the *condictio* only where there had been a direct conveyance of a certain sum or thing by the plaintiff to the defendant. All the cases suggested above were thus arbitrarily excluded. In the later law recovery was allowed even where the benefit conferred on the defendant did not result from the conveyance of a certain sum or thing (*condictio incerti*), but, here as elsewhere, the extension was made by piecemeal alterations of classical texts, and the limits of the remedy are therefore not clear. It was left to the Civilians, and especially to the German jurists of the nineteenth century, whose work is embodied in the German Civil Code, to make the *condictio* a workable general remedy for unjust enrichment.

But there have also been other routes within the Civil law tradition by which the principle of unjust enrichment has entered modern systems. We have seen that *negotiorum gestio* was excluded where the person claiming to be *gestor* had mistakenly thought that the 'affair' was his own, and also where, though he knew that the 'affair' was that of another, he had acted entirely in his own interest. In these cases some Roman texts allowed an action to the extent of the principal's enrichment only. In later centuries many civilians were prepared to extend this *negotiorum gestio utilis* even to the case where the principal had forbidden the *gestio*. The language is still that of *negotiorum gestio*, but so flat a rejection of a fundamental principle makes it obvious that what has in fact emerged is a general remedy for unjust enrichment.

Elsewhere, notably in French law, the remedy has taken a different, though still ostensibly Roman, form, but whatever

[1] See above, p. 135. *Specificatio* presents the same problem (p. 137).

the form taken, it has usually been kept within bounds by an insistence on the Roman requirements of directness or of lack of cause or by a close definition of enrichment. This is reflected in a preference for the term 'unjustified' rather than 'unjust' enrichment.

V

LAW OF SUCCESSION

WE have so far been concerned with the legal clothing which a man wears in life—his rights and duties. Any system of law must make some provision for the disposal of that clothing when life ends. The provision may indeed be crude. A primitive system, which sees a man's property as merely physical objects, may make provision for the disposal of those objects only, allowing his intangible assets and his liabilities to lapse. Again, a primitive system will usually dispose of the legal clothing according to fixed rules—by dividing it among the children for example, or by giving it to the eldest son, or by allowing some of it to lapse to the dead man's overlord. And it will not usually give any recognition to the dead man's wishes.

This part of Roman law is chiefly remarkable in three ways—for its precocious recognition of the dead man's last will, for the bulk and complexity with which the lawyers endowed it in its maturity, and above all for the rigorous application of the principle on which the whole structure rested, that of universal succession.

Of the early appearance of the will and of its later development more must be said later. Here it is enough to notice that it was to this institution that the law owed its bulk and complexity. A quarter of the Digest, and an even larger proportion of the Institutes, is devoted to succession on death, all but a small fraction being concerned with one aspect or another of the law of wills. Various reasons can be found for this predominance of succession on death. On the one hand there is the lawyers' robust belief, characteristic of their class and time, in the virtues, indeed the inevitability, of a liberal system of private property, of the right of every man to do as he will with his own. On the other hand, here more than anywhere else one meets the lawyer's essential conservatism and his reluctance to embark on any extensive systematization or simplification of the law. Old institutions were allowed to survive alongside newer (usually Praetorian) devices, even though these devices had been introduced precisely because the old institutions were not in keeping with new needs and new values. But duplication of this kind accounts only for part of the complexity of the law. In a developed system the law of wills is inevitably complicated, as English law shows. Questions of construction and interpretation are as varied as the ingenuity or ineptitude of testators, and these questions give full scope to that delight in details and fine distinctions which was as much a feature of the Roman lawyer's mind as his reluctance to systematize and to simplify. Our concern here, however, is with the essential framework of this elaborate structure, and first of all with its foundation-stone, the principle of universal succession. (The term itself is modern.)

I. GENERAL PRINCIPLES—CIVIL LAW

Universal succession. By this is meant the succession of one man (or several jointly) to the sum of the rights and duties of another. The legal personality of the one is merged in that of the other. This simple statement needs however some qualification. There are some pieces of a man's legal clothing which, at any rate according to ideas which we share with the Romans, can be worn by no one else. Marriage provides an obvious example. Less obvious perhaps are other rights deriving from the law of persons, such as *patria potestas* and *tutela*. There is, in short, succession only to 'patrimonial' rights—those rights which are included in the law of property and the law of obligations. Even here some exceptions must be made. Whether or not Roman law ever went through the primitive stage, mentioned above, in which only tangible property passed to the successor, some of the obligations arising out of delict and an unimportant handful of those arising out of contract retained a personal character to the end. And, in the law of property, personal servitudes were by their very nature incapable of surviving. On the other hand, and this was an important factor in the early centuries of Roman history, the conduct of the family religious rites, the *sacra*, also passed to the universal successor.

Universal succession might occur in several ways, by *adrogatio*, for example, or by the acquisition of *manus* over a woman already *sui iuris*, but by far the most important is that with which we are here concerned, universal succession on death.

Any treatment of this subject must ultimately fall into two

parts according as there is or is not a will, but some fundamental notions are common to both.

Heres, hereditas. The universal successor on death is the *heres*, and the complex of rights and duties (the *universitas iuris*) to which he succeeds is the *hereditas.* The *heres* may be appointed ('instituted') by will, or if there is no will he may be designated by law, but a *heres* there must be. Without a *heres* no succession can take place. For the prime purpose of the Roman will (and of the rules of intestacy) is to ensure the devolution of the *hereditas* as a whole. It may also effect a distribution of property, but this, if it occurs, is only a secondary consequence.

A glance at modern English law may make this peculiarity clearer. An English will usually appoints an executor (or executors) to wind up the estate and to carry out the wishes of the testator, but the executor is only superficially the counterpart of the *heres.* On the one hand the appointment of an executor is not essential. If none is appointed or none of those named is willing to act, the court will appoint an administrator; but if a Roman will omitted to institute a *heres*, or the instituted *heres* refused to act, the will was void and an intestacy resulted. On the other hand the modern executor is not a successor in the Roman sense. There is no merger of the two legal personalities. The executor is merely a personal representative appointed to carry out the wishes of the testator, and he is therefore neither liable for debts of the testator in excess of the assets, nor entitled to any surplus not expressly disposed of by him. The *heres*, on the other hand, takes both burden and benefit. Thus, the *damnosa hereditas* (in which the liabilities exceed the assets) presents, as we shall see, a stock problem to the Roman lawyer. Equally, the right of the *heres* to any undistributed surplus is fundamental to the idea of universal succession. It is, for example, implicit in the maxim that a man cannot die partly testate and partly intestate,[1] i.e. that a man cannot by will dispose of only part of his estate, allowing the rest to pass, as it would in English law and in other systems, to those entitled on intestacy. Thus, if a man makes a will in which he institutes X his *heres* to the extent of half his *hereditas*, and says nothing of the other half, the law, seeing only one *heres* and holding that a *heres* can

---

[1] 'Nemo pro parte testatus pro parte intestatus decedere potest.'

only succeed to the whole *hereditas*, will accord to him the whole. (The logical alternative was to declare the will void for lack of a *heres*, but the Romans had, as we shall see,[1] a deep-rooted dislike of intestacy.)

Nor was the possibility of appointing several *heredes* to different shares any contradiction of the principle of universal succession. They succeeded not to separate parts of the *hereditas*, but to undivided shares of the whole. Thus, if X was appointed *heres* to a quarter, and Y to three quarters, each was joint owner, in those proportions, of everything comprised in the *hereditas* (and was liable for the debts in the same proportions). The ownership was divided, not the things themselves: if the *hereditas* included a four-acre field, X was entitled, not to one acre, but to a quarter share of the whole field. Any joint *heres* could call for a division of the common property, and in historical times this was no doubt what usually happened, but the principle of the unity of the *hereditas* persisted.

This continuation of the dead man in his *heres* or *heredes* probably had its roots in social and religious rather than in economic considerations. It manifested the continuity of the patriarchal family and ensured that there should be someone on whom the duty of maintaining the family *sacra* would devolve. Thus the first principle of the early law of succession is that the inheritance devolves on the dead man's children. Their joint succession is, as Gaius puts it, *legitima simul ac naturalis*—derived on the one hand from man-made law but on the other hand expressing the natural continuation of the *paterfamilias* in his children. The idea that the children *in potestate* of the dead man have, as it were, a vested right in the inheritance survives long after the agnatic family and its *sacra* have lost their hold on men's loyalties. But this is to anticipate.

Types of heres. Though all *heredes* are alike in that they are universal successors, they differ in that some acquire the character of *heres* automatically—without their consent and even without their knowledge—whereas others do so only if and when they make a voluntary act of acceptance. Three types must be distinguished—

    (*a*) *Sui heredes.* The *suus heres* is the 'family' *heres* who has just

[1] Below, p. 251.

been mentioned. He must now be more accurately defined. He is any person in the *potestas* or *manus* of the dead man who becomes *sui iuris* by his death. The principle is exclusively agnatic. The wife *in manu* takes her place along with the sons and daughters *in potestate* and with any adopted children. They are all jointly *sui heredes*. Conversely, emancipated children or children given in adoption are excluded.

It is the *sui heredes* who are primarily entitled on the death of the *paterfamilias*, and their vested interest in the family property in early law is reflected in their name. They are 'heirs to themselves'. As Gaius puts it, even in the lifetime of their father they are in some way already owners of the family property. In this we hear an echo of the conception of the *paterfamilias* as the transitory head of a self-perpetuating organism, as the trustee of the family property rather than the absolute owner. This conception had of course long since disappeared and had been replaced by that of the *paterfamilias* as Gaius knew him, an autocrat enjoying in his lifetime untrammelled powers of alienation over the family property, and able by will to pass it quite outside the agnatic relationship. The notion of the vested rights of the *sui heredes* had become an anachronism, but, with many other anachronisms, it survived to complicate the law and to provide pitfalls for the unwary testator.

Since the *sui* succeeded to property which was in this vestigial sense already theirs, the succession took effect immediately on the death of the *paterfamilias*. The continuity of the family is reflected here also. There was no gap in the ownership of the family property or in the conduct of the family *sacra*. 'The King is dead, long live the King' expresses the same principle. The *sui*, moreover, had no power of refusal. They were *sui et necessarii*. The continuity of the family is more important than the interests of the individual.

The *suus heres* is the model of the universal successor. The others are formed more or less after this model, but it is only in the *suus* that the peculiarities of the Roman institution find their explanation.

(*b*) *Extranei heredes*. The *hereditas* might pass to persons outside the family—either by a properly drafted will or, in the absence of *sui heredes*, by the rules of intestate succession. These *extranei heredes* differed from the *sui* in that their succession was neither

automatic nor immediate. They had a choice (and are therefore also called *heredes voluntarii*), and they did not acquire
the character of *heres* until they had manifested their decision
to 'enter upon' the inheritance (*adire hereditatem*), either by a set
form of words (*cretio*) or by an act which could be construed as
showing that they had made such a decision (*pro herede gestio*). As
to this last there was much subtle argument, and the prospective
heres anxious to discover whether the *hereditas* was worth entering upon had to tread carefully.

(*c*) *Necessarii heredes.* If there were no *sui heredes*, the testator,
or at any rate the financially embarrassed testator, had to
reckon with the possibility that the *extranei* whom he had
instituted as his *heredes* might refuse to enter upon the *hereditas*.
There would then be at best an intestacy, and probably a posthumous bankruptcy as well, and neither prospect was welcome
to the Roman gentleman. The law met this difficulty by the
device of the *heres necessarius* (as opposed to the *heres suus et
necessarius*). He was a slave of the testator who was set free by
the will and instituted heir. As the name indicates, he had no
power of refusal, and, like the *suus*, became heir automatically
on the death of the testator. The possibility of an intestacy was
thus excluded, and though the risk of a bankruptcy remained,
it would be a bankruptcy of the newly emancipated slave.
Moreover the lawyers found a way of releasing him from the
material consequences of this bankruptcy. This is, however, only
one aspect of a wider topic— the inconveniences which followed
from the strict application of the principle of universal succession.

Devices to mitigate the inconveniences of universal succession. There
were three principal inconveniences: (i) the burden on the *heres*
of the *damnosa hereditas*; (ii) the converse difficulty of the heavily
indebted *heres* of a solvent man; (iii) the quandary in which the
heres extraneus might find himself, that it was difficult to discover
whether the inheritance was worth accepting without entering on
it. All these inconveniences derived directly from the principle of
universal succession, and any direct attack on them would have
struck at the root of the whole system. From such drastic
measures the lawyers were, as always, averse. The Praetor's
Edict could achieve the substance of what was needed, while
leaving the formal statement of the law unaltered. The devices

used are complicated and technical, but they provide a good illustration of the methods of Praetorian law reform.

(i) The burden of the *damnosa hereditas* falls on the *heres suus et necessarius* equally with the *heres necessarius*, but the means devised to relieve them differed.

(*a*) *Separatio bonorum in favour of heres necessarius.* As we have seen, the testator's usual purpose in instituting such a *heres* was to prevent the stigma of insolvency from attaching to his name. This would happen if the selling up of the estate by the creditors, which was the consequence and the public manifestation of insolvency, took place in the testator's name. It was important therefore that the sale should be of the estate of the manumitted slave, and that any actions brought in the course of getting in the estate should be brought in his name. This purpose of the testator's was achieved by the automatic entry of the heir on the inheritance, but there remained the other consequence that the heir was saddled with any debts which had not been satisfied by the sale of the inheritance. It was doubtless no part of the testator's purpose to confer this benefit on the creditors, and the lawyers saw no reason to insist on it. The Praetor's Edict therefore provided that the *heres necessarius* might ask that the assets which he acquired after the death of the testator, i.e. those which he acquired in his own capacity, should be kept separate from those which he had acquired by succession. In this way both the formal legal position that the heir was liable for the testator's debts would be maintained, and the substantial result of reversing the principle of universal succession would be achieved.

(*b*) *Relief of the heres suus et necessarius.* Here the Romans saw no reason why the *suus* rather than the dead man should bear the stigma of insolvency. The Praetor therefore gave the different relief of allowing the heir to 'abstain from the inheritance' (sometimes called *beneficium abstinendi*). The selling up of the estate took place in the name of the dead man, and the Praetor simply refused to grant any actions against the heir. The heir was thus able to abstain from the disadvantageous consequences of his position, but he was nevertheless still heir. In consequence the will still took effect as far as possible: the appointment of a tutor, for example, was valid, and if, when the creditors had been satisfied, there was after all a surplus, the heir and the legatees, if any, were entitled to it in the ordinary way.

(ii) *Separatio bonorum in favour of creditors.* The converse case presented a similar difficulty. The inheritance might be solvent and the heir (whether *suus* or *extraneus*) not. In this case the creditors of the dead man (and the wealthier a man the more likely he is to have creditors) might be unfairly disappointed of their expectations by having to share equally with the creditors of the heir. The device which the Praetor adopted was another form of *separatio bonorum.* The dead man's creditors could ask for the two estates to be kept separate until their claims had been satisfied.

(iii) *Beneficium inventarii.* The problem facing the *heres extraneus* was different. He could choose whether to accept or refuse the inheritance, but the choice might be difficult without an investigation of the solvency of the inheritance, and an adequate investigation might be construed as *pro herede gestio.* From this dilemma the law provided no escape until Justinian allowed the *beneficium inventarii.* If the heir made an inventory of the inheritance, which must be begun within 30 days of his knowing of his right and completed within a further 60, he would not be liable beyond the assets. This made, in effect, a fundamental alteration in the character of the *heres.* He now resembled the modern executor and residuary legatee. He was only liable for the debts to the extent of the estate, and he was entitled to any undistributed residue. But the parallel must not be pressed too far. He could still refuse the inheritance altogether, and then the rule that without an heir a will is void would still apply. And if he accepted but did not choose to take an inventory, or took it too late, the old law still held good.

In the different social conditions of the medieval and modern world the *suus heres* and the *heres necessarius* had of course no place, but the principle of universal succession was retained and with it the *beneficium inventarii* and the *separatio bonorum* in favour of the creditors. They still exist in French law, though the German Civil Code, while maintaining the principle of universal succession, has devised other means to mitigate its disadvantages.

Semel heres, semper heres. 'Once an heir, always an heir.' This maxim, coined by the commentators, expresses a last fundamental principle of universal succession. It is indeed implicit in much of what has gone before. The *hereditas* as a whole, or the quality of being *heres*, cannot be shifted from one person to another. This principle has two practical consequences: the *heres* cannot transfer the *hereditas* to another person; and the testator cannot provide that first one person shall be *heres* for a certain time (or for life), and then another person shall succeed.

(i) *Heres may not transfer hereditas*. He cannot, either before or after entry, make another person *heres* in his place, either by an act of transfer or by revoking his acceptance and allowing the person next entitled to enter. He could, and commonly did, sell the inheritance in the sense that he sold the corporeal things included in it, and transferred any rights by *cessio actionum*, but he was still *heres*, and so would still be liable for the debts. He therefore habitually exacted from the purchaser an undertaking by stipulation to indemnify him against any liability. Technicalities of the forms of action apart, he might then seem to have achieved the practical result of making the purchaser *heres*. The insolvency or disappearance of the purchaser would, however, show that he had not.

There was one exception to the inalienability of the *hereditas* (though not to the principle *semel heres, semper heres*). By the civil law the person entitled on intestacy if there were no *sui heredes* was the nearest agnate.[1] Gaius tells us that he could, before entry, convey the *hereditas* by *in iure cessio* (the method appropriate to such a *res incorporalis*) and would thereby make the recipient *heres*. This power was not however extended to the testamentary heir, perhaps because it would have enabled him to exclude the person next entitled under the will and thereby to defeat the intention of the testator.

The lawyers devised an ingenious method by which a testator could enable his *hereditas* to be transferred before entry. If he wished to give to X the choice of either entering on the inheritance or transferring it to someone else, he would institute as his *heres* not X but one of X's slaves. The slave was not of course capable of being *heres*, but would by entry acquire the *hereditas*, like any other property, for his master. Since, however, a *hereditas* included liabilities as well as assets, and since

---

[1] See below, p. 248.

a slave could not burden his master without his consent, the slave could make no effective entry on the *hereditas* without his master's authorization. On the other hand, since it was the slave and not X who was named in the will, it was the slave who must enter, and it would be the slave's master at the time of the entry who would acquire the inheritance. If, therefore, X sold the slave before he had entered, the purchaser would acquire not merely the slave but also the power to acquire the inheritance. He was in effect buying the slave together with an option on the inheritance, and this would of course be reflected in the purchase price. The *hereditas* could in this way be made freely negotiable.

(ii) *Testator may not appoint successive heredes*. From the principle *semel heres, semper heres* it also followed that a testator could not provide that X should be *heres* and on X's death (or after a certain time) Y should be *heres*. This meant that the common provision in a modern English will, 'to my wife for life and then to my children', was not in the old civil law open to the Roman testator. He could indeed partially achieve his object by giving his wife a usufruct of specific things, but even this would be restricted, until the recognition of quasi-usufruct, to non-fungible things. In the early Empire, however, the development of the *fideicommissum hereditatis*[1] did at last make possible the creation of successive interests in the *hereditas*.

2. PRAETORIAN LAW—*BONORUM POSSESSIO*

We have already seen that the Praetor intervened in some cases to mitigate the rigours of the civil law principles of universal succession. We must now consider the device of *bonorum possessio*, which enabled him to intervene in a much more general way and to create in several fields that duplication of institutions which does so much to complicate any presentation of the law, but which enabled the law to adjust itself to the changing needs of society. Here too the treatment must ultimately fall into two parts, according as there is or is not a will, but the main principles are common to both.

General principles of bonorum possessio. The Praetor could not change the Civil law. If he found, for example, that by their

[1] See below, p. 268, and above, pp. 145 ff.

exclusive emphasis on agnatic ties the provisions for intestacy laid down in the Twelve Tables denied the inheritance to cognates, who had, according to the ideas of a later time, an equal or better claim, he could not simply declare that such cognates were *heredes*. He could no more confer upon a man the quality of *heres* than he could relieve him of it. But he could authorize him to take possession of the property, and that possession would by usucapion ripen into ownership after a year. The Edict defined the classes of person to whom this authorization would be given, and the authorization was known as a grant of *bonorum possessio*. (This is rather misleading. Possession, being a matter of actual control, could not be created by a mere authorization. The grant was really of the legal means of obtaining possession from the present possessor. It also provided the *iusta causa* for the usucapion.) The position of such a *bonorum possessor* meanwhile was the same as that of any other *bona fide possessor* on the way to usucapion.[1] As against anyone except the *heres* he was secure, since if he were in possession no one else could show the title necessary to claim the inheritance from him, and if he were out of possession he had the usual Praetorian remedies. As against the *heres*, however, though he could obtain possession, the only advantage of doing so was that the burden of proof in the subsequent action would be on the *heres*. He would not ultimately be successful. *Bonorum possessio* was then described as *sine re*—the *bonorum possessor* could not keep the inheritance.

Bonorum possessio was not always *sine re*. If the Praetor wished to make it effective even against the *heres*, he could do so quite simply by giving to the *bonorum possessor* a defence (*exceptio doli*) to bar the action of the *heres*. The *bonorum possessio* was then said to be *cum re*. The *bonorum possessor* would be able to keep the inheritance. Moreover *bonorum possessio* was not given only to persons who were not *heredes*. The Praetor did not always correct the civil law; he sometimes merely supplemented it. The classes of person to whom the Edict promised *bonorum possessio* sometimes therefore included the *heres* himself. And the *bonorum possessio* of the *heres* was inevitably *cum re*, since there was no one who could take the inheritance from him under either civil or Praetorian law.[2]

---

[1] Cf. above, pp. 125 ff.

[2] It might seem that he had nothing to gain by applying for *bonorum possessio*

The position of the *bonorum possessor cum re* was not that of the *bona fide possessor* on the way to usucapion, but of the bonitary owner. For most—but not all[1]—practical purposes he was *heres*, and the true *heres* retained, as Gaius puts it, only the empty name.

Remedies of the bonorum possessor. Since the grant of *bonorum possessio* was only an authorization to take possession of the property of the dead man, effect was originally given to it only by a possessory interdict. This meant that the person to whom the grant had been made could only assert a claim to the *res corporales* of the inheritance (since they alone were capable of being possessed). Moreover, he could bring this interdict only against someone who claimed, rightly or wrongly, to be *heres* or against a mere interloper who made no attempt to justify his possession. He could not, for example, obtain possession of a *res corporalis* which the present possessor claimed to have bought from the dead man. Nor could he enforce any rights in *personam* (he was equally, of course, not liable for any debts). Once he had usucapted the *res corporales* he was, it is true, regarded as having usucapted the inheritance, but until then his title was of this limited and possessory character.

In the classical law, however, the *bonorum possessor* was so far recognized for what he in fact was—a Praetorian heir—that the ordinary actions were made available to him and against him, with the fiction that he was *heres*.

We must now consider the two ways—by will or by operation of law on intestacy—in which succession, whether by civil law or Praetorian law, might occur. As far back as our evidence goes there already existed a will of some kind, and all through their subsequent history the Romans regarded testamentary succession as normal—as the term 'intestacy' (*successio ab intestato*) itself shows—but what we know of other primitive systems, together with the peculiar character of the position of the *suus*

---

since he was adequately protected by the Civil law. The principal incentive was that someone else might claim if he did not. For example, a *heres* named in a civil law will was entitled to *bonorum possessio*, but if he did not claim it the Praetor would give it to the person entitled on intestacy. This *bonorum possessio* would be *sine re*, and the *heres* would therefore ultimately prevail, but he would have been put to avoidable inconvenience.

[1] See above, p. 127, n. 2.

heres, suggests (though this is much debated) that intestate succession is the older. It is therefore dealt with first here.

3. INTESTATE SUCCESSION

Preliminary notions. In the course of its history Roman law knew three main systems of intestate succession[1]—the old civil law which, subject to some modifications, remained formally in force until Justinian's time, the Praetorian system which was superimposed upon it, and finally the entirely new system with which Justinian replaced both, and which was not only to form the basis of much of the modern Civil law but also, through the Canon law, to exercise an influence on the English law. The exposition of these different systems may be simplified if certain fundamental common notions are explained first. The terminology in which these notions are expressed is part of the lingua franca of modern Civil law and has obtained some foothold in English law, but though derived from Roman materials, it is not itself Roman.

Let us suppose a system which offers the inheritance first to the dead man's children, sharing equally, and then to the nearest blood relatives, thus establishing two classes (*ordines*) of person entitled. Several questions will arise.

(i) Suppose that a man dies leaving two surviving sons, A and B. A third son, C, has died before him, but is survived by two sons, C1 and C2. What are the rights of C1 and C2? Three answers are possible. They may be denied any share, on the principle that 'the nearer[2] excludes the more remote', the nearer in this case being A and B. Or the principle of *successio per stirpes* or 'representation' may be applied: the inheritance will be divided equally between the three 'stems' (*stirpes*); C1 and C2 will 'represent' C, and will therefore be entitled to a one-sixth share each. Or, finally, the principle of *successio per capita* may be applied: the inheritance will be divided equally between as many persons as are entitled, and therefore A, B, C1, and C2 will each be entitled to a quarter.

(ii) If there are persons entitled in the class of 'children' but they do not choose to make any claim, are the nearest relatives entitled? If they are, there is said to be *successio ordinum*.

---

[1] Only the principal features of each are given in what follows.
[2] For the meaning of 'nearer', see immediately below.

(iii) If the nearest relatives do not choose to make any claim, are the next nearest entitled, and so on? If they are, there is said to be *successio graduum*—if one 'step' or degree within a class refuses, the next is entitled.

(iv) How are these degrees of nearness calculated? The Roman rule was to count up to the common ancestor and then down to the person whose entitlement was in question, each generation being reckoned as one step or degree. Thus, a first cousin is in the fourth degree, a nephew in the third. This method of calculation was adopted by the older English law, but the Canon law counts down from the common ancestor to both the dead man and the person whose entitlement is in question, and the longer of the two lines determines the degree of relationship. By this method both a nephew and a first cousin are reckoned to be in the second degree.

Finally, it must be remembered throughout what follows that succession to a Roman citizen was confined to Roman citizens and that therefore, for example, the issue of a marriage between a citizen and a *peregrina* without *conubium* could have no claim on their father's inheritance. Whether they had any claim on their mother's would depend on her 'personal' law.

Civil law. Until modified by imperial legislation, the civil law system was found in two clauses of the Twelve Tables with their *interpretatio*. The two clauses, as Ulpian knew them, ran: 'Si intestatus moritur cui suus heres nec escit, adgnatus proximus familiam habeto. Si adgnatus nec escit, gentiles familiam habento.'[1]

(a) *Sui heredes* have already been defined and the vested character of their interest explained.[2] It is only necessary to add that their shares were determined by the principle of representation (*successio per stirpes*). The opening words of the first clause show not only that by the time of the Twelve Tables the making of a will was normal, but also that the rights of the *suus heres* were taken for granted as part of the aboriginal customary law. The Twelve Tables merely make provision for the

---

[1] Literally, 'If a man dies intestate to whom there is no *suus heres*, let the nearest agnate have the property. If there is no agnate, let the members of the *gens* have the property.'

[2] Above, pp. 237 f.

destination of the property in the event of there being no *suus heres*.

(*b*) *Proximus adgnatus*. The entitlement of the nearest agnate, on the other hand, is usually thought to have been an innovation of the legislators. It is at any rate tied to a literal interpretation of the word *proximus*: there was no representation, and no *successio graduum*. If there was more than one *proximus* (e.g. two brothers, or an uncle and a nephew) succession was *per capita*.

(*c*) *Gentiles*. The nature of the succession of the *gentiles* and indeed of the *gens* itself is obscure, since even in the time of Gaius both had long been obsolete. The closest parallel to the *gens* is the clan, and in historical times the only positive mark of membership of a *gens*, as now of a clan, was the bearing of a common name. (Thus C. Iulius Caesar was a member of the *gens Iulia* and M. Tullius Cicero of the *gens Tullia*.)

This system naturally reflects the structure of early Roman society. In particular there is, in contrast for example to the older English system of succession to land, no notion of primogeniture and no preference for males over females. Primogeniture remained foreign to Roman law throughout its history, but in the later Republic when large fortunes were becoming common, discrimination against women made a hesitating appearance. No woman more remote than a sister could be entitled as *proximus adgnatus*. Women continued however to be entitled equally with men as *sui heredes*.

Bonorum possessio ab intestato. Such a narrowly agnatic system as that of the Twelve Tables was out of keeping with the ideas of the society which emerged from the economic and social upheavals of the second and first centuries B.C. Gaius castigates it for its injustice. In particular, it ignored the ties of blood as such—it excluded all relatives through females and therefore, *manus* apart, denied succession even between mother and child; and it excluded any child who had been emancipated. (A child given in adoption was of course entitled in his new family.) Moreover the decay of the *gens* must have made the restriction of the agnatic claim to the *proximus* increasingly inconvenient. By the time of Gaius, and probably long before, these defects had been largely removed by the Praetorian system of *bonorum possessio*.

The Edict offered *bonorum possessio* to four classes, and there was a fixed time within which each class must apply (*successio ordinum*).

(i) *Liberi*. These were children only in a limited and technical sense. The Praetor undertook no sweeping replacement of the agnatic *suus heres* by the cognatic 'descendant'. He merely ignored the artificial destruction of the natural agnatic tie by emancipation, and allowed those natural descendants who would, but for emancipation, have been *sui* to claim *bonorum possessio* along with the *sui*. The class also included, consistently with the same principle, those who had been *sui* but had been given in adoption and subsequently emancipated by their adoptive father; and conversely it did not include adoptive children who had been emancipated. *Liberi*, like *sui*, were entitled *per stirpes*, and the *bonorum possessio* was *cum re*.[1]

(ii) *Legitimi*. Whoever was entitled under the *lex* of the Twelve Tables could claim in this class.

(iii) *Cognati*. By giving *bonorum possessio* to the *liberi* the Praetor would, unless all the *liberi* were *sui*, correct the civil law; by giving it to the *legitimi* he would support the civil law; here he would usually be supplementing it. The *cognati* were the blood relatives, including of course agnates, and including even those who had become agnates by adoption, but only so long as their artificial relationship had not been terminated by emancipation. It was the nearest who was entitled (if several, *per capita*) with *successio graduum* to, usually, the sixth degree. The *bonorum possessio* was *sine re*.

(iv) *Vir et uxor*. Last of all comes the husband's entitlement to his wife's property and vice versa. To the modern eye the strangest

---

[1] There is one obvious injustice in this. Suppose, for example, that a man is survived by two sons, S, who was still *in potestate* at his father's death, and E who had been emancipated. S and E are equally entitled to *bonorum possessio*, but S, having been *in potestate* until his father's death, has no property of his own and all his acquisitions have been absorbed in the inheritance which E, who may have been given property on emancipation and has retained all his acquisitions since then, now claims to share. For instance, S and E may earlier have been joint-heirs under the will of a wealthy uncle. S's share will have passed automatically to his father, and the result of E's being entitled to *bonorum possessio* will be that he will not only retain his own share of the uncle's estate but will also be entitled, in effect, to half of S's share. The Praetor remedied this injustice by what an English lawyer would call a hotchpot rule (*collatio bonorum*). E would only obtain *bonorum possessio* if he undertook by stipulation to bring into account a proportion of his own property corresponding to S's share of their father's inheritance.

feature of the civil law system is the absence of any right of succession of a wife to her husband and vice versa. The Roman saw things differently. His idea of the family was different from ours. If the wife was *in manu* she was a *sua heres* to her husband; if she were not *in manu* she would be a *sua heres* to her father; if her father had emancipated her, though by the civil law she would have no claim, she would be entitled to *bonorum possessio* as one of his *liberi*. The Roman's idea of marriage was also different. As we have seen, he hardly thought of it as an institution creating rights and duties between the parties. The widow's portion (and, what was more important, the divorcee's portion) was provided for by the husband's duty to return her *dos*, or part of it.

Nevertheless the Praetor did make this ultimate provision for succession between husband and wife. It cannot however have been of great practical importance since it only took effect if there were not even a sixth degree cognate, or none willing to take. In this case too the *bonorum possessio* was *sine re*.

Bonorum possessio in these various cases was described as *unde liberi, unde legitimi*, &c., an elliptical term, the full version being 'bonorum possessio ex illa parte edicti unde liberi (&c.) vocantur'.[1]

This Praetorian system still had two serious defects. The relationship of mother and child was only recognized in the class *unde cognati*; and the *proximus adgnatus* was preferred even to less remote cognates. There was scattered legislation in the course of the Empire, but no coherent reform, and Justinian's Institutes in consequence present an untidy amalgam. Ten years later, however, Justinian initiated a remarkably radical break with the past.

The system of the Novels. In Novels 118 and 127 (A.D. 543 and 548) all vestiges of the *suus heres*, and of the distinctions between agnate and cognate and male and female, disappear and are replaced by the distinctions between lineal descendants, lineal ascendants, and collaterals. The order of succession was, in its main features, as follows (the nearer in each class excluding the more remote):

(i) Descendants *per stirpes*.

---

[1] '*Bonorum possessio* under that part of the Edict by which *liberi* are called (to *bonorum possessio*).'

(ii) Ascendants, and brothers and sisters. Children, but not grandchildren, of deceased brothers and sisters took *per stirpes* if there were a surviving brother or sister with whom to take (i.e. there was representation so long as there survived someone to keep the class of brother and sister alive). Subject to this rule of representation, succession was *per capita*.

(iii) The nearest other collaterals, *per capita*, with no representation, but with unlimited *successio graduum*. Thus if there survived an uncle, a first cousin (son of a deceased uncle), and a nephew, the uncle and the nephew would be entitled to half each, and the cousin to nothing.

(iv) The Basilica adds the same last resort as the Praetorian system—husband and wife.

If no claim were made the property went to the Treasury.

The unlimited *successio graduum* in the class of collaterals is in marked contrast to the modern English law which recognizes (after the surviving spouse, parents, brothers and sisters, grandparents) no collateral more remote than an uncle or aunt, but does allow unlimited representation of these. Thus, in an extreme case, a great-grandson of an uncle (sixth degree) could succeed, but not the son of a great-uncle (fifth degree). Most modern Civil law systems now limit the claims of collaterals to the sixth degree, or less. German law places no limit, though the system now in force is not Roman. The English rule no doubt reflects the relative weakness of family ties in this country.

4. TESTAMENTARY SUCCESSION

The complexity of the rules we have been considering must not blind us to the fact that intestacy was the exception, not the rule. Though there is no evidence of any 'horror' of intestacy, it is clear that the Romans considered it unfortunate and indeed reprehensible to die intestate. The story goes that the elder Cato, looking back on his life, had three regrets—that he had told his wife a secret, that he had made a journey by boat when he might have walked, and that he had lived one day intestate. No doubt not everyone was as conscientious as Cato, but the device of the *heres necessarius* and various rules of interpretation designed to maintain the validity of a will even at the cost of a distortion of ordinary legal principle testify to the lawyers' having thought likewise. To us in England indeed this may seem nothing very remarkable, since we also, though less markedly, look upon the will as normal, but in France, for instance, the majority are content to die intestate. For this there are probably two reasons. By French law a man may usually dispose by will only of a fraction of his estate, the rest being reserved to his family according to what are in effect the rules of intestacy;[1] and these rules correspond to what the ordinary man thinks to be the proper disposition of his estate. Much the same is true of Germany. In Rome, on the other hand, though from the beginning of the Empire onwards a testator's freedom was also restricted,[2] the civil law rules of intestacy were out of keeping with current ideas, and their reform by the Praetor or by legislation was partial and erratic. Moreover even where this was not so, as when a widower died leaving four meritorious sons all *in potestate*, it might well be wise, in order to prevent the parcelling up of the family land, to appoint only one of them heir and give the others legacies. And there would be other motives of a less material kind. So long as the old religion retained its hold, a man might wish to ensure that the performance of the family *sacra* should not fall into the hands of one who lacked the spur of *pietas*; and in later times he would often be drawn by the joys of posthumous generosity, particularly in the manumission of slaves. At any rate the Roman, with his individualistic attitude to property rights, would have had no sympathy for the attacks sometimes made in modern times on the whole institution of the will. It has been described, for example, as 'the expression of the will of a man who no longer has any will, respecting property which is no longer his property; it is the act of a man no longer accountable for his acts to mankind; it is an absurdity and an absurdity should not have the force of law'.

The Roman will is, however, even more remarkable for its precocious development. Elsewhere this development is late, but in Rome as early as the Twelve Tables there existed a will of some sort. This much is certain, but little else. In particular one must beware of assuming that the early will necessarily had all the characteristics of its mature successor. Of these the essential are four—(i) it appoints a universal successor, who may be someone other than the *heres ab intestato*; (ii) it may make gifts

---

[1] See below, p. 263.   [2] See below, pp. 261 ff.

(legacies) out of the estate, and may make other particular dispositions (appointment of tutors, manumission of slaves); (iii) it is 'ambulatory', or 'speaks from death' (e.g. the property disposed of is taken to include things which the testator acquired only after making the will, and a description such as 'my nephews' is taken to include those born since the will was made and to exclude those who have died since then (or rather their heirs)); (iv) it is revocable.

The early will. Gaius tells us of three early forms of will, but how many of these characteristics each possessed is much debated.

(*a*) *Testamentum comitiis calatis and testamentum in procinctu.* Both these were obsolete some time before the end of the Republic. The *testamentum in procinctu* ('in battle array') is a soldier's will, made before battle. The other is the more important. The *comitia curiata* met twice a year for religious business (probably in March and May and probably under the presidency of the *pontifex maximus*). This business included the making of adrogations (which may well have served, before any will existed, to provide a *heres* where no *suus* existed) and of wills, and when it was discharging the latter function it was styled *comitia calata* ('called together'). The parallel of *adrogatio* naturally suggests that the will was a legislative act, but there are signs that the function of the *comitia* may have been, or have become, limited to that of witnessing the act of the testator. Even if the former supposition is the right one, the important features of the will, granted the inability of a Roman assembly either to initiate or amend,[1] must have been its publicity and the control of the *pontifex maximus*, as guardian of the *sacra*. It was presumably ambulatory and revocable, and could apparently appoint tutors and manumit slaves, since the Twelve Tables refer to such acts as occurring by will. The parallel of *adrogatio* again suggests strongly that it could appoint a *heres*, though it has been argued that such interference with the customary rules of succession was as yet unthinkable and that the will was confined to particular dispositions. This might explain the peculiar form taken by the third form of will.

(*b*) *The mancipatory will* (*testamentum per aes et libram*). This was apparently a product of pontifical *interpretatio* after the

[1] See above, p. 5.

Twelve Tables, since Gaius speaks of the first two forms as having existed 'from the beginning' whereas this was added later, and for Gaius 'the beginning' would presumably be the Twelve Tables. It remained the normal civil law will until the fifth century A.D. As Gaius knew it, it had all the characteristics mentioned above, but Gaius tells us that it had undergone changes, as indeed is obvious from the contradiction between what it purports to do and what it actually achieves.

The testator first writes his will on wax tablets and then, having collected the usual five witnesses and a *libripens*, mancipates his property (*familia*) to a person called *familiae emptor*. It is, however, a mancipation with a difference. The *familiae emptor*, instead of the usual assertion of title, declares that he has the custody of the property subject to the testator's directions. Then follows a stage not found in the ordinary mancipation at all. The testator does not merely acquiesce but takes an active part by formally confirming the contents of his will and calling on the witnesses to bear witness that he has done so.

In Gaius' time this mancipation is a pure formality, the only purpose of which is to give validity to the contents of the wax tablets. The *familiae emptor* is a man of straw. The will takes effect only on death, and then the person who succeeds to the rights and duties is not the *familiae emptor* but the *heres* named in the will. And the will is revocable, though only, it is true, by the making of another one.

In its developed form, therefore, the mancipatory will was preferable to that made *comitiis calatis*, certainly because it was secret and because it could be made at any time and at any place where seven Roman citizens could be found, and possibly (if the comitial will lacked this characteristic) because it could freely appoint a *heres*. But clearly it was originally not a will but a device for getting round the difficulty or impossibility of making one. The history of other systems shows that such a conveyance *inter vivos* is commonly the precursor of a will. Beyond this all is conjecture.

Bonorum possessio secundum tabulas; the 'Praetorian will'. Whatever the original legal effects of the mancipatory will and whatever the course of events by which the *familiae emptor* was transformed into a man of straw, it is certain that the transformation was complete well before the end of the Republic. For we know from Cicero that already in his time the Praetor saw in the mancipation no more than an empty form: he promised *bonorum possessio* (*secundum tabulas testamenti*) to any person named *heres* in a written document sealed by seven witnesses, whether there had been a mancipation or not. His purpose in doing this was not to set up a new form of will but merely to recognize what had become the substance of the old. The five witnesses of the mancipation are now witnesses of the written will, and the *familiae emptor* and the *libripens* are added to their number. The will is written on one side only of two wax tablets which are then tied together, face inwards, and sealed by the testator and the seven witnesses. However this *bonorum possessio* was *sine re* until Antoninus Pius barred the claim of those entitled at civil law on intestacy.[1] Until then they had succeeded if they could show that the formalities of the mancipation had not been properly carried out. The practical effect of the Praetor's intervention had thus until then been merely to reverse the burden of proof, though the discharge of the burden might not be easy, particularly if the will recorded, as all surviving examples in fact do, that a mancipation had taken place.

This is now commonly referred to as the Praetorian will, and from the time of Antoninus Pius it was for most practical purposes as good as a will. In the late law, however, though it makes an appearance in the pages of the *Corpus Iuris*, the Praetorian will had in fact been superseded by other forms.

Later forms of will. The Praetorian will was Roman in its reluctance to make a clean break with the past. The external formalities of a will serve three purposes—to ensure first that the expression of the testator's wishes is verifiably his, secondly that those wishes were seriously intended by him as his last will, and finally that they are preserved complete. Thus an English will requires that the testator shall place his signature at the end of the document in the presence of two witnesses, who must then add their own signatures in the presence of the testator. The presence of the witnesses and the signatures serve to authenticate the document and to ensure that it is no merely casual expression of a wish; and the requirement that the signatures be at the

[1] Cf. above, p. 244.

end ensures that the document cannot be presented incomplete. In the Praetorian will the seals of the witnesses achieved all three purposes, the seal being both a 'signature' and a guarantee against the will being broken open. But if one asks why as many as seven witnesses were necessary, and why the testator himself did not have to authenticate the document with his seal, the answers can only be found in the original mancipatory will. The large 'cast' of a normal mancipation was probably needed not so much to prove that the act had taken place as to give it publicity, so that any defect of title (which in a small society would be likely to be known to the witnesses) could be investigated immediately. And the reason why the testator in the Praetorian will was not required to seal was presumably that in the mancipatory will he authenticated his act by the words he spoke. Neither answer makes sense, however, once the mancipation is no longer required. Moreover when papyrus or parchment began to replace wax tablets the seals no longer served so well to guarantee the completeness of the document. For this and other reasons there appears in documents of all kinds in addition to the old seal a newer mark of authenticity, the *subscriptio*. This is the nearest approach the ancient world made to, and is indeed the ancestor of, the modern signature. It is a sentence of varying length written 'under' (i.e. at the end of) a document, by the 'subscriber' in his own hand and consisting essentially of 'I, Lucius Titius . . . have subscribed.'

The common will of the late Empire, introduced in A.D. 439, requires this newer form of authentication from both testator and witnesses, but still without jettisoning the inheritances from the past. It is in substance the Praetorian will with the addition of *subscriptio* by testator and witnesses. Justinian puts this in a more elaborate way when he says that the law from which the requirements of the new will were derived is 'tripartite'—the will must be made in one operation and before witnesses (this comes from the civil law); the number of witnesses must be seven (Praetorian law, since by the civil law only five were witnesses); and to these requirements imperial legislation has added the *subscriptio*. From this analysis of its sources the will itself came to be called, not very happily, *testamentum tripertitum*.

The *testamentum tripertitum* has a direct descendant in the modern French 'mystic' (or secret) will, the *subscriptio* being replaced by its counterpart, the signature, and one of the witnesses by a notary. It is little used, however, and two other wills of the late Empire were of much greater subsequent importance —the public will and the holograph will. The public will (itself derived from the Greek law) was one which had been entered in the records of a court or deposited in the imperial archives. Its modern successor (the 'authentic' will) is made before a notary or a judge. The holograph will was simply written by the testator in his own hand. Justinian allowed it only in favour of children of the testator, but (with the additional requirement of the signature) it is in unrestricted use in Scotland and in Germany today, and is also recognized in France. It satisfies the layman's desire to be free of what he sees as the lawyer's artificial restraints, but, quite apart from the dangers of any 'home-made' will, it is criticized as being open to forgery or to secret destruction by the disappointed or the ill-disposed.

Internal requirements of a will. We have seen that the prime purpose of the will was to institute a *heres*, and that if it failed to do so, or the person instituted refused to enter, the whole will was void. As Gaius puts it, the institution of an heir is the source and foundation of the whole will. This being so, the institution had, to the formalistic mind of the early Roman lawyer, to be placed first in the wording of the will, and this reasoning was adhered to throughout the classical period. Out of *favor testamenti*, however, failure to place the institution first was not allowed to invalidate the whole will but merely those provisions (e.g. legacies) which preceded it. There were of course other more substantial requirements also. We have seen that the institution must be to the whole *hereditas*, though again *favor testamenti* led to a merely partial institution being construed as total. The institution must also be of an identifiable person (or persons). This made impossible, in particular, the institution of what we should now call corporate bodies, but which the Roman saw only as fluctuating groups of individuals (*incertae personae*). In this the lawyers were perhaps motivated by the fear of property accumulating in the hands of immortal bodies. That only Roman citizens (or peregrines with *commercium*) could be instituted followed from the 'personal' character of this whole branch of the law.

Moreover the whole will must be in Latin, and the institution of the heir, like nearly all the other important provisions which a will might contain (appointment of tutors, manumission of slaves, disinherisons, legacies) must be expressed in formal words. The institution must contain the word *heres* and must be imperative in form ('Lucius Titius, be you my heir' was the usual phrase, but 'I order that Lucius Titius be my heir' would do; not, however, 'I make Lucius Titius my heir' or even 'I institute Lucius Titius my heir'). Such distinctions, like the requirement that the institution came first, make pedantic reading and are obviously in detail difficult to support, but they have an underlying justification. Just as the external formalities of a will serve to ensure its authenticity and completeness, so also these internal formalities are intended to minimize the possibilities of ambiguity. The lawyer is accustomed to precision of language, and he may argue that when the time comes to interpret the will the testator will not be there to explain what he means, and that if he is not prepared to consult a lawyer when he is making his will he should not expect a lawyer to face the unenviable task of deciding between the conflicting claims arising out of an ambiguous provision. Even when such technical terms are used there will be scope enough for ambiguity—in the description, for example, of what is included in a legacy or of the persons for whom the legacy is intended. The later Empire, however, was out of sympathy with such verbal formalities, and in A.D. 339 Constantine abolished the need for any particular form of words. The use of Greek was not universally allowed until a century later.

Substitutions. (i) *Vulgar.* The only essential of a will was the institution of an heir, but it would be an uncommon will which contained nothing else. If the instituted heir were an *extraneus*, the next provision would usually be a substitution, i.e. a direction (in formal words) that if the instituted heir did not enter (and the wise testator would add a time-limit) some other person should be heir. There might follow other substitutions, ending usually with the substitution of a *heres necessarius*. The opening sentences of a will might therefore run: 'Lucius Titius, be you my heir and do you make *cretio*[1] within 100 days of your knowing

---

[1] This was a formal (and therefore unambiguous) oral act of entry on the inheritance. Cf. above, p. 239.

and being able to do so. If you do not thus make *cretio*, be you disinherited. Then be you, Publius Maevius, my heir and do you make *cretio*, &c. . . . Then be you, my slave Stichus, free and my heir.' These substitutions are called 'vulgar' (common, usual) and are in fact merely conditional institutions.

(ii) *Pupillary*. A child of any age could be heir, but not until the age of puberty could he himself make a will. This might present an unwelcome prospect to a testator. Suppose, for example, that he instituted his only son and that first he and then the son died before the son reached the age of puberty— the inheritance would then (since an *impubes* could neither have a *suus heres* of his own nor make a will) inevitably go to the nearest agnate. Apart from the general dislike of intestacy, the father might be reluctant to let the property go to the nearest agnate, and the lawyers therefore very early invented the device of the pupillary substitution to enable the testator to appoint an heir in case the son should die *impubes*. This, like the vulgar substitution, was in form a conditional institution ('Be you, my son Titius, my heir. If my son shall be my heir and die before reaching puberty, be you, Seius, heir'), but it obviously results in a shifting of the inheritance, in violation of the principle 'semel heres, semper heres'. First the son is heir and after him the pupillary substitute. It is probable that this was originally the limit of the breach with principle—that the substitute was looked on as the heir of the father and therefore took only that part of the son's property which he had inherited from his father—but in the classical law the breach was far wider. The substitute succeeded to the whole property of the son wherever it had come from, and therefore a will containing a pupillary substitution was in effect two wills—one for the father and one for the son.

Since the son might die before the father, a properly drafted will would include both a vulgar and a pupillary substitution, usually of the same person ('Be you, my son Titius, my heir. If my son Titius shall not be my heir or shall be my heir and die before reaching puberty, be you, Seius, heir'). If such a provision were included in the ordinary way in the father's will it would obviously provide a temptation to the substitute to ensure that the child never did reach puberty. The proper course, Gaius tells us, was to put the substitution in a separate sealed document, not to be opened unless the child died *impubes*.

Restrictions on the power of testation. The underlying principle of the Roman law, as of the modern English law, is that the testator may do as he likes with his own, but this freedom was restricted in two ways.

(*a*) *Formal—exheredatio.* As far back as our knowledge goes the rule existed that a *suus* must be either instituted or expressly disinherited. If this were not done, the will was void. This was a purely formal requirement. It did not prevent the testator from instituting whomever he chose (provided, of course, he was by the general law capable of being *heres*); it merely required him, if there was a *suus*, to make his intention doubly clear, positively by instituting the *heres* of his choice and negatively by disinheriting the *suus*. The original reason for the rule lay probably in the 'vested' character of the interest of the *suus*: since he was in a sense already owner, he could only be deprived of his title by an express provision. In the classical law, however, the rule was an irrational survival which served mainly to provide pitfalls for the testator.

If we use the word 'disinherit' we must not accord to it its English overtones. The father was not necessarily motivated by disapproval or dislike, and the disinherited *suus* was not necessarily 'cut out' of his father's will—he might well be a substantial legatee. It would often be wise in this way to prevent the parcelling up of the family estate—to give the whole to, say, the eldest son, subject to provision for his brothers and sisters. Moreover even if the father instituted all the *sui* he need not institute them to equal shares.

This part of the law is unedifying not only because it is an irrational survival, but also because its details are excessively complicated. The Praetor intervened by the grant of *bonorum possessio contra tabulas* (against the will) but the scope of his reform was very limited, his object being only to bring this branch of the law into line with his rules of intestate succession by requiring testators to institute or disinherit not only *sui* but all *liberi*, and to modify in detail the consequences of failure to do so. His rules were somewhat simpler than those of the civil law, but they still provided many pitfalls. One asks why the Praetor did not 'correct' the law more drastically. The answer lies mainly, no doubt, in the conservatism of the lawyers, but it may also have been thought that these rules did require a man, in however clumsy and inadequate a way, at least to consider his obligations to his children. This purpose could however be very much more effectively served by the newer device of the *querela inofficiosi testamenti* which we must now consider; but nevertheless the rules of *exheredatio* survived into the later years of Justinian's reign when they were finally confused with those of the *querela*.[1]

(b) *Substantial—querela inofficiosi testamenti.* The 'complaint of an unduteous will' is peculiar among the institutions of Roman law in being, in its early development at any rate, the product of court practice. It apparently originated, perhaps in the late Republic, in the centumviral court, a tribunal of perhaps some thirty or forty lay judges which provided an alternative forum to that of the single *iudex* for the hearing of, in particular, cases concerning inheritances. The relative stability of its composition and the narrower field of its jurisdiction probably made the development of a consistent practice easier for this court than for the multiplicity of single *iudices* whose cases concerned all branches of the law. The claim seems originally to have been made, as was a similar proceeding in Greek law, under the cloak of an assertion that the testator must have been insane, but the ground of complaint came to be simply that the will, by disinheriting the complainant or making inadequate provision for him, offended against the *officium pietatis*—the moral duty which a man owed to his family. It was thus probably in origin an appeal to standards more akin to those upheld by the Censor than to those enforced by courts of law. In one respect it long retained this discretionary character: the court had to decide whether the testator had a just ground for excluding the complainant, and no attempt was made to define a just ground until 542, when Justinian, with the lawgiver's dislike for unregulated discretion, promulgated a long list. In other respects, however, it gradually acquired the precise outlines of a legal institution. These must now be briefly considered.

The classes of person who could bring the *querela* were eventually settled to be (in this order): descendants (including

[1] See below, p. 263.

descendants of a woman); ascendants; brothers and sisters (though only if a 'base person' had been instituted). These persons could only claim, however, if in the particular case they were entitled on intestacy by either the civil or the Praetorian law, and then only if they had no other remedy. For example, the *suus heres* who had been passed over could proceed under the rules of *exheredatio* or could obtain *bonorum possessio contra tabulas*, and was therefore denied the *querela*.

The complainant must show that the testator had without just ground made no adequate provision for him. What constituted adequate provision came, under the influence of the *lex Falcidia*,[1] to be fixed at one quarter of what the complainant would have been entitled to on intestacy. This was later called his *legitima pars* or *legitima portio*—the modern 'legitim'. The provision need not have been made by instituting the complainant heir. If he had received his *legitima portio* by a gift out of the estate in any form his *querela* would fail.

The results of a successful *querela* varied according to the circumstances. As has already been said, the ostensible ground may in the beginning have been the insanity of the testator. If this was so, the result should have been to invalidate the will and produce an intestacy. And in the simplest case—where there was only one possible claimant and only one heir instituted —this was the result. The claimant took the whole inheritance (not just his *legitima portio*) and all subsidiary provisions of the will, such as legacies, were void. On the other hand, if there were several instituted heirs, the *querela* might be brought against only one of them, and then the will failed only to the extent of that one's share, legacies &c. being only proportionately invalidated. The logic of intestacy was thus abandoned, and the *querela* was treated as a suit against a particular heir. The principle that a man could not die partly testate was in effect abrogated.

The law was thus arbitrary and unsatisfactory. It appeared to say that certain persons had a right to a *legitima portio*, and yet the result of the testator's failing in his duty would usually be to give them a great deal more. Moreover it would often be difficult for the testator to make sure of complying with the law—the value of the inheritance might increase rapidly just before his death, or some members of a class might die and

[1] See below, p. 266.

thereby increase the *legitimae portiones* of the survivors. And the consequence of a small miscalculation of this kind might be to destroy the entire will. Finally, since the *querela* was only a last resort, there still existed all the complications of the law of *exheredatio*.

These defects were largely removed by interventions of Justinian. His earliest and most significant reform was to restrict the *querela* to cases where the complainant had received nothing at all under the will. If he had received something but it fell short of the *legitima portio*, he could only bring an *actio ad supplendam legitimam* to have the deficiency made good. The will was otherwise unaffected. In this way the testator was protected from the possibility that a miscalculation of his might enable the complainant to destroy the whole will and obtain far more than his *legitima portio*. Justinian later provided that any descendant or ascendant who was entitled to a *legitima portio* must be instituted heir. If he was instituted, but received (whether as heir or in any other way under the will) less than the *legitima portio*, he could only bring the *actio ad supplendam legitimam*. If he was not instituted, then the *querela* lay, but its effect was now only to replace the heirs instituted in the will by the successful claimant or claimants. In effect there was a will without an instituted *heres*. From this last reform it would seem likely that Justinian intended at last to combine the principles of the *legitima portio* with those of *exheredatio* and *bonorum possessio contra tabulas*, but it is not clear that this was in fact the result. Justinian also altered the *legitima portio* of children. If there were four or less, they were entitled to a third of their intestate share; if there were more than four, the fraction was a quarter.

Most modern Civil law systems have rules, derived sometimes from the *querela inofficiosi testamenti*, sometimes from the customary law, which are intended to strike a balance between the freedom of the testator and the claims of his family. These take the form either (e.g. in France or Scotland) of denying altogether to the testator the power to dispose of a certain proportion of his estate, which is therefore 'reserved' to his close relatives, or (e.g. in Germany) of placing no restriction on his power of disposal but allowing the relatives, if they wish, to claim a share. In either case the share is fixed and corresponds to the *legitima portio* of Roman law. By contrast, the English testator could in modern times give his fortune to his mistress and leave his wife and children destitute until, in 1938, Parliament allowed the wife (or husband) and children (but excluding adult sons and married daughters unless incapable of maintaining themselves) to apply to the court, not for a fixed share, but for 'reasonable provision'.

This contrast between the Common law and the Civil law not only helped to make intestacy far more common on the Continent than in England but also led, particularly in France, to a progressive parcelling up of family property and to the absence of that English figure, 'the younger son'.

5. GIFTS OUT OF THE INHERITANCE

To institute an heir and to devolve upon him the *hereditas* was the essential function of a will, but very early there developed other functions also—the manumission of slaves, the appointment of tutors, and especially the making of gifts out of the inheritance. Such gifts normally took the form of legacies.

Forms of legacy. There were four forms of legacy (*legatum*), two basic forms each with one variant. The basic forms only need be dealt with here. Each required appropriate formal words, and these must not precede the institution of the heir, upon which their validity depended. The two forms differed essentially in that one created in the legatee a right *in rem* in respect of the thing bequeathed, the other only a right *in personam* against the *heres* that he should convey the thing.

A *legatum per vindicationem* (for which the appropriate words were originally *do, lego*, 'I give and bequeath') vested in the legatee the ownership of the thing immediately on the entry of the *heres*. The legatee could then assert his ownership by *vindicatio* against the *heres* or anyone else in possession, without the need for any further act by the *heres*. He thus enjoyed the usual advantages of a right *in rem*, except that if the liabilities of the inheritance exceeded the assets or the *lex Falcidia* applied, the amount of the legacy was automatically reduced. The advantages of this form of legacy also, however, entailed restrictions on its scope. It was confined to things which could be the object of a *vindicatio*—specific corporeal things and *iura in re aliena*—and moreover only things of which the testator had the *dominium ex iure Quiritium* both when he made the will and when he died (i.e. things which he could himself have vindicated). A legacy of, for example, a slave of whom the testator had only bonitary ownership when he made the will but whom he had since then usucapted would be void. The only exception allowed, obviously for practical reasons, was that for fungible things (e.g. 'the wine in my cellar') *dominium* at the time of death was sufficient. A particularly important consequence was that a bequest of money, except in the very limited form of the coins held by the testator at his death, could not be made in this way.

A *legatum per damnationem* (for which the usual form was *heres meus dare damnas esto*, 'let my heir be strictly bound to convey') created only a right *in personam* against the *heres*, but had the advantage of much greater flexibility. Anything which could be bequeathed by legacy *per vindicationem* could be bequeathed in this way also, and without the need for *dominium ex iure Quiritium* in the testator. Indeed it was possible to make a legacy of something belonging to someone else. The *heres* was then bound to buy the thing for the legatee or to pay him the value of it if the owner would not sell. Moreover a legacy might be of 'future things' (e.g. 'the first child of my slave-woman'), of an annuity, of a fraction of the net inheritance, or it might be the gift of his *peculium* to a slave manumitted by the will; it might even be of an act to be performed by the *heres* (to build a house for the legatee, or to pay off his debts).

The restricted scope of the legacy *per vindicationem* and especially the requirement that the testator must have been quiritary owner of the thing both when he made the will and when he died made it a treacherous form in which to frame a gift. A *senatusconsultum* in the reign of Nero (A.D. 54–68) removed this pitfall. From this *Sc. Neronianum* was derived the rule that if a legacy was expressed in an inappropriate form it should be construed as if expressed in the most favourable form. As between the two forms with which we are concerned this meant that if a gift was void because expressed as a legacy *per vindicationem* but would have been valid *per damnationem*, it should be read as if expressed in the latter form. A legacy would thus no longer fail merely because an inappropriate form was used, but apparently a testator still had to use one of the recognized forms of words, until a constitution of A.D. 339 made even this unnecessary and one more of the hazards of the home-made will was removed. Justinian took the final step of subjecting all legacies to the same rules and allowing either the *actio in rem* or the *actio in personam* according to the circumstances.

A legacy, like the institution of an heir or the manumission of a slave, could be conditional, and a conditional legacy could serve many purposes. For example, if the testator wished to secure the manumission of a slave belonging to another person he could attempt to do so by giving to that person a legacy conditional on his manumitting the slave.

Restrictions on amount of legacies—lex Falcidia. Legacies were a charge on the *heres*—he was only entitled to what remained after paying the debts and satisfying the legacies. There was here a source of danger to the will. If a testator miscalculated the value of his property (or if, as is more probable, its value had fallen after he made the will), the legacies might absorb so much of the inheritance that the *heres*, if he were an *extraneus* and therefore had the choice, would not find it worth his while to enter. This difficulty was met by the *lex Falcidia* (40 B.C.). Legacies were not to be allowed to reduce what remained to the heir below a quarter of the value of the net inheritance (i.e. after deducting funeral expenses, the value of slaves manumitted, &c.). If less than a quarter was left, the legacies were reduced *pro rata*. If there were several heirs, each was entitled to a quarter of his share of the inheritance.

Donatio mortis causa. This was a gift made in contemplation of death in some particular eventuality (e.g. a dangerous journey which the donor was about to undertake), and only becoming fully effective if the donee survived the donor. Until then it was revocable either in the sense that no right passed to the donee (suspensive condition) or, more often, that the donee could be required to restore what he had received (resolutive condition). Like an ordinary gift (*donatio inter vivos*), it could be any voluntary enrichment of the donee by the donor, whether by the transfer of property, or the creation of a contractual right, or the extinction of a debt. In the later law there was no need for any immediate prospect of death, the gift being said to be made in contemplation of mortality rather than of death, and a man could in this way in effect make gifts out of his inheritance without the need of making a will or of satisfying any of the formal requirements of a legacy. Because of its substantial similarity to a legacy it was, however, subjected to some of the same rules. In general only those persons who could take a legacy could take a *donatio mortis causa*; by a constitution of Septimius Severus (A.D. 193–211) the *heres* could assert his entitlement under the *lex Falcidia* against a donee *mortis causa*; and, at any rate in the law of Justinian, the gift could be reduced by the claims of the debtors of the inheritance, and would be taken into account in calculating the donee's *legitima portio*.

Fideicommissa. Certain classes of person were incapable of being either *heres* or legatee. These included peregrines (who, it must be remembered, might be close relatives), Junian Latins, 'uncertain persons' (including what we should call corporate bodies and persons not born at the time of the will), and, under Augustus' legislation for the encouragement of marriage and the bearing of children, most unmarried adults (*coelibes*) and married persons who were childless (*orbi*—they were allowed to take only half of whatever they were given). In order to circumvent these and other restrictions on legacies the practice had grown up before the end of the Republic of requesting a validly appointed heir or legatee to make over the whole or some part of what he received to the person whom the testator wished to benefit. Such a request was without legal effect: its fulfilment was 'committed to the faith of' the heir or legatee. In a few special cases, however, Augustus ordered the consuls to intervene administratively to give effect to them, and thereafter they rapidly became a recognized legal institution. They remained, however, outside the formulary system and the jurisdiction of the Urban Praetor, and were enforced under *extraordinaria cognitio* by a specially appointed *Praetor fideicommissarius*. They are thus not a Praetorian but an imperial creation, elaborated by the jurists, and provide an illustration of the changing basis of the constitution. The *fideicommissum* in its developed form was an astonishingly flexible institution which was allowed to ignore a number of fundamental principles of the ordinary law of succession. Neither writing nor formal words were necessary. It was sufficient that the intention to make a request was clear. The person charged with a *fideicommissum* (*fiduciarius*) could be anyone who took any benefit from the inheritance, even the *heres ab intestato*, so that it was now possible to make a bequest without a will. The scope of *fideicommissa* was as wide as that of legacies *per damnationem* and in one important respect wider: there could be a *fideicommissum* to buy and manumit a slave belonging to a third person. The original advantage, however, that the beneficiary (*fideicommissarius*) could be someone who was incapable of being *heres* or legatee was gradually whittled away so that by the time of Gaius the only substantial category left was that of the Junian Latin.

The most important use of the *fideicommissum* was not, however, to provide a more flexible substitute for the legacy of individual things, but to effect a transfer of the *hereditas* (or part of it). The *heres* was requested to transfer the *hereditas* to the *fideicommissarius* either immediately or (and herein lay the importance of the device) at some later date or on the occurrence of some future event. Since a *fideicommissum* could be imposed even on a *fideicommissarius* and (originally) in favour of persons not yet born, the Roman could satisfy the common human desire, until now frustrated by the rule *semel heres, semper heres*, to 'tie up' his property—to control it beyond the hands of the first recipient, perhaps in perpetuity. He could make his son his heir, or give him by legacy or *fideicommissum* a piece of land, subject to a *fideicommissum* requiring him to preserve it and on his death to transfer it to his eldest son, who would in turn be required to transfer it to his son and so forth. Attempts to create such 'perpetuities' present a difficult problem to the lawyer or lawgiver—that of striking a balance between the claims of the living and the dead. The satisfaction of a man's natural desire to ensure that his property will serve certain purposes even after his death entails the disadvantage to his successors and to society as a whole that the adventuring of capital is thereby restricted. Whether for this reason or not, Hadrian forbade the making of *fideicommissa* in favour of 'uncertain persons', and testators were left to the device of forbidding alienation outside the family, but even such family settlements seem to have been restricted to persons alive at the testator's death and the first unborn generation. Justinian, however, once more allowed *fideicommissa* in favour of 'uncertain persons'. His purpose was probably to encourage gifts to charities, but the result was also to make possible un-restricted perpetuities. Faced later with just such a case, he decreed in a Novel that thereafter property could not be tied up for more than four generations. This is a very long period indeed by the standards of English law, but it remained the rule in most systems derived from Roman law, often until modern times. 'Fideicommissary substitutions', as they were called, were sufficiently popular among the French nobility for the period to be reduced by legislation in 1560 to two generations, and one of the early acts of the reformers of the French Revolu-tion was to forbid such substitutions altogether. This prohibition was repeated, with very limited exceptions, in the *Code Civil*, and reappears in almost all the codes derived from it. The modern German law takes a different route. It still allows the appointment of successive heirs, but in general declares void any such appointment which has not taken effect within thirty years of the death of the testator.

There are obvious affinities between the *fideicommissum* and the English trust. The *fideicommissum* cannot however be created *inter vivos*, and the position of the fideicommissary is different from that of the trustee. On the one hand, where the *fideicom-missum* requires the immediate transfer of the property his posi-tion is merely formal and transitory, and on the other hand where the *fideicommissum* creates a settlement he acquires a full beneficial interest. It seems, however, that, at any rate in Justinian's law, the fideicommissary could, like the beneficiary of a trust, claim the property from anyone who had taken it with notice of the *fideicommissum*.

Assimilation of fideicommissum, legacy, and donatio mortis causa. Justinian declares that legacy and *donatio mortis causa* have become almost indistinguishable, and that he has wholly assimi-lated legacy and *fideicommissum*. The wish is to some extent here father to the thought. A handful of differences remained. As between legacy and *fideicommissum*, for example, it was still the rule that a gift of freedom to a third person's slave could only be by *fideicommissum*, and therefore the slave still became the freedman of the *fiduciarius* and not of the testator, as he would have been if the gift could have been made by legacy. And as between *donatio mortis causa* and legacy, it was still the rule that a *donatio mortis causa* vested immediately on the death, not on the entry of the heir.

Codicils. The English codicil is merely a postscript to a will which differs not at all, in the formalities required and often in substance also, from a will. The Roman codicil, however, differed both in form and in substance from the will. It was an informal document (literally 'little book') dealing with the disposal, in any way other than by instituting an heir, of the whole or any part of an inheritance. It is mentioned here because, though codicils and *fideicommissa* have no necessary connexion, the two were in their origin and in their subsequent history closely related. We are told that one Lentulus when dying in Africa wrote codicils, which he had confirmed by anticipation in a will, requesting Augustus by way of *fideicommissum* to do something. Augustus carried out his wishes and then asked the lawyers whether codicils were consistent with the law. Opinion was in favour, the argument of convenience being adduced that it was difficult when abroad to satisfy the formalities of a will, and when Labeo made them there could be no further doubt of their legality. The developed law distinguished between codicils which had been confirmed by a will, either subsequently or by anticipation, and those which either had not been confirmed or were directed to the *heres ab intestato*. The former were taken to be incorporated in the will and could do anything which a will could do except institute or disinherit an heir; the latter could only create *fideicommissa*. The later law tended to require witnesses for codicils as for wills, Justinian fixing the number at five.

SELECT BIBLIOGRAPHY

HISTORY AND SOURCES

H. F. JOLOWICZ, *Historical Introduction to the Study of Roman Law* (2nd ed., 1952), gives a masterly account, both learned and readable. It provides a balanced discussion of controversial issues with full references to the literature (3rd ed., 1972, by B. Nicholas).

ELEMENTARY TEXTBOOKS

The three most commonly used are:

W. W. BUCKLAND, *Manual of Roman Private Law* (2nd edn., 1939).
R. W. LEAGE, *Roman Private Law* (3rd edn. by A. M. Prichard, 1961).
R. W. LEE, *Elements of Roman Law* (4th edn., 1956).

MORE ADVANCED TEXTBOOKS

W. W. BUCKLAND, *Textbook of Roman Law from Augustus to Justinian* (3rd edn., 1963), is the standard work of reference in English. Buckland had an extraordinary mastery of the texts, and this book, though too closely packed to be easily readable at length, contains an immense amount of information. There were few questions which escaped Buckland's notice.

W. W. BUCKLAND, *Main Institutions of Roman Private Law* (1931), is a difficult but perceptive book which has a great deal to offer to the student who already has a good grasp of the subject.

F. SCHULZ, *Classical Roman Law* (1951). Schulz was one of the outstanding figures of the German school of radical critics of the texts, and this book sums up the main conclusions of a lifetime devoted to the isolation of the classical law from later accretions and distortions. It is an elementary book in the sense that it is confined to the main institutions of the law, but it is not a beginner's book. On many questions it is a vigorous and stimulating statement of a point of view rather than a balanced account, though it is for that reason invaluable for the skilled reader. It is also marked by an ability to see the wood rather than the trees and to evaluate the Roman achievement.

EDITIONS OF TEXTS

The standard English edition of the Institutes of Gaius is by F. de Zulueta (2 vols., 1946, 1953). Vol. i gives the text and a translation, and vol. ii a commentary.

The Berlin edition (by Mommsen and Krueger) of the *Corpus Iuris Civilis* will be found in most law libraries. There are English editions of the Institutes by J. B. Moyle (5th edn., 1912) with a translation in a separate volume (2nd edn., 1889) and by T. C. Sandars (8th edn., 1888). The notes to both these editions are often out of date and unreliable. R. W. Lee's *Elements of Roman Law* (see above) incorporates a translation of the Institutes.

There is a translation of the first fifteen books of the Digest by C. H. Monro (2 vols., 1904, 1909).

There are also several editions, with translation and commentary, of individual titles of the Digest. F. de Zulueta, *Roman Law of Sale* (1945) and F. H. Lawson, *Negligence in the Civil Law* (1950) also include other relevant texts.

OTHER BOOKS

W. W. BUCKLAND and ARNOLD McNAIR, *Roman Law and Common Law* (2nd edn. by F. H. Lawson, 1952), provides a perceptive comparison of the leading rules and institutions of the two systems.

F. SCHULZ, *Principles of Roman Law* (1936), identifies and illustrates certain broad characteristics of Roman law, such as a tendency to abstraction or a respect for tradition.

F. SCHULZ, *History of Roman Legal Science* (1946), is a thorough and critical study of the forms of juristic literature and the transmission of the texts. Not all of its more radical conclusions have been accepted.

This list makes no mention of the large literature on Roman law published in languages other than English, or of more specialized works in English. References will be found in the larger works listed above.

INDEX

(Where more than two references are given under one heading, the principal references, if any, are shown in **heavy** type.)